PRAISE FOR *STAND UP, SPEAK OUT*

'Monica McWilliams' memoir is her compelling story of growing up as a gutsy girl in a small village near Derry, coming of age as a student, teacher and activist in Belfast in the midst of the Troubles, and all she did to help end them.'

HILLARY CLINTON

'This is a stunning read … Throughout her life Monica McWilliams has remained a fearless champion for equality, human rights, and equal political participation.'

BERTIE AHERN

'Monica McWilliams has given a voice to those marginalised and isolated individuals living with coercive control either at home or within our communities … This memoir recalls the challenges faced by a woman determined to make Northern Ireland a better place to live for all of its people.'

SANDRA PEAKE, CEO, WAVE TRAUMA CENTRE

'Monica McWilliams traces her personal and political maturity as she moves from girlhood to academic and political activist. Decades of experience within feminist groups and the trade union movement … contributed to her effectiveness as a leading figure in the Northern Ireland Women's Coalition. The misogynistic underbelly in Northern Irish political life is revealed at its most unedifying and mercilessly recalled by Monica as women enter the peace process.'

MARGARET WARD, HISTORIAN AND AUTHOR

'This memoir couldn't be more timely in demonstrating the costs involved in trying to break the impasse between the diversity of views within Northern Ireland and the people of the Irish Republic and the UK … A moving and fascinating account.'

ROY GARLAND, POLITICAL COLUMNIST AND AUTHOR

'Mo Mowlam holds a special place in the heart of the people of Northern Ireland and her place is properly acknowledged here. I and countless others owe a deep gratitude to Monica McWilliams and the formidable women in the Women's Coalition for refusing to bend to their detractors and for helping to drive peace forward.'

LOUISE HAIGH, SHADOW SECRETARY OF STATE FOR NORTHERN IRELAND

'Monica McWilliams writes from the perspective of not just the witness at the scene, but as a contributor to the events and the voice heard is all the more authentic.'

BRETT LOCKHART, QC AND MEDIATOR

'It's the grit, sweat and sheer willpower that makes women the best peacebuilders. Monica is one of them. The girl from Kilrea could never have imagined that she would bring so much knowledge, hope and humour to so many women the world over.'

COLLEEN DUGGAN, FORMER STAFF UN HIGH COMMISSIONER FOR HUMAN RIGHTS

Stand Up, Speak Out

Monica McWilliams

·THE·
BLACK
·STAFF·
PRESS

Grateful acknowledgement is made to: Arlen House, for permission to quote from Ruth Carr, 'David Manson's School Room', from *Feather and Bone* (2018); Templar Poetry, for permission to quote from Jean Bleakney, 'Jean', from *No Remedy* (2017); Clodagh Hayes, for permission to quote from Maurice Hayes, *Minority Verdict: Experiences of a Catholic Public Servant* (Blackstaff Press, 1995); Carcanet Press, Manchester, UK, for permission to quote from Eavan Boland, 'Child of Our Time', from *Eavan Boland: New Selected Poems* (2013); W.W. Norton & Company, Inc, for permission to quote from 'A Litany for Survival'. Copyright © 1978 by Audre Lorde, from *The Collected Poems of Audre Lorde* by Audre Lorde; Faber & Faber Ltd, for permission to quote from Seamus Heaney, 'Station Island VII', from *Station Island* (1984); Granta Books, for permission to quote the excerpt from *Call Them By Their True Names: American Crises (and Essays)* by Rebecca Solnit, © 2018 by Rebecca Solnit; Blackstaff Press on behalf of the Estate of John Hewitt, for permission to quote from John Hewitt, 'The Coasters' and from 'An Irishman in Coventry', from *John Hewitt: Selected Poems*, eds Michael Longley and Frank Ormsby (2007), and from 'After the Fire', from *The Collected Poems of John Hewitt*, edited by Frank Ormsby (1991). The publishers also acknowledge the support of the Linen Hall Library, Belfast, which holds an extensive archive of materials relating to the Northern Ireland Women's Coalition.

First published in 2021 by Blackstaff Press
an imprint of Colourpoint Creative Ltd
Colourpoint House
Jubilee Business Park
21 Jubilee Road
Newtownards BT23 4YH

With the assistance of the Arts Council of Northern Ireland

arts
council
of Northern Ireland

Printed and bound in Great Britain by Clays Ltd, Elcograf S.p.A.

A CIP catalogue record for this book is available from the British Library

ISBN 978 1 78073 322 7

www.blackstaffpress.com

For my sisters
Mary, my soul companion,
and in memory of Noeleen

Contents

Preface

The title of this memoir comes from a time when I was told to shut up and sit down by an elected representative in a public forum. Now, after lengthy consideration, I have decided to tell the stories of what can happen when you stand up and speak out. The events recorded here are the recollected memories of an eventful and, at times, controversial life. In recounting these, I have tried to be as accurate as possible, relying on diaries and multiple notebooks that I kept over the course of those years.

My story begins in the small market town of Kilrea: in the cattle mart, in the fields, and in the kitchen of my home in New Row. My parents were the source of many important lessons, as were the opportunities to participate in sports, drama and debates at my two convent schools. The campaign for civil rights in Northern Ireland, which began when I was a teenager, was a turning point in my life, and then came the turbulent years of the Troubles.

My years as a student at Queen's University were eventful – among some of my best but also some of my worst because of the ongoing conflict. In my early twenties, I found myself in Detroit – a city that was as infamous for racism as Belfast was for sectarianism. My feminism and passion for community action began in the mid-seventies and when I returned home, I came together with others to set up the Northern Ireland Poverty Lobby; became involved in the campaign for nuclear disarmament; joined the trade union movement against sectarianism; and threw myself heart and soul into the women's rights movement.

In the turbulent years of the 1980s, I juggled raising a family and working as a lecturer at the University of Ulster. I had the good fortune to see my research on domestic violence lead to changes in legislation and policy. The stories I tell here give an insight into what it was like to live in a country that was awash with weapons, with women more vulnerable as a result. The names in the chapter on domestic violence have been changed to protect the identities of those involved.

When the political landscape began to shift in the mid-1990s, I co-founded the Women's Coalition and was elected to the peace negotiations, aiming to bring a different perspective to the process. Those two years I spent at the negotiating table finally resulted in the Good Friday Agreement on 10 April 1998. That made me a joint signatory to a peace accord – something that very few women in the world manage to be. The weeks leading up to the referendum on the Agreement and the initial years of the Northern Ireland Assembly turned my life into a roller coaster. It was no different during my time as Chief Commissioner of the Northern Ireland Human Rights Commission, with the ups and downs of the various court cases and investigations, and the drafting of the required advice on a Bill of Rights with my fellow commissioners.

The period covered in this book is cloaked in many tragedies that I witnessed personally. In recounting these I have tried to ensure that this memoir is not unduly overshadowed by sadness and loss; I have had to remind myself that 'that was then and this is now'. None of us comes through a transition from conflict without being changed both personally and politically. I have lived long enough to see that redemption is possible for all of us. A new space opened up in 1998 and I feel it is important to celebrate the gains as well as to record the mistakes that were made. I am honoured to have stood on the frontline with human rights defenders not just here in Northern Ireland but in conflict regions across the world, and the lessons I learned as well as the inspiration that I found are an important part of my story.

My intention with this book is to leave behind my record of those times and also to correct some of the inaccuracies that I have found in a number of other accounts of the peace process, particularly those of male commentators and historians, who do not think what women did was important enough to document. I hope this book will help people to gain a deeper understanding of the work of peacebuilding: why it matters to have women at the table and how seeing the humanity in each other can lead to transformation.

1

The Early Years

'Already, at ten, in your element
totting up numbers
taking each problem apart
to solve inequalities –
a mission to make things balance.'

Ruth Carr, from *'David Manson's School Room'*

By 1959, when the children in our family lined up in the morning for our daily doses of cod liver oil and rose hip syrup, there were five of us waiting in line. First were John (9) and Terence (8), who were born just a year apart, then Mary (6) and me (5), and then Noeleen (3), the 'wee pigeon', carried to bed at night on my father's shoulders. Mary and I were Irish twins, born eleven months apart. Even before Noeleen arrived, having four under the age of four was tough on my mother and not helped by my non-stop crying. The midwife kept telling my mother she was giving me too much to eat, but I was ravenous and needed my nourishment.

My parents had seven children in all, but my youngest two sisters died at birth. Had that not happened, perhaps Noeleen could have had a sister as close to her as I was to Mary. All of us were born in hospital as that was supposed to be best, but it didn't turn out that way for Dymphna, who died choking with the umbilical cord around her neck, and Deirdre, who was stillborn. My mother had baptised them alone in the hospital because she knew they were going to be taken away immediately. The babies were taken from her and buried in unconsecrated ground, limbo land, which was in the top corner of the graveyard, beside the back wall

1

of Drumagarner chapel in Kilrea. My mother had to stay behind in the hospital; my father never mentioned whether he had attended the burials, but it wouldn't have been the custom to go. It was painful for her not to know where her babies' graves were, but we remembered Dymphna and Deirdre each night as we said our prayers in the kitchen. A few years later, my father bought a plot in the graveyard and put the family name on the headstone. When I walked past it each Sunday, I thought it was odd to have a grave with no one inside. I wanted it to stay that way forever.

My mother, Elizabeth McKenna, was born in 1915, the fifth child in a family of nine. The family lived in Tirkane in the parish of Maghera, close to the Sperrin mountains. She was left-handed and had had her knuckles rapped with a ruler by a teacher at school until she learned to write with the right one. She had experienced other kinds of cruelty, like the dentist who pulled all her teeth out in one day. By then she was a hardy young woman who had to ride miles home on her bike without a tooth in her head. That made the dentist a sadist in my eyes, but she didn't see it that way. I knew she was one of a kind, but I still hoped that some of those hardy genes would get passed on to me.

My mother had been an independent woman when, at thirty-four, she gave up a good job to marry my father. He first set eyes on his future bride at a wake when she was only seventeen, but their paths didn't cross again till more than a decade later. My mother had gone to Loughry Agricultural College to get her certificate in 'Dairying, Poultry Keeping and Rural Housewifery'. When she left, her friends gave her an autograph album with the following inscription:

> Never trouble, trouble,
> Till trouble troubles you;
> It only doubles trouble;
> And it troubles others too.

That was good advice for Lily in 1933 – Lily was what they called her then, but by the time she was my mother, she was only ever Betty. My father caught up with her when she was working in Ballyrashane Creamery, where she was applying her Certificate of Competency in Butter-Making. She was the only Catholic at the creamery but that didn't stop her from making great friends there. When they came to visit, they told us how good our mother had been to them and how much they had loved having her as their supervisor.

A marriage bar was in place when my mother got married – it remained until 1975 – which meant she had no choice but to leave her job. The sole breadwinner from then on was my father. My mother often remarked how difficult it was to leave behind the good wages and the craic. She was left with 'rural housewifery' from then on. She came to understand the meaning of the Russian proverb, 'I thought I saw two people but it was only a man and his wife.' That her role as a homemaker and mother came to define her life was the norm in the patriarchal society of the time, but it was good for us to see that my father deferred to her. He always told us, 'Ask your mother; she's the one who knows best.' That was his way of showing how much she mattered.

My mother did the listening whilst my father did the talking. I was more like him and Mary was more like my mother. When we got together with our multiple cousins, the tears would run down our cheeks as my father told his stories around the fire. My mother was the opposite – she never wanted to attract attention; she was happy just to hear him regaling us with his tales. She also had few expectations about needing things for herself. Each time she returned a gift he'd bought for her, I wished she'd kept it. She would tell us to make sure that when we grew up we had a bit of money to call our own.

My mother had got her driving licence at a time when a driving test wasn't required. In her case, we wished it had been since she didn't know how to use her wing mirrors. On trips out, Mary and I functioned as the indicators, sticking our arms out the windows, since having to switch them on was one job too many for her. She crawled through the villages, but she still asked if she should slow down. When Aunt Mary was with us, she would reply, 'Betty, if you go any slower, this car will come to a halt.' We would clap when we arrived at our destination, even when she reversed into a gatepost trying to park the car. She held her nerve for a year and then packed it in, which meant we didn't see our cousins as often as we would have liked. To keep us safe in the car, she made us all say prayers, a role that later fell to Mary even though she was a much better driver.

My father's father had gone to America to work on a sheep farm in Utah and came home in 1899 with enough money to buy a farm outside the town of Swatragh. At the bottom of a long lane, in front of a river, he built the family home at Stranagone. It was an ideal place for children to grow up, but any money my grandfather had made soon disappeared in the pub. The pony and trap knew its way home without him. It wasn't long before the bailiffs were at the door. His daughter Sadie kept them at bay while his son Patsy acted as the magician, riding the horse, their prime asset, as fast as he could out of their sight. My father Owen was born in Stranagone in 1914 – the fifth in a family of seven children. He would have loved to have stayed at school but had no choice but to leave at the age of fourteen to start milk rounds to bring money into the family. It didn't take him long to gather up some savings, from which he bought his first cattle. He quickly became successful as he could read the animals very well, was a good negotiator and never stopped working. Pretty soon he had a herd of some of the best cattle in the land and eventually became known the length and breadth of Ireland as one of the best in the business.

My parents married just after the war, in 1949. They paid £34.12.8 for their wedding breakfast at the Montague Arms in Portstewart. Both of them, and all their brothers and sisters, abstained from alcohol so the one bottle of champagne listed on the bill probably remained unopened. The accepted practice on both sides of the family was to take the Pioneer pledge in the belief that the family genes for 'the drink' were passed from one generation to the next.

After the reception, all the guests joined them on the first day of their honeymoon in Carrigart, County Donegal. However, my mother's mother didn't go to the wedding; she didn't go to any of her daughters' weddings. If she had any reservations about my father, they soon disappeared. My grandmother loved that he brought my mother to visit her each week in the homestead at Tirkane. And before long they were bringing a gaggle of grandchildren there as well.

It was the boys who were expected to go with my father when he worked outside the house, but I always wanted to go too. If he went to the fields when the dogs were worrying the ewes, he would bring me along with his gun. We would lie in wait and if the dogs appeared, he would fire a couple of shots. He never set out to hurt a dog but if he wounded one, we would follow the blood trail back to its owner who would be furious at my father for taking a shot at their dog – and also start making excuses. The exchanges were hot and heavy at the start, but it was good to see my father and the owner come to an understanding, with my father insisting that the dogs stayed in during the lambing season. I did other jobs for him, like watching the sow to make sure she didn't harm her suckling piglets. When my father used the expression, 'That person would eat their young', I knew what he meant. He was good at handing out advice, telling me to stay with the flock and not to be running after the stray. That meant that I was not to get distracted; the wanderer would come back by itself.

I loved going to the cattle mart with my father. I stood beside him when he and the other men sealed their deals by spitting on their hands and then slapping them together. I was fond of those cattle dealers and they were fond of me. They often gave me a luck penny, whispering, 'That's for yourself because your father was so good to me.' They would give me a sixpence each time I mentioned my birthday, no matter how many pretend birthdays there were, and would take me to buy bagfuls of sweets and Love Hearts in Scullions. I got a mouthful of fillings in return.

After the mart was over, I would sometimes go with the cattle dealers to Dempsey's pub in Kilrea. As a lifelong Pioneer, my father never set foot in licensed premises, but I wanted to sit beside the dealers up at the counter and be allowed to bet on the horses. On Grand National day in 1961, I picked out Nicolaus Silver as a winner, placing a pin on his name in the newspaper. I got lucky with that spectacular white horse, and Mrs Dempsey gave me a wink, promising not to tell my mother that her seven-year-old had been gambling. One of the dealers who sometimes worked for my father was known for getting worse for drink on a fair day. On occasions, when he'd start roaring and the police would be called, he'd hide in our backyard. I'd watch as the police took him away with a blanket over his head. If he'd dropped his hat, I would keep it safe and give it back to him the following week. Cattle dealers never went anywhere without their hats. My father's has pride of place on my bookshelf.

From quite an early age, my father asked me to help him with his accounts, and I loved the idea of being his bookkeeper. Deciphering his writing was always a challenge so matching what was going out with what was coming in was like a jigsaw, and took time to figure out. We had a few rows, but I soon learned from him that for every problem, there had to be a solution. He had stub books that read, 'No Damaged Stock Taken or Confusion Marks on Ears'. I wonder if that was some kind of subliminal message for later.

He was generous to a fault – known to buy cattle for men who didn't have the money at the time of the purchase. He didn't care how long it took for them to repay him. His generosity came easy and I wanted to replicate it. It appeared to me that it was those with most money who had the hardest time parting with it, even when it was for a good reason. Mean people would say they were tight for money when it wasn't the case, and my father would tell me he could see them coming from a mile off.

Wherever we went, if he heard that someone had fallen on hard times, he would stop at the house to see if he could help. I liked being part of that. When our cattle broke out of a field, his kind-heartedness to our neighbours was reciprocated and people came quickly to lend him a hand. One evening our heifer fell into a swamp and locals turned up with their ropes. They could see the animal's distress and worked quietly in the field. I felt moved as I watched them in the cold evening light with no one saying a word. When they finally pulled the animal on to dry ground, I put a blanket over her, hoping she wouldn't die from the shock since I knew the cost of losing a healthy animal. Witnessing that sense of responsibility that the men felt towards my father, their neighbour, left a lasting impression.

My father was often worn out from travelling to cattle auctions in the west of Ireland. He had a habit of going to bed when we were playing in the backyard, and if someone started screaming, 'Leg Before Wicket' during a rounders match, he would shout out the window for us to be quiet. Noeleen was usually standing quietly in the corner and would tell us to do what he asked so he wouldn't have to come down. But if he came home from the marts and we were watching TV, his first question was always, 'Have you nothing better to do?' He worked around the clock and didn't like to see us idle, since, according to him, there was nothing but filth on the screen. He thought *Burke's Law*, an American detective series, was much too advanced for us. That meant going to Mrs McIntyre next door to watch it as she didn't care if the girls were running around in bikinis. One night, when we were fighting over which programme to watch, he reached for the TV to throw it out the back door, but my mother managed to calm things down – as usual – and put it back in its place.

My father was at his most content when he was fishing, and the local fishermen called him 'the old man of the river'. In the summer evenings I would watch him casting out his line and reeling it in. Our neighbour Sean Donaghy once caught eleven salmon but my father outdid him by catching one more. His long waders weighed him down and he couldn't swim, but I could see that he was at his happiest up to his waist in the water. He thought it was fun to reverse his car at the edge of the Bann, pretend the gears weren't working and say to me that the car was sliding in. I woke up at night dreaming of drowning but I think he had no idea how scary it was for me in the back seat, closest to the river. As well as fishing, he loved playing bridge and studied the game for hours in his armchair in front of the fire. I found the *Laws of Duplicate Contract Bridge* for him, as he was a stickler for checking the rules to see who was right. His partner, Patsy McNicholl, was the local road sweeper, and the two of them were hard to beat.

He didn't have the same kind of patience in the yard or the fields. We called him John Wayne as he steered his green Rover like a horse, banging on the side of the door as he drove through the fields, shouting for us to 'cap' the cattle in the right direction. When he moved, we moved too, at speed. I had no fear of those big beasts and weaved my way through them until we got them safely home. We all became long distance runners and champion sprinters because of that experience.

Football games brought the worst out in him. When my brothers were playing, we slid down the seats to avoid the embarrassment – he thought he was the referee, telling whoever would listen what the decision should have been. During one match with local rivals at Ballinascreen, he got especially worked up, and I tried to remind him that it was only a game – but he still jumped over the fence to remonstrate with the referee. Before the All-Ireland GAA final at Croke Park in 1958, in which our cousins were playing on opposing teams, we all prayed that he wouldn't do the same. Sean O'Connell, my mother's nephew, was on the Derry team and Padraic Haughey, my father's nephew, was playing for Dublin. Everyone was relieved to see that my father was less invested than when his own sons were playing. Dublin beat Derry, and on the way home we laughed to be told by the Haugheys that Dublin would never be beaten.

My mother was good at working with my father, and he was rarely short with her. I often stood up to him, following the advice he always gave me – 'Don't let anyone walk over you' – but he didn't mean for me to apply that to him. He once sent me to get chips for the fishermen and then marched into the shop to find out why I was taking so long. The other customers nodded in agreement when he told the owner that he should take down his 'fast food' sign and give it to somebody else. They thought it was funny, but I didn't and when we were back in the car I told him so. I walked for miles to get home after he put me out of the car. The good thing was that neither of us held a grudge and we were back on speaking terms before long.

My father often had a few men working for him, and we came to know some of them well. Jimmy O'Kane rescued me the day I took off on my bike to get out of doing the dishes. I lost control going down the hill after Church Street and as I fell on to the road, my hand got caught in the spokes of the bike. Jimmy found me and carried me home in his arms with a missing bit of my finger in his handkerchief. I spent three weeks in hospital recuperating and getting tetanus injections in my bum. My mother had told me to bless myself with Holy Water before each injection as she believed that was just as important as the medical treatment. The other children saw me diving under the covers and I heard one of them say, 'She's gone for her holy dip.' The nurses stuck me in a cot when there weren't enough beds in the children's ward. Visitors compensated with gifts like a toy accordion, but I was affronted to suffer the indignity of a cot at nine years old. When I came home, my mother sent me for piano lessons in the room behind Peden's sweet shop, hoping they would help straighten out the artificial bit of finger. I passed the preliminary exam in pianoforte, playing in the Presbyterian church hall in Coleraine, where the judges presented a certificate to the girl with the crooked finger. But my enthusiasm didn't last – I stopped playing and my finger never got straightened out.

Card games were a regular occurrence in our house but gambling for money wasn't allowed so we played for matchsticks instead. We loved the winter nights when the cattle dealers came to play cards in the kitchen. They hid sixpences for us children to find in the morning and since I was an early riser I was the one who got the most money. Pat McGlinchey, who worked for my father, lived in our house and was the source of much fun for my brothers and cousin Bob. They'd steal his milking stool and take advantage of the times when he'd had too much to drink, which was often. On his way to bed, he would fall over the tripwires they had set across the stairs. But no matter how late Pat came home, he was up at dawn eating porridge at the kitchen table beside me. He told me that the woman he wanted to marry had turned him down but that he still kept the ring in his pocket. When he passed away, my mother gave me his ring, but I didn't need it to remember Pat – he was one of a kind.

We said our prayers all together each night and mine was the fourth decade of the rosary. I said it like a mantra from a kneeling position on the kitchen floor. My mother fasted on the first Friday of every month. She called them her good Fridays and said good Fridays would be good for me too. During the parish Stations, the priest would come to the house to say Mass and hear the neighbours' Confessions. I was the one who kept the record of the donations in the book. The amount that each neighbour gave was treated with more discretion than at funerals and at the Mass, when the priest called out how much each person had given, in effect showing the pecking order of the parish. The customs were carefully observed – the housekeeper who worked for the parish priest had to sit in the back seat of his car, reflecting her gender and status. Each Easter Mrs Rafferty made us a new outfit: my favourite was a yellow suit and matching hat. We built Easter huts, pretending they were real houses, where proper manners had to be observed, like expecting my father to wipe his feet on the mat before entering. Cousin Caroline at Stranagone made no exceptions for her dozen siblings or the five of us who climbed in and out of hers.

The names we were given at baptism came from the saints, unlike Protestants, who I thought could choose any name they wanted. The names made it easier for strangers to work out your religion. Felix was on my father's birth certificate, which would have confused some people, but he used Owen and that made him more of a 'left footer'. When people asked my name, they found they couldn't settle the question easily and then had to move on to the next one: 'What school did you go to?' I learned early that the foot you kicked with, just like the spade you dug with, meant you were either a Catholic or a Protestant. Whenever I asked why the foot mattered, I would be told: 'catch yourself on'. It really did matter and came up time and time again throughout my young life.

My christening took place on Saint Monica's feast day and that was how I got my name – Monica was the long-suffering mother of Saint Augustine, a reformed reprobate. According to my mother, I was no saint, and struggled to be like my namesake. She called me Tom Thumb – the nickname made me want to behave more like my sister Mary, but I didn't always manage it. I should have been doing what my mother needed me to do, but instead I did what I wanted. I would take the Hoover and lie under the bed reading my book, a picture of George Best – my favourite footballer – by my side, when I should have been cleaning upstairs. Mary could have told on me, but she didn't, and that's one of the many reasons I loved having her as my sister.

A few years before he was married, my father bought a house in Kilrea. He had managed to save a decent amount over the years and, because he was a successful cattle dealer, he was considered to be good for a loan from the bank. It was a large house with lots of barns and sheds out the back – a perfect place for a family home. At the start of World War II, American soldiers requisitioned the house as they needed accommodation during their stay at Aghadowey aerodrome. The officers rearranged the rooms to suit their requirements and built a hatch between the kitchen and what became their breakfast room – we kept its name but we never ate there, opting instead for the kitchen table.

When my father first bought the house, there was a railway line at the bottom of the street, and the address was Railway Place. In 1950, the railway closed and our address became New Row. My father had used the railway to transport his cattle but when that all stopped, he turned to cattle lorries instead. On quieter days, the old station house, with its booking office and waiting room, was where we played at being conductors and guards.

The kitchen was the heart of our home. Most days, the kettle swung from one side of the Aga to the other as my mother made tea for the men. The men were my father, the workers, the lorry-men, cattle dealers and anyone else who crossed our door on a fair day in their big yellow boots. It was a lot of hospitality and a lot of work so when we were all small a housekeeper came to stay to help my mother.

At dinnertime on fair days, I would go to the pantry to feed my dolls while waiting for the kitchen to get back to normal. Before long, I'd had enough of the dolls and decided to ask Santa for a typewriter. I searched the house for weeks until I found where the toys were hidden and made a scratch on my present. The discovery that Santa wasn't real taught me to be careful about what I wished for and an early lesson that you'd always be disappointed if you put your faith in a fantasy.

My mother knew to keep me busy: encouraging me to wind skeins of wool and to sew and knit while I was reading. That's what we girls did – multitasking even if we didn't know it. We stored the wool in a cubbyhole, and the bats loved the darkness of it as well as the sleeves of my coat. The pulley for airing the clothes on the ceiling worried me as much as the bats. For years, I lived in fear of it falling on top of one of us until it did just that, landing on my mother. She knew she was fine, and wasn't the type to get into a panic – there were five of us already doing that. I begged her to get rid of that pulley, feeling sure it would kill her someday. It stayed where it was for years, but it's gone now and is much missed, like my mother.

My mother had a great conviction that being outdoors was good for you. When she was growing up, not everyone in the family got a place on the pony and trap, the only form of transport, so she frequently had to walk miles to get anywhere. She was a firm believer that we ought to be out in the fresh air as much as possible, not least because it helped her to get on with her work in the house, and frequently told us to get out from under her feet. The day we took her at her word, we were gone for hours. We were found later, miles from home, eating honeysuckle and sucking blackberries on the road to Swatragh. We had a knife to protect us and used it to cut branches for sticks, along with a rope, in case we were attacked. I was seven years old and at the rear, while John, the oldest, led from the front. After that escapade, my mother made sure to ask us where we were going. If she left home without us, I would ask where she was headed and always got the same answer: 'Timbuktu or Kalamazoo.' When I eventually got to those places myself, they were much further away than I had been led to believe.

Generally in our house, I got the easy jobs and Mary got the hard ones. Shaping yellow butter into tiny balls was one of mine, as was getting the buttermilk out of the churn. The smell of it turned my stomach but the pancakes my mother made with it made me forget that – they disappeared from the griddle on top of the Aga as quickly as she could turn them over. The chickens in the backyard were also disappearing, but for a different reason. If my mother showed up with a brush in her hand, those chickens knew what was coming. They scattered as she picked one out, twisting its neck as it screeched. Mary plucked and gutted the carcass; I did the singeing with methylated spirits to get rid of the stray feathers that wouldn't come out.

We enjoyed those dinners, and the times when we had rabbits and hares, snipe and pheasants – shot by my father. We knew where the food came from. If we turned our noses up at whatever was on offer, my mother would say, 'No force, no flatter; if you don't like it, it's no matter.' It was different when we went to stay at my father's homeplace in Stranagone. There was no fuss allowed as my uncle and aunt who lived there had thirteen children. Most of them had been born at home and after each of the births Aunt Martha was on her feet the next day, in the field with her toddlers running alongside the pram. We didn't dare turn up our noses at the Stranagone table and when we went to bed, we slept like spoons, all squeezed in together without complaint. All in, I had eighty-six first cousins – some of them in families with over a dozen children. Five would go on to become priests, and my cousin Anne became a nun.

In our own house back in Kilrea, my brothers tried to boss us because they were older and they thought that was what boys did to girls. They expected me to do their fetching; I would tell them they were useless so-and-sos and that they could get whatever they wanted themselves as they had legs of their own. The gender divisions were clear but I always had lots to say for myself and I was determined they weren't going to walk over me.

Although I was outspoken and much less biddable than Mary, my mother only put me across her knee once. Someone had been stealing from the milkman, and a neighbour had seen me buying sweets by the dozen in a few local shops. I wasn't the thief; it was the girl down the street who asked me to share her takings, and I accepted without asking any questions. My mother said she was sorry for not believing me. It was another of life's lessons: if something seems too good to be true, then it usually is.

My outspokenness meant that I was the one who started the rows. My mother was always begging us to 'keep the peace'. When she was planning a treat for my sisters, she often arranged for me to stay with Mrs McIntyre or the McKays out the road. That meant she and my sisters could have a few peaceful days on the beach at Portstewart. What was going on became clear when the breadman called at the house where I was staying and spilled the beans that my sisters had gone off on a holiday and must have forgotten about me. They were in Kelly's boarding house where high tea was on the menu. High tea sounded really special, so I complained to my father, arguing that they were getting more than me. He had a soft spot for me and brought me to Portstewart, where my sisters were wandering up the prom, licking cones of Morelli's ice cream. In order to be allowed to stay, I had to promise not to start any rows. If I did, I would be sent back to Kilrea, but if I stuck to the rules the reward was high tea at Kelly's for two whole days. My Cinderella days were over, but the experience was a formative lesson on how to use the carrot and the stick.

I was sent to be company for my grandmother during the summer holidays from the age of ten. Her home in Tirkane at the snout of the Carn wasn't far from Maghera – it felt to me like it was in the middle of nowhere but it was only ten miles from home. My grandmother was confined to bed because of an amputated leg and lived with her son, my Uncle Patrick, who wasn't married. My job was cooking: I made the Complan, a fortified energy drink, as well as fried eggs, bacon and spuds, and a custard dessert, and, since we ate the same things every day, I became an expert. My uncles David and Patrick ran the farm, and they drafted in more help during the summer. When they did, I knew to cook more of everything. Every so often I rang home from the red phone box at Tirkane; our house at Kilrea was one of only four with a telephone, so it was easy to remember the number – Kilrea 204.

There was no electricity at my grandmother's and only an outside latrine. I had a chamber pot in my room as I didn't want to go out in the middle of the night with only a Tilley lamp to light the way. I thought 'chamber pot' was a very grand name given what it was used for.

On the days my cousins came to visit, we headed to the river. Stepping stones and a deep pond provided the fun for our clan from the Bann. We thought we'd learned to swim by splashing around in the trout hatchery at Portna, near home – but we hadn't, so it was a miracle that none of us drowned. If the eels in the Bann at Portna looked like snakes, whatever was in that pond looked just as scary.

When the cousins departed, I only had the antiquarian books up the stairs to distract me. At home I had twelve volumes of the *Encyclopædia Britannica*, which I buried myself in, but the books in Tirkane were hard going for a ten-year-old. The magazines that came from the missionary orders took my mind to faraway places – I wasn't to know then that I would travel to them on missions of my own.

The house at Tirkane had a post office and I loved being the postmistress. My uncle supervised me until I learned to dispense the payouts from a stool behind the counter. It was the perfect training ground for my future role as my father's bookkeeper. I got an orange ten-shilling note for my efforts at the end of the summer. When the van arrived each Friday, I bought the groceries, including digestive biscuits – a luxury to be taken with a cup of tea once I had cleared up after dinner. I was alone most of the time, sitting by the grandfather clock, listening to it tick while I read. But I never felt lonely. The sense of independence that came with being in charge, especially in the post office, was what I enjoyed most at the ripe old age of ten.

When I felt I needed to be in touch with someone closer to my own age, I sought out a pen pal from *Ireland's Own* magazine and chose a girl who shared my first name. Monica Donaghy lived in Bishop Street in

Derry and that was far enough away for me. We wrote to each other for years and sent presents at Christmas. It was exciting to hear what city life was like as I was living at the bottom of a mountain and had never been to Derry.

The stories my grandmother told me were fascinating, and I loved the time I spent with her. The only thing I worried about was the phantom pain from her amputated leg. I still have the letter that I wrote in 1965 to my uncle, Father John, when he was the parish priest in Rotherhithe, in London, asking him to pray for her.

He got around his working-class parish on a motorbike, which caused a stir since he was a big, lanky man like all the McKenna family, known locally as the *Faidhes*, the Irish for long ones. When he came home each summer, he would walk over a hundred miles to Lough Derg to join my mother for a pilgrimage. He would complain about the rain and the midges but could stay up fasting and praying for three days and two nights. My father had said, after the time he'd joined them, 'I prayed that if I ever got off that island I would never be back again.'

My uncle came from a long line of Father Johns in Tirkane. The first was born in 1793, five years before a United Irishman turned up at their door. Watty Graham, a Presbyterian from Maghera, had been trying to escape to America and was hiding from the yeomen who came searching for him. When they couldn't find him in the house, they burned half of it down. Watty Graham was hanged five years later, in 1798, but his memory lives on in the house. My grandmother told me how, in the 1820s, the next Father John escaped from a window in the bedroom in which she now lay. It was against the law to say Mass at that time, and he had been reported for conducting this sacrament at a nearby Mass rock. My grand-uncles in Tirkane spoke Irish, like many others who lived there, as the 1911 census confirms. There was still no peace for my grandmother, who recalled how the Black and Tans put bullet holes in her wall in 1921 when they went on the hunt for fugitives opposed to the partition of Ireland.

I would go from time to time with my uncles to the mountain to check on the sheep. Each time I saw the pile of stones at the top of the Carn left there by emigrants on their way to Derry to catch the ship to New York, I was reminded of my father's sisters, brave young women aged seventeen and eighteen, who went to America in 1930 as third-class passengers on the SS *California*. My father was meant to go with them but he was refused passage when it was discovered that he was only fourteen, so he ended up having to wave farewell from the quayside. Instead of disembarking with the rest of the passengers, Aunt Mae stayed on Ellis Island for three weeks to help her sister, my Aunt Sue, recover from an illness she had contracted on the journey across the Atlantic.

The American cousins and aunts came back to visit us in 1960. By then my father's mother was wearing widow's weeds – my grandfather had died a decade earlier and she had come to live beside us. I liked to watch her as she gathered up her long black skirt to form a basket to carry groceries home from Henry's shop across the street. His shop was the place where I got a penny for each empty lemonade bottle and then doubled my money by taking the same bottles from the rear of the shop and handing them back across the counter to him. When Patsy Henry realised what I was doing, he told my mother I would go places; she scolded me and told me I wasn't that hard up for money. That put an end to my entrepreneurship. Patsy was a kind man, and he kept a tick book on the counter for hard-up wives to write down what they owed him for their messages. They paid him what they could whenever they could. I knew how stretched these women were, married to men who queried the price of a pound of bacon but never the price of a pint.

Although my grandmother's husband, Charlie, had been no stranger to the pub, and had done enough drinking to last the family a lifetime, my grandmother still enjoyed her bottle of stout. I would be the one sent to the pub with her order and would bring the stout home in a brown paper bag. My father didn't approve of her drinking, but he could live with it if she didn't go to the pub herself. We didn't believe him when he told us 'the drink is in the blood,' passed on from one generation to the next, but it turned out he was right.

To get to the pub, I would dander through the town with its black stone fronts. Kilrea was Cill Ria, meaning the church on the hill. Catholics outnumbered Protestants two to one, but the number of churches was in reverse, with three for Protestant denominations and one for Catholics. The location of the Catholic church meant getting a bus or facing a three-mile walk each Sunday. The town reminded me of the line in the nursery rhyme 'Rub-a-dub-dub' – 'the butcher, the baker, the candlestick maker'. The difference was that we had two of everything – one for Catholics and one for Protestants.

The Diamond was the gathering point each evening for a group of older men from round about. In centuries past, it had held a pump where rival factions fought over which side's emblems should be displayed. That rivalry, over orange and green, carried on – between the loyal Orange orders and the ancient order of Hibernians.

The public library was next to the Diamond, in Church Street above a garage. The two women librarians allowed me to sit on the floor, where I pored over what was on offer. When I told them how great it felt to be surrounded by books, they winked at each other and asked if I wanted to do the stacking. I could see the war memorial from the library window, and I used to pass it every morning on my way to school. The names of the war dead were listed along with the places where they had fallen. I knew the Paul and Bolton families, whose relatives had been killed in Ypres and Gallipoli. The Spanish flu that followed World War I also affected our town, taking the life of young Dr Hegarty as he tended to his patients in Kilrea. That war and disease could have such an impact on my own small community was something I never forgot.

Saint Patrick was said to have paid a visit to Kilrea in the fifth century. When I was much older and people would insist to me that they were the true natives of Ireland, I would remind them of our patron saint's mixed heritage. The other famous visitor was King James I in the seventeenth century, who put the town on the map. He granted the townlands of Kilrea to one of his Worshipful Companies, the Mercers, who established themselves on a site at the River Bann just outside the town. The Honourable The Irish Society was given the rights to the river. Hundreds of years later, my father had to pay an exorbitant fee every year if he wanted to fish there for salmon. The fees went up as fast as the fish stocks went down. The Irish Society placed its nets at the Cutts in Coleraine, taking most of the salmon off to London. My father renamed it the 'Dishonourable Irish Society' as it was left to the local anglers to build their own hatchery to replenish the stocks.

We also had 'Big House' unionists. They were the local landed gentry, like Dame Dehra Parker, the grandmother of James Chichester-Clark, Baron Moyola, who became MP in 1960 and prime minister of Northern Ireland in 1969. She had a big house in Bridge Street. When it was Kilrea's turn to host the Twelfth of July in 1962, Chichester-Clark came to visit. People passing our house asked Mary and I where the field was located, and we had to admit to not knowing. They replied with curses and insults – we were both under ten.

Each Twelfth of July, we liked to sit on the windowsill and watch the men from the Orange Hall next door go past. I had been listening to them practising on their bagpipes for months and knew they never caused offence, but it was a different story with the flute band from Bovedy. We peeped out the window, hearing their shouts of 'Kick the Pope' as they came to a halt just before they disbanded at the Orange Hall. They got red in the face as they hammered their big drums under the banner of King William of Orange, who was displayed on a white charger just like Nicolaus Silver, the horse I'd won a bet on in the Grand National. I asked my mother what the men were shouting about; she turned away and said quietly, 'the least said the better'. I had left the town by the time a cross-community festival was founded – there were none when I was growing up – and named after the fairy thorn tree that we loved to play under. I felt at a loss to understand how we could be neighbours but hardly know each other.

Our neighbours, the Kerrs, were Protestants and when my parents were away for the day, we held a competition with the children in that family to see if what they said was true – that because they were Protestants they were better off than us. We took turns to bring things from our house to show them off on the street. There was little between us until I found a box of chocolates, which sealed the deal and the Kerrs went home disappointed. My mother was mortified when she came home and found us carting everything back into the house. She sent me to apologise and I did as she asked. Saying sorry wasn't that hard; I was more put out that the Kerrs weren't asked to do the same.

Many Protestant farmers refused to sell land to Catholics; my father got around the problem by slipping some money under the table so someone else would do the bidding on his behalf. He knew the importance of owning land and would often tell us it was the one thing

18

they weren't making any more of. He valued it since it had been so hard for him to buy his own land in Kilrea.

The hay field was one of the few places where some 'mixing' took place. As soon as the combine harvester arrived to do the rounds of the local fields, it was all hands to the mast to bring in the hay. It was my job to make jam sandwiches for the workers and fill the milk bottle with hot tea, twisting newspaper into the neck to stop it leaking. I loved walking to the fields, and watching the hay stack up as the long, hot days wore on. We used the baling twine we'd collected to make swings that we tied to the rafters in the hayloft and organised games to see who could jump the farthest between the bales. Our loft was the place to be. Even the Kerrs came to join us when they saw the fun we were having. The day that we loved the most was the last Sunday of September when the whole town, Catholic and Protestant, would head off to Portstewart to celebrate the hay being in for another year.

Few families could afford to pay for education in the days before the Welfare State, but I was a beneficiary of the free system established in 1948, providing me with opportunities that my parents could only have dreamt of. My brothers went to St Columba's boys' primary school, and my sisters and I went to the girls' convent, St Anne's. I couldn't wait to get to school and I loved it when I was there. In my first year, my teacher was Sister Marie Therese, who I thought looked like one of the saints from the magazines in Tirkane. My job was to carry the milk up to her classroom at break time and, as my reward, I got the bottle of Sukie orange juice that was tucked into the middle of the crate.

On May Day we put on our white veils and joined the nuns in a procession around the convent lake. When I was seven years old, singing Ave Maria and holding bluebells in my hands, I felt like an angel. I went to the oratory beside the school every morning for seven o'clock Mass and knelt by myself in the front row. The nuns were in a closed-off area beside the altar, but they could see me. That was all part of being an angel, and I was hoping that being seen this way was starting to work.

When I was eight years old, I moved to Sister Claire's classroom, where there were three different age groups. That gave me an excuse to play up. I was no angel the day I managed to pull her veil off, and I can still hear the gasp from the class. I hadn't really meant to be that bold and Sister Claire knew that. Rather than punishing me, she realised that I was a child who needed to be kept busy. She moved me to a desk beside her budgie and I became an angel once more. Sister Claire played the piano in the classroom, so we would gather around her to sing. She would lower her chin, and that was my cue to turn the page. I thrived on having things to do and Sister Claire piled them on. I was the page-turner when she played the piano, the budgie's little helper, and would run messages between the classrooms for her. She and I became such bosom pals that I chose Claire as my confirmation name. She was delighted when I told her. The Mercy Order to which she belonged had a motto, 'When sleeping women awake, mountains will move.' I loved the idea of moving mountains but knew I needed to find a way to do it without having to become a nun.

The opposite of Sister Claire was Sister Alphonsus – Phonsie to us. We dreaded moving up to her classroom when we turned nine. If she caught one of us eating sweets, she made the offender stand all day on a chair beside her desk. She was a bully, who seemed to enjoy humiliating her pupils, but she didn't petrify me the way she did other girls in the class. My sister Noeleen was so scared of her when she got to her class that my mother used to keep her home from school.

Phonsie went a bit easier on me than on some of the others – I don't know whether she could see that I wasn't terrified of her, or whether she enjoyed taking credit for the fact that I was a good pupil who sometimes won prizes. I entered a writing competition and won a platinum pen and a certificate signed by Ruth Dudley Edwards, a journalist at the *Sunday Independent*. Years later when we came across each other again, we clashed and she certainly wouldn't have been awarding me any prizes by then.

One day, one of my classmates told Phonsie that she'd lost thruppence, and Phonsie immediately assumed that one of us had stolen it. She said that we should approach her desk one by one, and whoever had stolen the thruppence should slide it under a book that she had placed there. When it was my turn, I placed a three-penny piece from my own pocket under the book because I was so fed up with her making our school life miserable. She wanted to humiliate one of us, but I didn't give her that pleasure. She knew I wasn't the one she was looking for, so her bamboo cane stayed where it was.

Joining her class marked the end of the fun at school, and the last couple of years were marred too by the run-up to the eleven-plus. If we passed, we could go to grammar school, and I'd been named as one of the girls who might just make it. The preparations for the test were on Saturday mornings. Classes on drawing, knitting and writing took precedence the rest of the week.

Multiple-choice questions were coming out of our ears and we also had to write a long essay. We all dreaded the exams and couldn't wait to put the whole experience behind us. I wasn't able to take the second test because I was sick on the day, so I took a supplementary paper at the local Protestant primary school, which was the designated retake centre. I did my essay under a picture of the Queen. That was different from the picture I was more used to – the Sacred Heart. The school's playground had swings and climbing frames instead of our empty yard at St Anne's. I wanted to pass – I had used fancy words like 'silhouette' in my essay. Sister Claire told my mother not to worry but I still had to wait for months to see how it would turn out.

On the day the results were due, there was a postal strike but Sister Claire, in her role as school principal, strode through the town in her long, black habit and demanded that the post office hand over the letters. Her girls had waited long enough. I followed her to the school gates where my two friends were waiting to see the size of the envelopes because that told us if we'd passed. Jill and I were handed fat ones but Dymphna got a thin one, which meant she would not be coming with us to Loreto Convent in Coleraine. That took some of the shine off the day for me and Jill.

When we finished the eleven-plus, we got a few days off school and went to pick potatoes. The farmer would collect us in a cart and bring us to the field where we waded in to face the endless rows of spuds. It was dirty work, but I liked the money in my pocket at the end of the day. They paid the boys more than girls because the farmer thought they were able to pick more potatoes. I hated the idea of being paid less and complained to him and anyone who would listen about it. One of my suggestions was that the boys should stay at home one day so that the farmer would see the girls could do just as good a job, but the boys just laughed. I seethed even more when I saw one of them putting stones in his basket to fill it up faster.

I gleaned important lessons from those years: from my family and friends, young and old; from the nuns at school and the men at the marts; at home in Kilrea; in the house at Tirkane; and on the many farms where I went to stay. They were the seeds for what was to come later.

2

Getting Educated for Civil Rights

'When the masses start to read, the establishment
is in trouble – when they start to count, the game is up.'

Maurice Hayes

The mantra in our house when I was growing up was that education was the way to better yourself – it was free and it was the ticket to wherever we wanted to go. My parents were determined that we would make the most of the opportunities that were on offer for us and that hadn't been available to them.

I started at Loreto Convent in September 1965. Mary had already been there for a year, so she knew the ropes. We got up at half past six, and it was so cold in the winter that I put on my uniform under the bedclothes. My mother had made porridge the night before and left it in the Aga – both it and her Ulster fry helped to fortify us for the freezing cold wait for the bus on the Diamond.

Loreto was a big change from my small primary school in Kilrea. When I arrived, I was told that I had been placed in B class, where we were to do domestic science. About a week into term, I discovered that the girls doing real science were in the A class, so I asked to be moved – A sounded better and I definitely didn't want to be stuck in a stream that was learning to cook and sew. I told the nun that my friend Jill McNamee from Kilrea needed to move too, since she was good at maths, just like me. The two of us trotted off to 1A and we never looked back. As we marched into the room, Eileen Fisher thought I looked like a cheeky skitter and she hoped that Jill would take the empty seat behind her rather than me. She changed her mind after I invited her to stay the night at our house. From then on, we were friends. Eileen came from a family of ten children, and when I went to stay at her house, the loving care the siblings showed towards Louise, their youngest sister who had cerebral palsy, stayed in my mind for days afterwards. It was the first time I had spent time with someone with a disability.

At the end of the first term, Miss Rafferty wrote in my report, 'Has potential but is too easily distracted.' She was right – I was playing Jacks whenever I could, in pairs or groups of four on the classroom floor. According to the teachers, I was also distracting the girls in Class 1A, and the head nun constantly had to remind me to wear my beret at the right angle when she inspected us as we lined up for the bus. She asked me one day why I couldn't be more like my sister Mary. What she didn't know was that Mary was a 'messer', but she was better at hiding it than I was. She was enjoying life with her friends, mostly talking about the facts of life, which were certainly not talked about inside the classroom. We would pore over *Jackie* on the bus and compare notes on what we knew. My mother soon realised that Mary and her friends didn't know much, so she sat me down and told me what was what. The information she gave me made more sense than the biology class at school, in which Mother Consilio skipped the relevant pages. The doctor I went to see about the monthly migraines I was suffering told me they'd disappear once I had babies, and handed me some pink and yellow tablets with the advice, 'You can take these – they might help until then'. Alexander Pope's poem 'A Little Learning' was on the school curriculum, warning that a little bit of knowledge was a dangerous thing – that we should drink deeply of it or not at all. That was the kind of advice I needed to hear.

When I was thirteen, Miss Murray taught us Henry Reed's war poem, 'Naming of Parts', and she mentioned that she needed a gun to explain it properly. I knew how to dismantle my father's gun from all the times I had seen him do it, so I brought it to school in my hockey bag and set it on her desk. Miss Murray was known to be highly strung and seeing the gun set her off. In a high-pitched voice, she demanded to know which one of us had brought in the gun. I owned up, claiming it was a favour to her, and asked if I could describe the parts to my classmates before she sent me home. The girls thought that was a good idea and we got to do the poem. I phoned my father from the head nun's office and he advised me to come home on the bus. I put the gun under a chair in the bus station cafe as I sat there waiting. The cafe sold single cigarettes and you could ask for one at the counter, but I decided that I'd better watch myself – I was a girl on the run with a gun.

Music and drama were the subjects in which I didn't get distracted. Mr Burgess was the only male teacher, and he understood that although I was good at acting, I couldn't hold a tune to save my life. But he still gave me a good part in *The Arcadians*, the school opera, which we performed, accompanied by a full orchestra, in front of a large audience of important people. When I told my father about my nerves, his advice was to get up there and stop worrying about who was looking at me. Like Alexander Pope, he was a wise man, and I did as he said. On the final night, we all bowed together on the stage, having acted our different parts, no matter whether singing or dancing. Each night of the performance, I changed out of a jockey outfit into a ballgown for my different roles, learning early in life to throw myself into the job with a passion.

It was the same story on the sports field where Mrs Ford, the PE teacher, gave up her Saturdays to take us for hockey and netball and drive us to faraway places, like Belfast, for athletics. Sister Elizabeth – Lizzie to us – acted as referee, racing around in her black habit with a whistle in her mouth. I started keeping a diary at around this time, and I wrote 'crap' in it each time we lost a match, which was not infrequently. What wasn't in the diary was the incident after a game the day that Mrs Ford wasn't able to bring me home. I was hitching a lift – which was something we did all the time, although I wasn't usually on my own. A man stopped and I got into his car, but as we got further up the road, he turned to me with a smirk on his face and said, 'If you make it worth my while, I'll take you all the way home.' My brain went into overdrive. A hundred yards further on, I knew he would have to slow down at the fork on the road and that's when I jumped out. Once I got out, I wanted to slam my hockey stick hard into the side of his car but instead I trailed my bag all the way to the Salmon Leap, my cousins' pub outside Coleraine, and phoned my father from there. He said how wise I was not to be taking lifts from strangers when I was alone on the road. I didn't say a word as I felt I was the one who had made a mistake. Deep inside I think I knew it was the creep who was to blame, but that didn't stop me from feeling angry at myself. At the age of fifteen, it was another of life's lessons. After that, I didn't feel as invincible.

When we brought our sporting trophies home, my mother would say, 'You have a gift from God and be thankful.' She gave all the praise to God in the belief that any gifts we had came from Him. She also believed self-praise was no praise and had little respect for those who puffed themselves up. I absorbed all this, and if someone complimented or congratulated me, I would reply, 'Sure, that's nothing.' I didn't know then that taking pride in my achievements would have been good for my self-esteem – that was a term I had yet to learn.

My mother would always advise: 'Walk humbly, do justice, love tenderly.' I watched her put those words from the prophet Micah into practice herself when John went off to St Columb's College in Derry. He hated it there. I wrote him long letters to cheer him up, telling him how lucky he was to be getting a good education. John didn't think he was lucky to be stuck in a dorm instead of being out in the fields with the cattle. My mother wasn't prepared to see him so unhappy, and he didn't go back to St Columb's after Halloween.

Having read Enid Blyton's books and the *Bunty* comic strip about the 'Four Marys' at St Elmo's school, my sister Mary decided that boarding school must be exciting. She was dreaming of midnight feasts, but when it didn't turn out like that, she also came home by Christmas and that was the end of that nonsense.

When the head priest at St Patrick's in Maghera, the school both my brothers attended, was making decisions on which boys were fit for the grammar stream, my mother was told that Terence was heading for the intermediate stream. She wasn't having any of that and made the unusual decision to move him, first to a school in Ballymoney and then to the Protestant grammar school at Dalriada, where she believed he would get a better education. As a result, Terence and I ended up in the same school year. It was lucky that he had already made his Confirmation before he got to Dalriada – at the time there was an outlandish rule that children couldn't be confirmed if they were attending a Protestant school.

Even if it had come about by default, Terence benefited from his integrated education. There was little difference between his Protestant school and my Catholic one. We were both good at sport, and neither of us cared whether the game we were playing was English or Irish. He was on the rugby and GAA teams; I played hockey and camogie. It also turned out that our schools' curricula were identical, even down to history, in which any mention of Ireland was missing. The only difference was that I learned Irish for the first three years – which meant I had more craic than he had at the Gaeltacht each summer. When we tried to study together, he would put on Led Zeppelin; I preferred Leonard Cohen. There were non-stop rows over which music was better.

When it came to choosing O levels, I decided to take all three sciences, but since Mother Consilio hadn't a clue, we ended up teaching ourselves. Only four girls – I wasn't one of them – ended up taking science to A level, and had to walk down the road to the Coleraine Academical Institution – we called it 'the Inst' – for all their classes. Unless we were prepared to do that, we couldn't do science. I chose English, Geography and French so as not to close off any options. I wasn't sure what I wanted to do, but I didn't want to be restricted to teaching or nursing, which were the most popular career choices for girls at Loreto.

In my last few years at school I studied hard during the week and played hard at weekends. I wrote 'shattered' in my diary each Saturday morning after another Friday night out. I turned night into day, averaging about four hours' sleep. I had still enough stamina to write in my diary, 'Got up like a lark to go and play hockey' but by the end of the same day I wrote, 'Must get more sleep.' I was lucky to be a teenager during the golden age of the Irish showbands. As Mary and I and half a dozen friends gathered together in our bedroom to get ready on a Friday night, the Marian Hall across the street might as well have been Las Vegas. Brian Coll and the Plattermen, Big Tom and the Mainliners and, best of all, the Miami Showband all came regularly. Mary had a sewing machine and ran up the latest fashions – making the best dresses that I always wanted to wear. The night that she wouldn't lend me one, I cut a piece out of her culottes and the ensuing row went on for so long that my mother told us that we wouldn't be going anywhere unless we stopped fighting. Even with the arguments over what to wear, the prepping was more fun than the dances. We could watch the crowd from our window and work out the best time to make our entrance.

By the time we got to the hall, all the girls were already lined up on one side, waiting for someone to ask them to dance. The charge from the lads came at the break in each set, with a surge that could push us backwards into the ladies toilet. Standing in the front row, I would hear, 'Would you like to dance?', but I was never sure who was being asked. If a lad had overdosed on Dutch courage and slurred, 'Would you like an orange juice?' I would usually reply, 'No thanks, I'm on solids now.' The skill was to decipher what he was saying in the first place. There were fisticuffs when a lad looked the wrong way at another man's woman – their main aim was to show how tough they all were. No matter how much I looked forward to each Friday night, my diary entries of 'Bored' and 'Yuck, yuck, yuck' tell a different story. The church was complaining that the mad craze for dancing was turning us girls into a seething mass of emotion but that wasn't the case for me.

My brother Terence's best friend was Martin O'Neill, who came to the dances occasionally but, because he didn't ask anyone to dance, the closest I got to him was watching him from the sidelines on the football pitch. He was one of the shy ones, but not so shy the day he and my brother played for the Derry GAA minors and lost the All-Ireland final at Croke Park in 1969. A few years later, in 1971, when he was in England playing soccer for Nottingham Forest in the First Division, my schoolfriend and I ended up staying with him on our way to our summer jobs in London. He brought us to a nightclub in Nottingham, which was a step up from Kelly's in Portrush, the one we'd gone to at home and that my mother referred to as 'a den of iniquity' because it served alcohol.

The other entertainment on offer close to home was the picture house in Kilrea, where the sound of the rain beating on the tin roof often meant that we couldn't even hear the film. The usher, Paddy Park, had a torch that he shone on courting couples in the back row. Each time we saw his light go on, we would turn around to get a good look – the action was always better there than on the screen.

Jones's Café was more exciting and had a jukebox. The night my mother came rattling her ring on the window, we had just paid to hear Nancy Sinatra singing 'These Boots are Made for Walking', but she was gesticulating that we better walk our boots smartly down home. Although my parents were much more liberal than many of my friends' parents, it was always us girls and not the boys who were asked to do everything in moderation. The boys were given much more freedom while we were expected to behave like modest convent girls. I went beyond moderation when, at the age of fifteen, I smuggled bottles of cider from Coleraine to have before the dance in the Marian Hall. My friend Jill and I drank a can each inside the ladies' toilet beside the cattle mart and then headed to the dance, chewing gum as we walked past Father Deery, terrified he would smell the drink on our breath. We only did it the once – it wasn't worth the effort. Whenever we went to a dance away from Kilrea, and arrived home late, my mother's words were always the same: 'Thank God you are safe, I haven't slept a wink all night,' even when she had been fast asleep.

Mary was the goody-goody and was dating a guy who was just the same. He was a boarder at Garron Tower, and we could have guessed then that one day he would become a bishop. I was going out with Liam O'Kane – he had a car and was able to take me to Kelly's. His family was known as the 'Pope' Kanes. That was because a relative wore a coat that looked like a pontiff's cape – but there was no chance of my date becoming Pope.

When we were teenagers, there were even fewer opportunities to mix with Protestants than there had been when we were younger. We danced in different halls and went to different schools. For the seven years that we shared the same bus every morning, we rarely exchanged a word. The Protestant boys attended the Inst; we went to the convent. They called us 'the Virgins on the hill'. The nuns made sure it stayed that way. I wanted to know what it would be like to date a Protestant boy but I could only dream about that. From my bedroom window I could see the fun that the girls and boys were having at the Young Farmers' Club dance in the Orange Hall. Fraternising was permitted between the sexes but not between the two religions, and there was zero tolerance for anyone who mixed up the rules.

In 1969, I began to read about violence on the streets of Derry. The *Irish News* described it as 'the worst flare-up since the 1921 Troubles'. What I didn't know then was that members of my extended family had been affected by this earlier violence. My father's eldest sister, known to

us as Aunt Sadie, had joined Cumann na mBan during the 1916 Easter
Rising. She had met her future husband, Johnny Haughey, when he was
a fugitive hiding from the Black and Tans, the auxiliary force recruited
by the British army who were sent out to round up IRA members. It was
Aunt Sadie's job to bring Johnny Haughey messages 'on the run' and
to warn him about the soldiers. They knew where he lived because his
house was the one with the white marble crosses on its chimney. When
they came to arrest him and couldn't find him, they shot up the crosses
instead.

A year after the Anglo-Irish treaty was signed in 1921, the young
couple left the six counties, and moved to Mayo on the southern side
of the border. General Michael Collins knew they would have been in
trouble had they stayed – the pogroms against republicans had already
started in Northern Ireland – so he commissioned Johnny Haughey into
the Free State army. As the years progressed, my father listened to what he
always called 'the Athlone news' on RTÉ to hear how his nephew, Charlie
Haughey, was faring in the Fianna Fáil party in Dublin.

My mother's side of the family was also affected. Her cousin, Dan
McKenna, had been the commander of the IRA's second northern
division. He too had had to go south, where he also joined the Free State
army, later becoming its chief of staff while his brother, John, became a
colonel. My parents didn't talk about what had happened to their relatives
– but they took a keen interest in local politics. My father never missed
a news bulletin.

Those events in 1921 were a foreshadowing of what we were about to
live through. Joan Baez came in 1969 to the Marian Hall and sang the US
civil rights anthem during one of our Friday night dances. With violence
breaking out around us, Father Deery wanted us to hear about civil rights
from Joan Baez. When she sang 'we shall live in peace someday' and 'we
shall overcome', I didn't know which would come first.

People in our rural area weren't receiving much help from the state
and had decided, back in 1963, to start a cooperative movement,
moving things up a notch to form a co-op farming enterprise on land
they acquired at Swatragh, County Derry. The idea of starting a co-op
to benefit local people had originated in Glencolmcille, Donegal. The
movement was going from strength to strength with its livestock market

and auction, giving locals a sense of ownership of their own enterprise. John Hume promoted the idea of credit unions the following year, in the hope that they would help to save people from loan sharks. My father thought it was a good initiative and kept telling the people in the town that they would increase their savings by dying, as the credit union doubled the savings of the person who had died and paid for the funeral. Our neighbours in Kilrea thought that was reason enough to join – they were the generation who remembered the shame of their relatives being buried in unmarked paupers' graves.

In 1965, our cousin Charlie Haughey was in the Fianna Fáil party when the taoiseach, Seán Lemass, came to Northern Ireland to meet Terence O'Neill. It was the first time the leaders from each side of the border had met since the partition of Ireland in 1921. The meeting was televised and we watched with interest because of our family connection.

By the late 1960s, the opposition to the unfair system of government in Northern Ireland – unionist control and one-party rule – that had continued for almost fifty years was reaching boiling point. An *Irish News* headline at the time read 'Diabolical discrimination'. Many felt that nationalist politicians hadn't challenged the unionist discrimination against Catholics strongly enough, so were toppled from their elected roles by independents like Ivan Cooper and John Hume. A similar contestation was taking place on the unionist side, resulting in the overthrow of Terence O'Neill, who was forced to resign on 1 May 1969. His resignation followed the planting of a bomb at the Silent Valley reservoir that was blamed on the IRA, but was in fact put there by loyalists from the Ulster Volunteer Force (UVF), with the express aim of getting rid of the unionist leader, who they felt was making too many concessions to Catholics and working too closely with his counterparts in the south.

I was watching the protests of the US civil rights movement on TV and listening to Martin Luther King saying, 'We will not be satisfied until justice rolls down like water and righteousness like a mighty stream.' I felt as though he was speaking to us. When the *Sunday Times* referred to Northern Ireland as 'John Bull's political slum', I thought of the place in Kilrea known as Kabul, the very poorest housing in the town. In nearby Rasharkin, a housing estate was known as Tin Town because of its corrugated roofs. Catholic families were living in these conditions long after housing reform had begun. The infant mortality rate was among the highest in Europe and one in four houses was unfit for human habitation. The only slum clearance that had happened in Northern Ireland was by default – when the Luftwaffe dropped its bombs on areas long scheduled for redevelopment. It was a shameful record for the Northern Ireland government. Working-class people began to raise these grievances on both sides of the community divide but it was Catholics who were suffering the most since they lived in the areas in which there was little to no investment.

There were additional grievances because of the actions of the RUC and the way its officers policed Catholic communities. We had direct experience of this when, in 1967, the B-Specials, a notorious section of the RUC, stopped our car outside Portglenone. One of them pulled a small statue of the Virgin Mary off the dashboard, asking my mother, 'What's that thing doing there?' and then threw it on to the ground. It seemed to us that night that the police could do what they liked under the Special Powers Act. I subsequently learnt that even the apartheid regime in South Africa didn't have such extensive powers as the ones that existed in Northern Ireland after partition. Local Catholic communities didn't trust the government or the police because they hadn't proved themselves trustworthy. We were seen as extreme when all we expected was equality of treatment for all citizens living under the UK government's remit, whether they were in Kilrea or Kingston upon Thames.

The demand for equal rights led to one of the first meetings of the Northern Ireland Civil Rights Association, which took place in 1967 in Noone's Hotel in Maghera, not far from us. Both Mrs Noone and Kevin Agnew, the hosts of the meeting, were well known locally. The meeting initiated a call for an end to discrimination against Catholics in employment and in public-sector housing; an end to the Special Powers Act; and a franchise for local elections to put a stop to gerrymandering. In June 1968, nationalist MP Austin Currie organised a civil rights picket in Caledon to bring attention to the discrimination in housing. Emily Beattie, a nineteen-year-old single Protestant woman, and the secretary to a local unionist politician, had been allocated a new council house ahead of the Catholic Gildernew family, who were at the top of the housing waiting list. The nepotism and discrimination couldn't have been more blatant.

The chairperson of the Campaign for Democracy in Ulster, Paul Rose, was an MP at Westminster at the time. He told Austin Currie in 1968 that 'no British government – including this Labour government – will intervene to remedy injustice in Northern Ireland unless you people there force it to do so.' A doctor and his wife from Dungannon, Conn and Patricia McCluskey, decided that's what they had to do, so they set up the Campaign for Social Justice (CSJ). Prior to the founding of the CSJ, Patricia McCluskey was one of sixty-seven people, mainly women, who founded the Homeless Citizens' League, in response to the heartbreaking stories of young homeless families that Conn heard about while working as the local GP. Their first marches had taken place in Dungannon in 1963. When they later wrote a book about their experiences, Dr McCluskey sent me a copy with a note that said, 'People have forgotten that the civil rights movement was started exclusively by women.'

As the civil rights protests continued, I watched momentum build, people taking to the streets in their hundreds, men and women from all walks of life. Members of the Civil Rights Association felt they had had enough of sending letters to Westminster that were sent straight back to Stormont to the very minister who had been the cause of the complaints in the first place. On 5 October 1968, a public protest in Derry City was part of a change in strategy. The journalists and TV cameras recorded the event. Pictures went out that evening on the television showing terrified civilians forced off the streets by the police. People were running to seek shelter from the onslaught. One man was pictured screaming, having been struck in the groin by a police baton, and Gerry Fitt, the SDLP MP, was shown bleeding profusely from his head. John Hume's strong words against the police brutality brought him to international attention. The world's media flocked to Northern Ireland from that day on.

On 4 January 1969, a neighbour of mine from Kilrea, Maureen O'Kane – the niece of Jimmy, who had saved my finger years before – joined the student march from Belfast to Derry with members of the People's Democracy. Maureen was on the home straight when she was caught in an ambush at Burntollet Bridge, not far from Derry City. Maureen could see Ronald Bunting, the leader of the Ulster Protestant

Volunteers, who was well known for his anti-Catholic rhetoric, leading a mob that was armed to the teeth. Some of the marchers were hit with nail-embedded cudgels and pushed towards the river. A number had fallen in, unconscious. Maureen showed me her injuries when she got back home. We were outraged that no one was to be charged with assault. I sensed that things would never be the same again.

In 1969, when I was fifteen, I attended my first meeting of the Northern Ireland Civil Rights Association in Drumagarner hall, near Kilrea. Before I left that evening, Kevin McCorry, the secretary of NICRA, handed me my blue membership card. In February of the same year, Ivan Cooper came to Kilrea as he was running for election as an Independent MP. He needed all the support he could get – he had been denounced as a traitor by many in his own Protestant community for being a leading member of the civil rights movement. Our family in Kilrea hoped he would win – and on 24 February 1969 he took the seat from Paddy Gormley, who had been the nationalist MP since 1953. I supported Ivan Cooper because of his demands for reforms. As it turned out, by the time some of these were introduced, it was too little, too late.

By August 1969, there was growing violence and unrest. In Derry City, from 12 to14 August, there were two days of non-stop rioting. Television pictures showed the Battle of the Bogside during which Citizens Defence Association members wore facemasks soaked in lemon and vinegar to counter the CS gas fired by the police. Petrol bombs entered folklore when a story circulated about a milkman getting a note in a bottle that said, 'No milk today please; but leave me 200 bottles.' When the dairy counted their stock later that week, it discovered that 43,000 bottles were missing. The most intense violence occurred in Belfast, with many businesses and homes burnt out. Thousands of people fled and we watched on television as families sat perched on lorries surrounded by their bits of furniture. They had become refugees in a war zone. The British army arrived under 'Operation Banner' that same month and were welcomed at first in the belief that they would be able to restore order and protect families in Catholic areas. But it wasn't long before those perceptions changed.

At home in Kilrea we met soldiers on the roads with boot-polish-blackened faces searching people as well as their cars, both night and day. In County Derry where I lived, Catholics felt the soldiers had become one sided in their support of the unionist politicians. Because the soldiers didn't recognise the names of local towns, they struggled with names like Maghera or Magherafelt. We would be held up at the checkpoint until a superior on the other end of a walkie-talkie was able to decipher the name, and give the go-ahead for us to proceed. When the soldiers stopped us close to home and asked where we were going, we'd reply, 'Still Kilrea'. That's what got written down, as though it were a real placename. The soldiers hadn't a clue we were going somewhere else in the same town.

The 1970s didn't start too well for us when, on 6 May 1970, the news broke that our cousin Charlie Haughey had been dismissed as minister for finance in the Irish government over the allegation that he had plotted to supply arms to the Provisional IRA, along with another of his cabinet colleagues. It turned out he had been following cabinet directions to procure weapons for the Irish Army that potentially could be needed to protect Catholics against the pogrom that Northern nationalist MPs were warning of in 1969. He was acquitted later in the same year, but the trials cast a long shadow, not least for our family in the North.

Shortly after the trial ended, loyalists painted sectarian graffiti on the walls of the toilets in the Salmon Leap, our cousins' pub in Coleraine, and later came back to spray the bar with gunfire. No one was injured but we asked ourselves who would be next, deeply worried that a member of our family would be targeted again. Police arrested the perpetrators and one of them claimed that his motivation for the attack was a thirst for revenge, in the belief that Charlie Haughey had run guns into Northern Ireland. I came across this man many years later and heard him say, 'It was a very cruel time when morality went out the window.' It was a miracle none of us were killed.

By 1970, we were witnessing the emergence of militant republicanism and loyalist paramilitarism. I saw how quickly ethnic and political identities became entrenched. The peace walls dividing the two communities grew in number in response to the demands from locals for increased safety. The coverage of the Falls Road Curfew during the summer of 1970 was the first time I saw women in action in large numbers. When word had gone out that the British Army was preventing food vans from getting into the area, three thousand women formed a platoon, putting supplies into prams for the curfew zone. They said they wanted to show their solidarity with the women affected, but for some the additional incentive was to defy the British Army.

That same year, Prime Minister Ted Heath asked Reginald Maudling, his home secretary, to visit Northern Ireland. On his return to London, Maudling was reported as saying, 'For God's sake bring me a large Scotch. What a bloody awful country.' After internment was introduced the following year I felt we had become an awful bloody country. On 10 August 1971 at 6 a.m., Catholic homes in Kilrea were raided by British army combat units who kicked in doors to drag two of our neighbours from their beds. As time went on, news started coming in that some of the men were being subjected to inhuman treatment – referred to later as the 'five techniques' of torture – and the language of human rights began to seep into my vocabulary. Police intelligence was so poor that many of those arrested were known locally to be opposed to the IRA whilst others had no connection to the organisation. The police didn't include IRA women in their internment net. That reflected the stereotype that the combatants were all male. That was soon to change.

When loyalists started getting arrested in February 1973, most nationalists believed it was a sop to make the whole thing look more even-handed. My cousin Declan McCotter was arrested around this time – the family was relieved when he returned home that same evening. Internment was a public relations disaster and alienated the army from the nationalist people. Given the state's inability to reform, it wrote the script for more conflict. It led me to conclude that if any government denies its people justice, they may deny it peace. The polarisation and systemic abuses led us to a very dark place.

A civil disobedience campaign began against internment. A rent and rates strike started, during which people – including our family – were asked to withhold their payments to the government. It became a widespread campaign of peaceful resistance. The first demonstration against internment that I joined was on Magilligan Strand on 22 January 1972. On that bright sunny day, there were men and women that

I recognised from all different walks of life among the four thousand protesters heading up the beach. The organiser shouted on a loudhailer that, despite the march having been officially banned by state authorities, we were not breaking the law since a treaty existed between the UK and Ireland that allowed us to walk inside the tideline. I had no idea what he was talking about but I took him at his word and hoped the army had also heard of this treaty. We were empty-handed on a sandy beach, so there was no risk of stones being thrown at the army. Above the sand dunes, I could see the Nissen huts that had been purposely built for internment – some of those being held there were climbing on to the roofs to see the march.

Behind me on the beach, Mary was walking with my father who, at fifty-seven, was going at a slower pace. I was glad our local GP, Dr McGurk, was beside them after I saw people ahead choking on CS gas. Word was out that the gas that the soldiers had been firing was coming in our direction but because of the strong wind, it blew back into their faces. They hadn't been wearing gas masks and were scrambling to put them on. Chaos was breaking out all around – and I was shocked when the person next to me collapsed, having been hit by a rubber bullet. John Hume stepped forward to tell the army commander that he should be ashamed of himself for giving the command to fire at peaceful demonstrators at such close range. The soldiers seemed undaunted, walloping marchers with their truncheons, which prompted yet another complaint from John Hume. He was the elected Member of the Westminster Parliament but was being told by a British Army commander from the Parachute Regiment to go home.

I had become separated from my brother Terence who, it turned out, had gone to get a closer look at the 'men behind the wire' – he wanted to see if any of our neighbours from Kilrea were among the internees on the roof. When I finally caught up with him, he could hardly walk as he had stepped on a nail sticking out of a plank. I had little sympathy since it meant we had to carry him back across the dunes. An army helicopter was still hovering above us, with its loudhailer informing us that the march was illegal, but as darkness was falling we shouted to the pilot to keep his spotlights beaming on us since we needed them to find our way back to the car park. When I got there, I could see young lads breaking into the Magilligan dance hall and taking chocolate bars out of the slot machines. They knew the dance hall owner had assisted in the construction work at the internment camp and they felt some kind of satisfaction in vandalising his property. It was a stupid thing to do as these were the kinds of actions that tended to make the news, rather than the peaceful conduct at the marches. As it turned out, the reports that followed focused on the Parachute Regiment's atrocious behaviour. I wrote in my diary, 'When will this ever end?' If the army thought their actions that day would prevent future marches from going ahead, the reverse was the case.

At school on Monday morning, my friend Ann O'Hagan passed around a rubber bullet that she had taken from the beach as a souvenir. Everyone was shocked to see it – it was shaped like a very thick pencil with a silver spike at the end. Our school friends speculated that we could have been blinded or maimed. When the teacher asked if any of us had been wearing our school uniform, I didn't know if she was concerned that we would bring the school into disrepute, or if she was trying to work out if the army could have known that there were school girls among the marchers.

The following Sunday, 30 January 1972, Terence got a lift to the march that was taking place in Derry. My friends and I had been turned back, so I watched it on TV with my parents. When we saw a priest we knew, Father Edward Daly, waving his white handkerchief in front of a casualty, we knew something terrible had happened. The agony on people's faces was stark and by six o'clock, the news came through that thirteen people had been shot dead. Terence still hadn't come home so my mother kept saying her prayers until he showed up. At the funerals three days later, our hearts went out to the families. Our brother was home with us but, because of the actions of the Parachute Regiment, relatives of theirs were being buried.

We waited to hear if there would be a day of mourning after Bloody Sunday. I wrote in my diary, 'Lot of bitter feeling. Paratroopers were disgraceful. But the school still isn't closed.' By Tuesday I wrote, 'Big row at school. Demands for a National Day of Mourning.' By Wednesday, the bishops had said that all schools should close, but when we returned on Thursday, my friend Ann O'Hagan ended up getting punished for causing disruption in the school earlier in the week. According to my diary, she was 'kicked out until Monday'. Calls for a Civil Disruption Day came from the Civil Rights Association – people were to take to the streets again to protest against the army's actions on Bloody Sunday. It was supposed to be for one day but civil disruption would continue for the next three decades.

The week after Bloody Sunday I was driving to a French evening class with my friend Grainne when a car slammed into me, causing me to skid across the road, go into a ditch and overturn into a field. I found it hard to climb out the car's front window as my collarbone was broken. After my father had brought me home, we were getting ready to leave for the hospital when the phone rang with the caller on the other end asking my father if he had a scrap car for sale. It was suddenly clear that it had been no accident: the other driver had deliberately crashed into me. When the police came to take a statement, they said my attackers were probably the same men who had damaged two other cars in the town that night. There was silence when I asked – because of the cars that had been targeted – if the attack was sectarian. I spent useless weeks looking at cars to see if there was cream paint from my father's on any of them. The culprits were never caught and I bucked myself up and got on with life.

I had recovered enough from the crash for my father to take me to Newry the following weekend for another protest. I wrote in my diary, 'Hope there won't be any trouble today.' As we set off to walk, I could see a line of women leading the march. Ann Hope, who would later become a friend of mine, was on the front line with a bandage around a head wound she'd sustained on Bloody Sunday. A helicopter that was hovering above came down close to us. Its loudhailer informed the thousands of demonstrators that the march was illegal and that we were liable to be arrested. I had heard the same thing on Magilligan Strand. As locals handed out tea, I noticed black flags flying from their upstairs windows in memory of those who had been killed on Bloody Sunday. By the time we reached the field, it was getting dark. There was already a sea of people, silent and united in grief. I wondered if this was how life was really meant to be.

On 1 February, Prime Minister Ted Heath announced that a public inquiry into the events of Bloody Sunday was to go ahead, and it was to take place in a building near my school in Coleraine. My desk was beside the window on the second floor and I was able to watch the helicopters coming and going each day, bringing whoever was needed to represent the government side. The tribunal was one of the shortest in history – it didn't take too long for Chief Justice Widgery to conclude that the soldiers had been fired on first and there was 'no reason to suppose that the soldiers would have opened fire otherwise'. It became widely known as the 'Widgery Whitewash'. I was watching the last vestiges of allegiance to a system of justice disappearing. It drained the spirit out of the civil rights movement, but it wasn't the end to the search for justice. I didn't know then that I would be wearing a very different hat when a fresh inquiry into the events of Bloody Sunday was declared.

I wrote again and again in my diary, 'Troubles go on.' When the British introduced direct rule, my entry for 24 March 1972 was 'Stormont is gone. Heath's proposals coming in.' But four months later, on 21 July 1972 – a day that became known as Bloody Friday – the political situation deteriorated into chaos when the IRA exploded nineteen bombs in Belfast, killing nine people and wounding over a hundred. It blew the heart out of the city centre and it blew the heart out of me. I didn't think things could get any worse, and then three no-warning IRA bombs exploded in the village of Claudy, in my own county of Derry, killing nine people, including an eight-year-old child.

The bombing campaigns continued, and, again, an entry in my diary – 'Bomb scares galore' – shows that they had become a frequent occurrence. That same summer of 1972, we stood outside the Marian Hall in Kilrea one Friday night until the bomb squad declared that it was safe for us to go back in. But next time, it wasn't a hoax. Two hundred pounds of explosives went off in the phone exchange across the street from our house. I felt the blast just before a broken pane of glass knocked over my inkwell, covering me in ink. When I came downstairs my mother thought that I had been badly cut and was covered in blood, but the cause was my fancy red ink. Although the milk bottles were still intact on the windowsill, the roof tiles and windows were in smithereens on the street. I stuck Sellotape on the replacement glass to see if it would stop the panes from shattering the next time. Once again, we moved on with our lives.

Each time, the bombs seemed to get bigger – one contained 750lb of explosives and caused extensive damage to the town: six shops had to be demolished and six families' homes were destroyed. I woke up when the house began to shake. Aunt Mary was staying in my bedroom and I knew of her fear of thunder – when she heard a clap begin she would sprinkle Holy Water and say the words, 'Be gone, Satan.' We found her under the bedclothes that evening, saying her prayers. When I told her a bomb had gone off in the town, she replied, 'Thanks be to God – I thought it was thunder.' Bombs were becoming ordinary everyday events. I wrote in my diary, 'The dance is going ahead on Friday night. Bomb damage expected to cost one million pounds.'

During the long summer holidays after I finished school, I headed off to London for a summer job. I was happy to say goodbye to Portrush's Lido cafe, where I had spent a few weeks working for a minuscule wage. There was better money to be had in London and I enjoyed the novelty of not being asked to show a security man what was in my handbag every time I went into a shop. The only flat that was affordable for six of us – Mary, me and our four friends – was in Clapham Common. It meant commuting into Victoria Station by train and catching two more buses to take us to the Littlewoods store at Marble Arch. As we travelled the final leg of our journey home one evening, a man flashed at us from inside the carriage. We sat in silence until I decided to give him a rendition of 'Faith of our Fathers'. The other thing we hated about that train was having to fork out for the tickets. Money never seemed to last until Friday pay day, when we each got a little brown envelope with pound notes sticking out of one corner.

In spite of the lack of money, it was a great summer – the last one I spent with my school friends. The A level results had arrived in August and it was time to head back to Northern Ireland – I had got the grades I needed to get into Queen's.

3

Belfast, Detroit and Beyond

'Injustice anywhere is a threat to justice everywhere.'

Martin Luther King, Jr

I came to Belfast in September 1972 to study for a degree in Social Sciences. I found a flat on the Lisburn Road with my sister Mary, who was training to be a PE teacher at Jordanstown. We'd left the search for somewhere to live so late that we were the beggars who couldn't be choosers. The flat had been lying vacant because no one wanted to live beside the UDA drinking club next door. In spite of where we were living, I liked the city and was looking forward to becoming more independent. The next years were among the best for me but, because of the Troubles, they were also the worst.

In my first year I had chosen to study geography, psychology, sociology and anthropology; all four subjects kept me busy. In Freshers Week, I signed up for hockey in the winter and athletics in the summer. I was working hard and playing hard, but unlike at school, I was out every night rather than just Friday. By November, I was enjoying myself so much that I was staying in Belfast every weekend. It helped that I was on a full grant, so I only had to work during the Easter and summer holidays and not during term time.

Belfast students stayed in a clique, which meant that those of us from the country did the same. But that quickly changed for me when I met Deirdre, Sheila and Maria, who'd been hanging out in the Students' Union in their last year at school in Belfast and knew their way around. I was eighteen years old and finally getting a chance to discover whether

Protestant boys were any different. It turned out that all boys were the same: fixated on cars and football. There were certainly some students who seemed determined not to mix with anyone from 'the other side of the fence', but I wasn't one of them and neither was the law crowd. Their names told you which foot they kicked with but Norman and Alistair were pals with Rory and Eamon. I wrote in my diary that 'the boys brought me flowers for my birthday, stolen from the garden at Queen's.' My other good friends were from the hockey team, but I wasn't happy the day one of the players ran on to the pitch shouting, 'For God and Ulster.'

Patsy Hennessy took up some space in my diary in that first year and I was still missing him on my birthday after we broke up. Although I was enjoying meeting new people, I was completely shocked when I heard a young woman say she had come to Queen's to find a husband. I couldn't understand why anyone would want to settle down so young – I had read somewhere that young women would go to university to get a Mrs Degree, but I wasn't one of those.

If the walls of the Students' Union could talk, what would they say about those years? There was a Young Unionist club, a Republican club and a Labour club, and all were flourishing. Some students sorted themselves out by geography, faith and politics. I was there to broaden my mind. I had heard enough dogma and I didn't want to hear any more from the cynics who thought that 'right' was all on one side. Others were withdrawing from politics altogether because they didn't like any of it. They were already suffering from 'Troubles fatigue' and switched off when the subject came up.

Sunday night was the chaplaincy Mass followed by drinks in the Union bar. I wasn't the only one who was expected 'to keep the faith' when I was away from home. Like most mothers, mine asked me on the phone each Sunday night what time I'd been to Mass. The chaplaincy at the university was like a sanctuary: a place to rendezvous before another busy week. Around that time, I began to read about liberation theology, which brought challenging messages on taking the part of the most vulnerable rather than the most powerful, and making it clear that working with the marginalised was much more liberating. I wanted to get involved in that. For me, parity was better than charity since it meant a more equitable outcome; to others in the church, this smacked of socialism. I was reading Paulo Freire's *Pedagogy of the Oppressed* with its simple message: support should start from the point the potential recipients are at. That's what I wanted to do next – I was young and the world was my oyster. The theories were challenging but I was just as interested in their application.

University was not just a time for self-analysis; I had plenty of work to get on with. When I wrote my assignment on 'The Geographical Implications of The World Population Growth' I stated, 'the simple expansion of food production will not provide a way out of the world's dilemma. We need birth control, contraception and family planning to deal with the problem.' I had concluded that 'one of man's biggest problems is learning to control himself.' I was hoping the tutor wouldn't take that personally. He gave four words of feedback: 'You are writing concisely.' Perhaps he was offended or couldn't be bothered to extend his very short sentence along with his B++. More constructive feedback would have been welcome. In all the subjects that I had chosen, it was the study and description of women's roles that particularly interested me, whether it was Margaret Mead's study of the influence of culture on Melanesian women, or John Bowlby's maternal deprivation theory. This theory argued that mothers in waged work deprived their children of affection. It had sunk into most people's heads, even when I was a student, that a woman had to give up her job once she was married. Both Protestant and Catholic churches helped that thinking by insisting that a woman's primary role was as a housewife and a mother. Working-class men were obsessed with keeping 'their women' at home in order to keep up with the Joneses, even when they couldn't afford to lose the women's wages. It was a no-win situation for women, just as it had been for my mother when she gave up her job, and independence, to marry. Years later, these thoughts were still in my head when I came to convince the state that a child out of a nursery meant a woman out of a job.

On 2 October 1972, Military Reaction Force undercover operatives disguised as workers for the Four Square Laundry were attacked by an IRA unit following the disclosure that the laundry had been set up to gather intelligence on the IRA. Dr Gill Boehringer, who was known as one of our best sociology lecturers, had been doing research in the same part of Belfast; he and his student researchers were also accused of gathering information for the British Army. By the time that was found to be untrue, it was too late – he had already given up his job at the university to return to Australia. I got the feeling that there were agents everywhere especially when I saw an IRA poster with a picture of a man half in civvies and half in a British Army uniform, with the warning, 'This Soldier Could Be Standing Beside You. Watch What You Say.' From then on, when we talked about politics, we spoke in a whisper.

My diary that month read, 'Shooting outside tonight. What a place to have a flat.' At first we'd thought it was fireworks but then we realised that it had to be real shots since fireworks were banned. We crawled to the back of the flat and stayed there until it went quiet. This became a regular occurrence. Later that month, when a bomb was placed in the UDA drinking club that was next to us, soldiers came to tell us to evacuate the flat. When we shouted through the window that we were in our pyjamas, a soldier replied, 'Well, hurry up but take your time.' Chris and Rose Burke, friends from home who shared the flat with us, bounded down the attic stairs with Mary and me, taking out hair rollers as we went. The bomb was a hoax, but the one the following week, in the supermarket a hundred yards down the road, was the real McCoy. We were evacuated again and were made to stand much further down the street. The explosion blew cans of food high into the air and we gathered as many as we could carry back to the flat.

On 31 October 1972, James Kerr was shot on the opposite side of the Lisburn Road to where Mary and I were riding our bikes. A policeman nearby had seen what had happened and caught the gunman as he ran past us down the street. It turned out that he was a member of the Red Hand Commando and had told the policeman that he had killed 'a Fenian bastard'. At the inquest that followed, the victim was described as 'being in the wrong place at the wrong time'. I was to hear that too many times. James Kerr was a seventeen-year-old Catholic working as a garage attendant and his workplace was the right place for him to be. In 1989, the republican armed group, the Irish People's Liberation Organisation (IPLO), killed the gunman Stephen McCrea with an Uzi sub-machine gun as he sat in a pub on the Shankill Road after his release from prison.

They claimed it was a reprisal for James Kerr's murder. The sectarianism continued; the only thing that had changed was the size of the weapons.

I became friendly with Peter Gormley through the athletics team. By the time I met him, I was already aware that he had suffered a terrible tragedy. On 27 November 1972, Peter's father, who was an eye surgeon at the Mater, had been taking his younger sons to school. He had changed his route because of a road closure and was taking a shortcut when three loyalists attacked the car, riddling it with bullets and killing his brother Rory. Another brother and Peter's father were also wounded. The boys had been wearing their St Malachy's school uniform, which identified them as Catholics. The gunman was said to be about fifteen years of age, a year older than Rory. What Peter and his family had gone through always stayed with me.

To get away from it all, I applied for a summer job in the States in 1973. I decided to go with my friend Deirdre Kennedy, and we saved up for our tickets from what was left over out of our student grants. We went as part of a student visa programme that provided us with a list of employers offering summer work. When we arrived in Manhattan, although we'd put our watches back by five hours, we felt they were light years ahead. The stresses of Belfast took a while to wear off, and we jumped each time we heard a car backfiring. But as time went on, the tension subsided and we soon began to enjoy our newfound freedom, zooming around the streets of Manhattan. We didn't want to leave New York city, but we didn't have the money to stay.

We bought tickets for the Greyhound bus and headed for Asbury Park on the Jersey Shore and our first US jobs. The first thing we needed to do was find somewhere to live – we rented a bedroom at the top of a four-storey wooden house. We weren't to know it when we looked around, but it turned into an oven on summer nights. The fire escape was our only relief and we sat there for hours looking at the wondrous wooden houses along the street. Asbury Park had a huge amusement park and we worked in the arcade, where I spent long hours shouting into a loudhailer, 'Roll up, roll up! A dime a time!' My Irish accent boomed across the arcade, leading to enquiries about the length of my drive from Ireland and compliments about speaking English so well. When the park closed at midnight, we spent our time in a pub listening to live music.

The band asked Deirdre and myself to come with them on their coast-to-coast tour. It was a tempting offer, but I could hear in my ear my mother's loud questions, 'You are going where and with whom?'

After three weeks, we'd had enough of working twelve-hour shifts, seven days a week, so we caught another Greyhound bus, this time to Wildwood, further south on the Jersey Shore. We knew there would be jobs there because two of our friends had staked it out the year before. By the time we hit its boardwalk, the town was buzzing and living up to its name. The first night in our new boarding house we discovered that the man who was living in the attic could only access his room through ours, via a door behind a curtain. The landlady had mentioned that there was a room above us but we didn't know that the only way to it was through our bedroom. It was the strangest way to meet Tony Novosel from Pittsburgh, a man who became a good friend when we needed one, and remains so until this day.

We worked hard for a week as hotel chambermaids, only to be told that our hospital corners on the beds weren't up to standard. We moved to jobs on the boardwalk where the shop owners were up to all kinds of tricks. There was no tax on clothes in New Jersey, but they didn't tell customers that. We found a new apartment where we were jammed cheek by jowl with ten others. We barely had any more privacy than before, but it didn't matter to me – I was out every night and felt as free as a bird.

In that time of great fun and happiness, a terrible thing happened. We were all out one night when a man we'd met asked one of our friends to go to his house to pick up some things for the party we'd invited him to. When she got home that night, she told us he had raped her. We were all devastated but supported her decision not to report it as we were in a foreign country. We stuck to each other like putty after that, looking out for each other, especially at night.

That summer, young men were still being drafted for the Vietnam war. I knew what the draft meant because my cousins, all brothers, were in New York – they'd gone over to work for one of my father's sisters, who had emigrated in 1930. My cousin Richard hightailed it out of New York and back to Ireland as soon as he got his call up, and cousin James made it home too but cousin Charlie got conscripted. They were not to know that President Carter would in years to come pardon draft evaders of the Vietnam War and that I would later share a platform with him, and hear him say that this pardon was his way of showing mercy.

After we left Wildwood, we hired a car and visited the sights in Washington DC, including Arlington cemetery. While I was there, I saw soldiers in white uniforms carrying a coffin, wrapped in the stars and stripes, and worked out that the soldier must have been killed in Vietnam. I remembered doing an essay at school with the title: 'Ask not what your country can do for you but what you can do for your country.' As the pallbearers passed by, I wondered what they would have said. Nixon was still sending soldiers to Vietnam when he already knew that he couldn't win the war. At the boarding house back in Wildwood, I had met a recently returned veteran. He told me how much he valued the Supreme Court's judgment when it ruled in favour of the *New York Times* and the *Washington Post* for reporting that intelligence agencies had been wrong not to disclose that the USA was losing. Even so, the media was still getting the blame for the loss of support for the war in Vietnam. I was in the States again the following summer when President Nixon resigned because of the Watergate scandal. It was good to see him finally held to account.

We were back in Belfast in time to start our second year at Queen's by September 1973. Mary and I were sharing a flat this time with my schoolfriends Eileen, Chris and Kate – although our bedroom had a leaking roof, the flat was an improvement on the previous year's. We paid £14 rent each month – I didn't have enough money to have my glasses fixed but I'd enough to go to the Students' Union, where life at night went on much as before. A debate between Ian Paisley and Merlyn Rees created some excitement and afterwards I wrote, 'debate excellent', but I wrote the same thing in my diary the following week when comedian Frank Carson appeared. I also managed to get to the poetry and short story readings. But my diary also records the pandemonium that was going on outside the Students' Union. On 12 November 1973 the entry reads: '21 bombs went off in Belfast. Really loud and frightening. Never heard so many before.' On 7 January 1974, I wrote, 'Shops bombed again. Very little left of them.' When I arrived home to find soldiers had surrounded the flat, I wrote, 'Army found guns and explosives in a garage opposite.' What should have been extraordinary was becoming very ordinary.

For a weekend's fun, Mary and I would occasionally hitch a lift to Dublin. One Friday, we got into a car with three men who turned out to be going to a Sinn Féin meeting. On the Sunday, on the way back, we took a lift, again with three men, but this time they turned out to be in the RUC. We pulled in for a bite to eat at the Border Inn between Newry and Dundalk, not knowing that a Provisional IRA commemoration was being held there. I realised something was up when the driver came out of the toilet, looking like he had seen a ghost. He shouted for us to head straight for the exit. Once we were on the road again, he told us that in the gents toilets he had seen a former prisoner whom he had interrogated at Springfield barracks. We were shocked by how much he told us – we probably shouldn't even have known that they were in the police; we had assumed they were rugby fans coming home from the match. It was risky for him to give us those details as we were strangers, but it was more than risky for men in the security services to stop at the Border Inn. I thought of the killings of three Scottish soldiers in 1971, lured out of Kelly's Cellars – a pub in Belfast city centre that was off limits to them – and shot by the IRA in the back of the head. Allegedly, women had been used for the 'honeytrap' plot. Beyond the tragedy of the killings, what also concerned me was that one of the soldiers was only seventeen, not eligible to vote but eligible to fight for his country. I must have had a good sense of what could have happened in the Border Inn as my diary entry for that Sunday evening reads: 'Glad to get home safe and sound.'

Before long, I was back in Dublin with the hockey team. I wrote 'great craic' in my diary after a pub crawl. Dublin seemed like a normal city when compared to Belfast. But that wasn't the case a month later when three car bombs exploded in the city on 17 May 1974. The UVF had detonated three 'no-warning' bombs, causing the deaths of twenty-six people and injuring hundreds of others. Ninety minutes later another car bomb went off, this time in Monaghan, killing six people and injuring another, who later died. It was the highest number of casualties in a single day of the Troubles at that time. The victims, most of them young women, were aged from five months to eighty years. The UVF had taken its war into the Republic and the border area had become a danger zone. My cousin Charlie, from Stranagone, was a customs man at Newry. It wasn't a good place to be working during the Troubles, given that the IRA had blown some of his close colleagues to pieces inside the customs huts. I wondered whether he had been at work the day the UVF men drove past with explosives in the back of their cars. Preventing this kind of attack was supposed to be the job of the security and intelligence services, but they said they didn't know a thing about it. In the aftermath, questions were flying around about how they could have been in the know about so many things but completely missed the plans for these major attacks.

The last two weeks of May that year were like fourteen days of hell. The Ulster Workers' Council (UWC) called a strike in protest against the Sunningdale Agreement, which was proposing power-sharing with nationalists and a cross-border Council of Ireland. The strikers envisaged it as opening the door to a United Ireland – they produced a poster with the words 'Dublin is only a Sunningdale away'. Ulster Unionist David Trimble, who would go on to be First Minister in 1998, subsequently said that at the time he was the UWC's 'cerebral backroom boy'. Ships were prevented from entering the port at Larne and loyalists took over Ballylumford power station, causing electricity to be cut off for long periods. Farmers were forced to pour their milk down the drains as it couldn't be processed and food was wasted because extensive loyalist roadblocks blocked its transportation. The UWC's aim was to bring Northern Ireland to a standstill and they succeeded. The Secretary of State, Merlyn Rees, declared a State of Emergency. Belfast was like a war zone, and I wrote in my diary, 'No electricity, heat, light or food.' The strikers gave out permits for petrol and decided which workplaces provided essential services. Stuck indoors during the blackout, I wrote, 'This atmosphere is not conducive to studying. Not much stewing last night.' I was struggling to prepare for exams by candlelight. We made fires in the street to boil water for tea. At the rare moments the electricity came on, we ran to the kitchen to heat up whatever we could find in the cupboard.

During the strike, Mary had an exam at Jordanstown, so we drove there together. We were stopped at a roadblock by a fifteen-year-old brandishing a baseball bat and shouting at us to pull in. He had a squeaky voice that Mary knew immediately from her teaching practice in his school. When he recognised her, he waved us through, saying, 'No problem, Miss.' Suddenly he was a polite young man in a balaclava, wishing her good luck that morning. When we finally reached the PE college, the notice on the door stated that all exams had been cancelled because of the strike. I was delighted for Mary but annoyed that Queen's hadn't done the same for us. We turned the car around, hoping our baseball bat friend would let us through again, which he did, although he didn't offer to escort us back home. Mary drove like a dervish, knowing there were no police or soldiers anywhere on the roads. The fifteen-year-old on the Shore Road must have had the time of his life in his balaclava as the constitutional stoppage went on for two weeks.

By far the worst news I got was when I heard that my close friend, Michael Mallon, had been murdered. Mickey, as we called him, was part of our school clan, made up of boys from Garron Tower and girls from Loreto. He had been in Toomebridge for the weekend and had been hitching a lift back to Queen's – which we all did at the time but would never do again. One of the cars that picked him up, rather than bringing him safely to the university, took him to a loyalist club on the Donegall Road where the UDA men interrogated him before shooting him dead. His body was found near Shaw's Bridge, close to the university playing fields, where we'd both played sports each Wednesday afternoon. I wrote in my diary, 'Who could have done such a terrible thing?'

Mickey and I had been in the same statistics class, and, not long after his murder, I had to take the exam. The seats in the Whitla Hall had been set out alphabetically. I had desk 261 and Mickey had been allocated 260. When the invigilator saw the empty desk, he asked where Mickey was. I told him; he advised that I get on with my paper, but it was hard to concentrate. It was Mickey's mop of blonde hair that I saw as I stared at his empty seat. When I got home that evening, I made another diary entry: 'What a country. Serious thoughts of emigrating. Northern Ireland has gone to hell.' The only concession to the strike from Queen's was to reduce the pass mark to 35 per cent for all students that summer. I heard later that the criminal injuries award to Mickey's family had been cut from £1,582 to £82 to cover only the funeral expenses.

The march to Parliament Buildings on 28 May 1974, led by Ian Paisley and others, marked the end of the strike, and the end of devolved government. The Stormont parliament remained prorogued until 1998.

I left for England that summer to complete the research for my sociology thesis. It wasn't quiet there either since the IRA was setting off bombs in Birmingham, Guildford and Woolwich. The focus of my study was 'The adaptation and assimilation of Irish immigrants into a London suburb', so I lived among the Irish residents and worked in the McVitie's biscuit factory in Harlesden. The Irish women said they had come to work for a few months in London, planning to earn enough money for their weddings. After their big days back home they returned to the factory, comparing wedding dresses during their breaks in the canteen. I knew they wouldn't be going back home; they were here to stay for years because of the lack of work in Ireland for them or their husbands. It was a hard life, since emigration was the alternative to poverty in rural areas. We also talked about the amount of tax they were paying – many thought it was too high, not least because they were often doing two jobs to make ends meet. I said that their taxes paid for the National Health Service; they said that if they got sick, they were going back to Ireland, but I thought they probably never would. Interviews with Irish families living in Harlesden also formed part of the study. Dr Bob Millar, my lecturer at Queen's, wrote me a letter explaining how to choose individuals at random rather than self-select from a list. I used the parish register and selected every fourth address, but it didn't always go to plan when a different household to the one on my list turned out to be at the address. I was taken aback one day when an Englishman answered the door and told me, 'Go back to where you belong.'

There couldn't really have been a worse time for my study to take place – there was not a hope of Irish people in London assimilating when there were IRA bombs going off in England. I had studied Claude Lévi-Strauss in anthropology and he summed it up when he noted that assimilation was tantamount to saying, 'We [the majority] will refrain from vomiting you out if you let us swallow you up.' My experience in the factory showed me that ignoring differences did not lead to assimilation: Irish workers sat at one table; Jamaicans at another; and the English at a third. Assimilation wasn't going to work for reconciliation between the different communities in Northern Ireland either. I started working on the idea of inclusion instead, as I wanted to deal head-on with differences instead of wishing them into thin air. The study was an early introduction to themes that would loom large later in my life.

Not long after I returned to Belfast, I drove Mary to her first job interview for a PE teaching position at a Protestant secondary school in Ballysillan. When she had met the principal a few days before, he'd said she was the kind of teacher he was looking for. He was so encouraging that she was hopeful. The ten men on the school board whom she met at her formal interview had a different opinion. One of them asked her, 'What school did you go to?' and when he heard, 'Loreto Convent', that was it for her. She knew she wasn't going to get the job. Legislation on fair employment had still not been introduced in Northern Ireland, so there was no redress, even though she felt she had been discriminated against. The school governors had maybe done her a favour, though – I wrote in my diary: 'too dangerous a place to be working in'. Mary needed a job and went for another interview, this time at a Catholic school. Her application form stated that she'd gone to Jordanstown, so the interview panel asked her why she hadn't chosen St Mary's, the college for Catholic teacher training. That school didn't take her either because she hadn't followed the conventional path for Catholic teachers. She eventually got a temporary job, but after a year she packed it in – because she wanted to see the world, she got a job with Aer Lingus. All of the cabin crew staff were women, and they had to undergo a grooming check each day. Anyone considered overweight was put on a diet, and they all had to be single, good-looking and not wearing spectacles. When the airline's management declared Mary cosmetically unfit because she'd cut her finger on the lawnmower, I joked that she was working for Aer Fungus. One of the anti-discrimination posters at the time summed up the frustration of the female staff: 'Weigh my brain and not my body.'

While Mary was off seeing the world, my final honours year was proving the toughest so far – I was finishing my thesis and facing into my last term with eleven exams in front of me. I graduated from Queen's in 1975. It was the same month that the UVF carried out the brutal Miami Showband Massacre, killing three members of the band, including lead singer Fran O'Toole. It shocked me to the core because I'd seen the band play so many times. The UVF put out a statement describing it as 'justifiable homicide'. It was later that I learned that the Glenanne Gang, led by Robin Jackson ('the Jackal'), was responsible for these murders and also carried out at least 130 other sectarian killings in the 1970s and 80s.

I started my postgraduate degree at Queen's in town and country planning that September. I had worked out that planning was a career in which I could put into action what I'd learned so far. I was already interested in community planning, and I was hooked by studies such as Ron Wiener's on 'The Rape and Plunder of the Shankill'. At that time, new motorways were being planned, and there was real concern that they would divide the city of Belfast. I was aware that city planners were taking input from the army but did not consult local communities about how the decisions would affect their livelihoods and families. I'd seen the maps used by the army that were coloured in orange and green to help them distinguish between the two tribes. The already segregated city was becoming even more divided through redevelopment, shattering the old networks and leaving families, especially women, alone and isolated in the new public sector housing estates.

We were reading George Orwell's *1984* on the course as a way of looking to the future. The security influence on urban planning was described as a 'mini-Orwellian' portrayal of policy making. We argued over whether the abnormality of a violently contested society was being deliberately normalised through government decision-making. Street layout was to have sweeping cul-de-sacs to ensure that army vehicles wouldn't have to reverse in working-class areas. 'Peace walls' formed part of these plans, emphasising their permanence in the city landscape. They were designed to keep the two communities apart at pressure points so their name always seemed like a misnomer.

Part of our programme – led by lecturer Pat Braniff, who was a mentor to me – was to work alongside the communities, to help them to put forward alternatives that would work for them. I got to know Jackie Redpath, who was leading the 'Save the Shankill' campaign that, against the odds, managed to overturn the original decisions with technical advice from our town-planning department. He held meetings in the Methodist church hall late into the evening and kept the planners there until they had agreed that the residents' plans were as worthy as the official ones designed by the government's experts.

Liam Neeson appeared on the scene during my town planning year, when he was one of the actors at the Lyric Theatre. He impressed me when he said that the credit for his knowing how to treat women well was due to his sisters. I already knew them – I had been to his sister Bernadette's house and she could make a cat laugh. We went out for a few months and we had a great time together. I watched him in *Philadelphia Here I Come* and in Brian Friel's *Translations*. I felt that the playwrights, poets and actors were raising issues that society needed to talk about more openly. If Liam Neeson was expecting romantic evenings, I suspect I ruined them for him – I was talking politics most of the time. When he asked what I wanted to do with my life, I told him I wanted to bring about change. I asked him the same question and he replied that his plans were for Broadway. We wished each other luck with our dreams when we broke up at exam time. His calling card was cherry blossoms from University Avenue and I missed them after we parted.

There was a growing public abhorrence of the scale and impact of the violence. In early January 1976, Mary O'Dowd's family experienced a terrible tragedy at the hands of the Glenanne Gang. I knew Mary through my close friend Maura Lavery. The O'Dowds had been having a party at their home in Bleary, County Armagh, when men broke in, spraying the room with gunfire and killing her two brothers, Barry and Declan, along with her uncle, Joe. Mary and her sister, Eleanor, were unharmed, as was her younger brother, Cathal, but her father was badly wounded. Her other three brothers were out that night, otherwise they might have been killed too. The ambulance rushed Mary's father, Barney, to the hospital where the surgeon removed the thirteen bullets. Afterwards the family packed up and moved away, as Mary's mother, Kathleen, was terrified that something else terrible might happen to her other sons. The awfulness of what happened to Mary's family always stayed with me, and I will never forget what her beautiful, gentle father, Barney, told Susan McKay in her interviews with victims of the Troubles at WAVE, when he spoke about the impact of the attack: 'I wasn't half myself … I walked the roads some nights, all night, until daylight. It didn't go away from us as it just can't go away. Hate was being driven at you.'

Another Catholic family, the Reaveys, experienced the same sectarian hatred that night, when three of their sons were shot by the same gang. Two died at the scene and the third died later. The Reavey family asked that no retaliation be carried out in their name. The IRA attack at Kingsmills the next day, when ten Protestants were murdered on their way home from work, was seen as a reprisal but it is now known to have been planned some time before. Reason had gone out the window.

Later that year, on 28 May 1976, the Club Bar on University Road was attacked with a no-warning bomb by the UDA. It killed two young men and injured many others – the bar was packed with students that night, and it was lucky that we weren't there, as it was a regular haunt of ours. The UDA had previously attacked the pub, two years before, on 4 November 1974, killing the doorman, Ivan Clayton, whom I knew from evenings spent there. He was a Catholic from Finaghy, and Catholics owned the pub – it was clear it was a sectarian attack.

I went back to the States that summer, using the university travel scholarship I had won to study urban planning. It was the bicentenary of America's Independence in 1976 and the stars and stripes were flying high on the houses. During our time working in Wildwood, we had heard that there were vehicle sales companies that needed cars to be delivered from one part of the country to another – all we had to do was keep the car topped up with petrol and oil. Mary, Rosemary, Marian and I squeezed into a Pinto and headed off on a journey that would take us from Philadelphia to San Jose, California. We took in Pittsburgh, where we stayed with our friend Tony Novosel; Chicago to stay with a cousin; and crossed the mid-west to Salt Lake City, where we signed the Mormons' visitors' book. When I phoned home, my mother told me that two well-dressed young men kept calling to the house and seemed to be trying to convert her to their religion. When she said that she had asked if they were 'non-Catholics', I guessed that would put an end to their visits. She rang off, saying, 'Your father says it would be better if you didn't leave your address in those places.' We travelled on to San Francisco, Las Vegas, the Grand Canyon and even made it to Tijuana, where Mary drove the wrong way up a one-way street and got us all arrested. Our parents placed a great deal of trust in us – they had no idea about how far we travelled or some of the scrapes we got into.

The messages on the walls back in Belfast were a reminder of what we were coming home to. 'Don't be vague, Shoot a Taig' on one side was countered on the other by 'God made Catholics, but the armalite made them equal'. As I drove past the City Cemetery, I saw a poster telling the new secretary of state, Roy Mason, what Northern Ireland was like. It said, 'You will not break us, Stone Mason.'

In the second week of August 1976, a peace movement sprung up in response to the tragic circumstances of the deaths of three children. Joanna and John were out walking with their mother, Anne Maguire, who was pushing a pram with baby Andrew inside, when a car mowed them down. Its driver, an IRA man, had been shot dead at the wheel by a British soldier. Mairead Corrigan, the children's aunt, formed Women For Peace with Betty Williams. They brought together Catholics and Protestants from across Northern Ireland to make a stand against the ongoing violence. In Andersonstown, they led ten thousand down the Catholic Falls Road, and on 28 August 1976, their number rose to twenty-five thousand, this time on the Protestant Shankill. Northern Ireland came to international attention after the two women received the Nobel Peace Prize, but when the movement changed its name to the Peace People, it had a committee largely made up of men, and some questioned whether that was the reason it began to peter out. Others said it was because their plea for an end to the violence never succeeded in getting a response. Either way, the conflict dragged on.

The Troubles returned to our door in April 1977. I was standing in the kitchen back home in Kilrea when Kathleen Donaghy, our next door neighbour, came to tell us that loyalists had murdered her brother William. He owned a shop in Ahoghill and had answered his door late in the evening to somebody looking for aspirin for a sick child. He was known for his kindness and for helping anyone in need, but the two men were not there for aspirin; they were members of the UVF. It later became known that they were reserve police officers, unmasked and out of uniform, and part of the notorious Glenanne Gang. William Strathern was just how the speaker describes him in Seamus Heaney's 'Station Island': 'big-limbed, decent and open-faced ... the perfect, clean, unthinkable victim'. His ghost also appears in the poem and calls out the unmasked gunmen who shot him: 'shites thinking they were the be-all and the end-all'. We could see the murder had an impact on Kathleen for a long time after; it also left its mark on our family. My mother always remembered him in her prayers.

As I was coming close to finishing my postgraduate course in town planning, I applied for the University of Michigan exchange scholarship to study in the USA and later that summer I got a letter to say I had been successful. I was overjoyed – I was desperate to get away. In September 1977, I headed off to Ann Arbor and was looking forward to a new start. It was tough to say goodbye to my parents, as I knew I wouldn't see them again for some time. My mother said Detroit was a terrible place; I reminded her that we had survived a 750lb bomb the previous year in Kilrea. Where I was going had to be better.

The day I set off, Mary was working on the flight to Shannon airport on the first leg of my journey. I was miserable – we were Irish twins in every possible way and now I was going off for more than a year without her. We were both putting on a brave face but it was clear it wasn't working when the passenger beside me joked, 'Do you two girls know something about this flight that I don't?' The immigration officer at JFK looked up from his desk to stamp my papers with the word 'alien'. He told me to remember my 'alien' number as that was most important. He may have said, 'Welcome to the United States of America' but I don't remember that part.

When I arrived in Ann Arbor, my roommate Sue Duckworth couldn't have been kinder or more friendly to an 'alien' like me. My luggage was being held at the airport because it had Belfast written on the tag. Sue's father went to extract it for me and when he arrived back with it, he said, 'Your trunk is in my trunk.' Sue helped me with the registration process, which was computerised and worked like clockwork, but only if you knew how to use it, which I didn't as Queen's was a long way from having a system like that. By the time November arrived, I had started to settle in and loved my visit to Sue's family home in Buffalo for Thanksgiving.

The Indian summer was magnificent – the redbrick buildings on campus were surrounded by yellow and orange leaves and there were squirrels leaping across the square. I kept them in mind until green grass appeared again at the end of April, when I celebrated my birthday after the worst winter and worst blizzards in over two hundred years. It was a shock to be playing a hockey game on a grass pitch in temperatures of minus zero. I wrote to Julie Mackie, whose family had provided my Helen Ramsay Turtle scholarship in memory of their American mother, and said, 'Believe me, Belfast is like an oven compared to the weather here,' and added that students were going 'jogging', something I had never heard of. Conscious that my clothes made me stand out, I invested in a pair of American carpenter pants and would have loved to have seen Mary's reaction to my new look. I was very homesick that Christmas – I couldn't afford to go home – although comforted by my mother's fortnightly letters. Although the university exchange and scholarship covered most of my expenses, I was still very short of money. I sold the American football tickets that came for free as part of being a university student. Each time my fellow students went along to cheer for the Wolverines with 106,000 others in the biggest stadium that I had ever seen, I was disappointed that I was missing out, but relieved that my meals for the next week were paid for. I added these funds to the money I received as a teaching assistant. I learned to keep a straight face each time I called on Randy to answer questions in the architecture class on north campus. It was the other way round when I needed someone to explain what foxy meant when it was first said to me.

I'd never been away from home for so long before, but it turned out to be a hugely important time in my life, and I came to love Ann Arbor. It was my first opportunity to meet students from all over the world and to learn more about their culture and politics.

The students from Iran introduced me to their Persian poets and literature, and invited me to their homes to sample their cuisine, with its wonderful aroma and spices – a far cry from the Ulster fry. When they took to the streets to protest against the Shah, I decided to join them. They were under surveillance from SAVAK (Iran's secret intelligence organisation) so they walked with brown paper bags over their heads, with holes cut in them so that they could see out. I thought we should have tried that on our civil rights marches, but felt sure the Special Powers Act would have found a way to disallow it.

Students packed the halls for discussions about South Africa and listened intently as speakers described the harsh programme of state-sanctioned segregation and discrimination against the country's Black population. John Hendricks, my friend down the hall in the dorm, was from Cape Town and had been part of the boycotts before he left to do his doctorate at Ann Arbor. He described the racist behaviour he had experienced in the South African education system. When I asked him to speak Xhosa, he made me speak Gaelic in return. At Christmas, I went to his wedding in Toronto where I met his fiancée, Cora. She had travelled from South Africa and was staying with friends who had been forced into exile in Canada. They sang 'Danny Boy' around the piano just after I had phoned home to wish everyone a Happy Christmas. It was a poignant moment when I thought about the song and where it came from. It was even more poignant watching John and Cora exchanging their vows the next day, knowing their families from their homeland couldn't be with them. We toasted their future together and raised our glasses to the hope that one day they would be able to return to a very different South Africa.

When I returned to Ann Arbor in January, I watched the news each night in the common room. I was feeling far removed from what was happening back at home. On 17 February 1978, the IRA bombed the La Mon Hotel using some kind of napalm-like device. When the USA used napalm in Vietnam, there was no doubt in my mind that the same people who had placed that bomb in the hotel would have condemned its use in Vietnam. The 'Shankill Butchers', a UVF gang, drove around Catholic areas at night, seeking out innocent people so they could torture and kill them. The newspaper articles that I was reading in the States made Belfast sound like an abattoir. When a friend said to me, 'I suppose you'll never go back', I replied that I would as soon as my course was finished. Some of the other students didn't have a choice and couldn't return to their homeland, but I could. I had spent six years getting an education and it was time to give something back.

I was fortunate to find a mentor, Professor Jim Chaffers, during my time in Michigan, when I was deciding what to do with my life. He had a motto that I have always remembered: 'Whatever you become a part of, it shouldn't be something that you alone gain from.' He would go on to have an instrumental role in the design of the Martin Luther King, Jr. Memorial in Washington DC but back then he was working against 'redlining' – a system that prevented people of colour from getting loans or mortgages against properties that were in the 'red' areas, which were typically neighbourhoods with large Black or minority populations. This made it impossible for people in these areas to buy or renovate homes. To counteract the discrimination, the US Congress had introduced the Community Reinvestment Act, extending credit and loans from banks to enable low- and medium-income families to buy houses, even in 'red' districts. When Jim Chaffers explained all this to me, I wanted to help him to change the system in any way I could.

An Irish-American group in Detroit asked me to speak a number of times about my thesis, in which I compared inner-city redevelopment in Belfast and Detroit. At one of these presentations, I displayed slides of Belfast followed by slides of Detroit to show the deprivation in both cities. I asked the audience to think about how groups could unite to challenge the laws that were creating such divisions. Some looked aghast at the idea of joining hands across the racial divide with their African-American neighbours. I wasn't invited back to give any more presentations since the comparisons I was making about poor people's lives, irrespective of whether it was the US or Northern Ireland, weren't going down well with the audience. But Fred Burns O'Brien, an Irish-American civil servant, was also in the audience and invited me to Washington DC to address the Ad Hoc Congressional Committee on Irish Affairs. President Jimmy Carter had commented on human rights conditions in Northern Ireland and was instrumental in getting the Committee established in Congress. The Congress members asked me to testify on unemployment at one of their hearings. When I arrived on Capitol Hill, I remembered how I had stood outside looking up at the building three years before as a student. Now I was standing inside, in front of a panel of Congress members, to give evidence.

I thought I was doing well until Congressman Mario Biaggi asked me to repeat a remark. I had said that the lowest rate of employment was 7 to 8 per cent, compared to other areas where it was much higher as a result of religious discrimination. He had thought I was saying 78 per cent. When I repeated the figure, I could see how relieved the Congress members were that the figure wasn't as high as they had first thought. Speaking at a congressional public hearing at the age of twenty-three was a formative experience. I left copies of my report for each of the attendees

– my strategy was to leave a 'fist of facts' on the table, showing that, in the decade leading up to 1978, over 97,000 people had packed their bags and left Northern Ireland. Unionists were arguing that Catholics not emigrating in the same numbers as Protestants was the cause of higher Catholic unemployment. I was able to show that wasn't the case as Catholics were also packing up and leaving in high numbers. I concluded by saying that the provision of equality for all was controversial in Northern Ireland. I should have added that my experience in Detroit had taught me they had the same problem in the USA.

My boyfriend at the time was Ali Riza Khomeni. He was a Turkish student, who was proud of his heritage and kept talking about Atatürk's Ottoman Empire, but who didn't like to be reminded of the Armenian genocide. No matter where we come from, we all have our blind spots. When Ali came to visit me the following year, my parents were most hospitable. When they spoke to him they paused after each word, not knowing that his English was perfect. They were relieved to hear that we weren't planning to stay together since Ali's scholarship mandated that he spend a number of years in the Turkish army. That was the end of a beautiful east–west relationship.

4

Putting Gender on the Agenda, in the University and in the Community

'In the writing of history, men are often present but where
are the women? ...They are there, ready to shoulder
almost any task, to take on any responsibility.
The lack of focus on women's history has been
a greater problem than the lack of sources.'

The Vasa Museum, Stockholm

Once I was back from the USA in June 1978, I needed to find a job. My summer gig peddling encyclopedias around housing estates in Dublin had come to an abrupt end. Nobody answering their doors was interested in buying a set since they had barely enough money to put food on the table. In previous summer jobs, I had made beds and cleaned toilets, cut bacon and packed biscuits in factories, picked strawberries and potatoes in fields, but flogging big volumes of books around doors topped the lot. I would have missed the job that was to become my future career if my mother hadn't been scanning the ads in the newspapers for me. The Ulster Polytechnic was looking for lecturers to join the new degree course in Social Policy and I got one of the jobs.

To make it look like I was worth the annual salary of £5,289, I tied my hair in a bun and put on my glasses, but no matter what I did to make myself look older, the security man still thought I was one of the students. Education campuses were subjected to bomb scares, hence the need for daily searches, and each time he searched my briefcase at the entrance to the polytech, he asked for my student ID card. The director of social sciences introduced me to my colleagues – all men – on my first day and then passed me a kettle, saying, 'Our new staff member can make the tea.' Mike Morrissey instantly became my friend when he took the kettle instead. We worked together for years, and there was never a cross word between us. Bob Osborne, John Ditch and later Frank Gaffikin made up the social policy staff and I couldn't have asked for a better bunch of colleagues. I wished all the men I came across were like them, but it wasn't the case.

One older lecturer in particular used to bother me, taking pleasure in undermining my confidence, telling me I should learn to have more fun and calling me a party pooper each time I left his company. Sexual harassment hadn't been heard of back then, but I could read the smoke signals. It was the problem with no name.

Faculty meetings were also a good training ground for later years as I learned that where the stakes are small, the higher the politics. The Dean's approach to faculty meetings veered from collegiate to inquisition. At exam boards, it was the done thing to score points off faculty members. We four musketeers in social policy ignored the games. Teaching students came first, and I loved every minute of it. The course involved social policy, political science, sociology, and research methods, and our students would go on to become social workers, youth and community workers, and to jobs in the government, since it was the kind of course that led you into the field of public service. The mature students were a joy to work with, bringing their own experience to us, the teachers. It was good to see the interaction between staff and students in the coffee bars or – after work – in the real bars.

The management had decreed that we should 'publish or perish'. This pressure increased when the polytechnic merged with the University of Ulster in 1984. With this emphasis on research, it was hard to ensure that enough value was placed on teaching and that our work was impactful in the local communities that were right outside the university's front door. None of this was made easier by the Conservative government's introduction of league tables that were created by people who didn't seem ever to have done a day's teaching or research in their lives. Each academic's worth was judged on how much money they were bringing in. It made the university feel like a market by forcing us to compete with our colleagues. Thatcher managed to stay in power from 1979 to 1990 – it seemed like a lifetime, and with each passing year our world of knowledge became much less collegiate.

Around this time, I also embraced the world of technology and was glad to leave behind the Gestetner, which covered me in ink when I ran off handouts. Computers and printers ended the need for any of that. I was completely self-taught when it came to computers and later discovered the magic of Ctrl+Alt+Del. I brought Angela Davis, the US civil rights activist, to Belfast as a guest speaker in 1986 when the University of Ulster was celebrating its twentieth anniversary. She told us that the day was near when we would be organising public meetings on mobile phones. Angela Davis was ahead of her time in predicting such a thing in 1986.

In our teaching we had to take on board the situation in Northern Ireland. The tangled web of the British-Irish problem was hard to unpick, but the curriculum we had designed meant we had to tackle it. The discussions went up several notches in the class I taught to members of the Amalgamated Transport and General Workers' Union, which included politically minded people of all persuasions. Plum Smith, a loyalist activist and former prisoner, was one of the most vocal in the class. The arguments of the opposing sides summed up the problem: those on the side of the union with Britain baulked at accepting anything other than an internal solution; those on the other side couldn't countenance that. For nationalists, the conflict was as much about the state's existence as it was about whether or not the state was fairly governed. The debates went on for hours. The question was whether the constitutional divisions would defy a resolution. As the arguments raged around me, I held on to my father's belief that for every problem, there has to be a solution.

About this time I met Avila Kilmurray at a community development conference in Corrymeela. She and Tom Lovett had founded a new course in Community Action Research Education at Magee, another campus of the University of Ulster. Her doctoral thesis had just been blown up in a bomb in Derry that had also destroyed the contents of her flat. As I would come to know, Avila never gives up, and she completed her thesis years later. She was an early advocate for action learning, as was I, having found the approach to be of great benefit during my postgraduate courses. I wanted to bring it into my teaching and to get my students out into the field as practitioners.

In 1985, Mike Morrissey and I took our students to Divis Flats in West Belfast to get them engaged in a project that was underway to have the high-rise blocks there demolished. The complex of 850 flats had been built in 1966 to replace the slum housing on the Falls Road. When responsibility for housing and redevelopment was transferred from Belfast City Council to the Northern Ireland Housing Executive in 1971, there were 61,000 families on the waiting list and Divis Flats were part of the new authority's efforts to rehouse them. The families who moved to the flats were at first delighted – the tin bath in front of the fire was replaced by a brand new bathroom with an inside toilet, along with central heating. It was that very heating system that turned out to be a nightmare – the fuel bills kept rising as residents tried to counter the condensation that was endemic in the flats, and it led to a vicious circle of debt, and the debts kept rising.

On the day of our visit, community workers Gerry Downes and Sean Stitt showed us around. Debris was overflowing from the rubbish chutes and children were playing among it on the high-rise walkways. Women had to cart their shopping up numerous flights of stairs because the lifts kept breaking down. There were burned-out cars and lorries lying beside two swings on what was supposed to be a playground. About ten years earlier, the BBC had screened a programme on the flats called *Internment in Divis*. When we were there, the women told us that was how it felt to them. As part of their protest at the conditions, they were preventing contractors from carrying out repairs, saying it was only a short-term solution. They were known as the 'petticoat brigade', a name given to women campaigners down through Irish history. The students thought the women were great.

On one of the high-rise floors above us, a soldier crouched, pointing his rifle over the balcony. An army helicopter was decanting heavily armed men on to the twenty-two storey tower block next to us, and a battalion of soldiers was driving around in armoured vehicles. This was one of the worst places to be during the Troubles. No one had ever forgotten nine-year-old Patrick Rooney who was killed in one of the flats in 1969 when a tracer bullet from a police machine gun went into his bedroom during a gun battle. It was still like a war zone when I brought the students there in 1986.

While the area was crying out for a play park and other community facilities, all Divis got was a betting shop. A local resident told us that, a few years previously, a band of men from a local IRA unit had approached a man coming out of the betting shop and brought him to one of the flats, where he was relieved of that day's takings. They left the man there until they had given each of the tenants the amount they owed in rent arrears – they had fallen behind because of debts accrued due to high fuel costs. The tenants paid the rent collector when he called later that day and their rent books were marked as being in order. The rent collector was heading for home when the band of men took the rent money from him and sent him on his way. They returned the money to the man from the bookies. The narrator told it like a Robin Hood story. According to him it was a victimless crime during which nobody lost any money and local residents' rent arrears had been settled. The housing authority thought differently but didn't press charges.

On the way back to the university, I realised the students were stunned, especially the more sheltered ones. The reality of the effects of poverty, poor housing and conflict on the people who lived in Divis every day of their lives had sunk in. I felt strongly that, if they were going to be working on social policy, they needed to see how it played out when things went wrong, but also how a campaign for rehousing could meet with some success. A few years later, in 1987, a decision was taken to demolish the flats. The students' own university experience in those years was not what you would call normal, with bomb hoaxes on campus becoming a regular event. The alerts came by way of codes telephoned in to the police by paramilitary groups, but their information on location and timing wasn't always accurate. The protocol was that students should leave their belongings and move quickly outside. The hoaxes were most frequent at exam time. On one occasion I was able to spare the students a resit by telling them not to speak to each other. Hordes of students stayed quiet as I herded them out into the open. They returned to their desks when the area was cleared and put their heads down once again. They got an extra hour because of the bomb scare, and cheered at finishing time. It was a mark of the times that students and staff were more worried about getting the exam done than we were about the prospect of a bomb.

But it hadn't been a hoax bomb three years before, on 4 November 1983 (nor was an earlier one in 1977) – a bomb, planted by the IRA, caused the deaths of three policemen, as well as injuring other officers, students and staff. I was also one of the lecturers on the police criminology course, but it happened that my colleague Paul Maidment, who was injured in the explosion, was teaching that day. The IRA knew there were police officers attending classes on the campus, so they made the university a target. We were sitting ducks because the class was always held in the same room and I had raised this concern at a union meeting. The university's concession was to undertake a full search of the room before each class – but they had missed the device that day because it was hidden in the ceiling. Some colleagues had already refused to teach the police; even more were reluctant to take the classes after the bombing, but I believed the police students deserved the same educational opportunity as any other student, especially when it came to the topic of domestic violence.

The lectures were moved to the police training college at Garnerville, near Holywood, and I went there each week instead. I was still going there in the August of 1986 when the IRA announced that any civilians working with security forces in Northern Ireland would be viewed as collaborators and could be attacked. I wasn't sure who was on their list. Each Thursday as I arrived at the entrance to the police college, a police officer holding a pole with a mirror at one end checked under my car. A few years later, in 1990, I became more worried when the IRA began using human proxy bombs, strapping explosives to drivers that were detonated at army barracks and police stations. Each Thursday, as I left the university to drive to the police college, I tried not to think too much about the risk.

When I entered the college, the first thing I noticed was the wall of pictures showing policemen (and they were all men) in old-fashioned uniforms. Judith Gillespie, who would go on to become assistant chief constable, was one of my students. She told me that when she first joined the RUC, she had to jump in and out of jeeps in her police-issue skirt since female officers weren't allowed to wear trousers. In 1985, Mrs X, a

tragedy increased our determination to get rid of the Payments for Debt Act. It was abolished some time later.

As time went on, I became more and more interested in gender issues like the feminisation of poverty. I wanted a 'kinder' politics that would benefit women and address the needs of the most vulnerable, like Rosie Nolan. I joined Gingerbread, a new organisation for single parents, set up with the aim to 'ginger' up the government for more bread. The social security system had been based on the notion of the man as the head of a two-parent family, and anyone who fell outside of that norm, for whatever reason, was affected by a drop in their income. We worked with widows, prisoners' wives, mothers who hadn't got married, and separated and divorced women from both sides of the community. The thing they all had in common was poverty. We helped claimants to navigate the bureaucracy so they could receive what they were entitled to. We also campaigned for the system to change. At that time in Northern Ireland, being a single mother was doubly difficult due to the conservative nature of society and the churches' emphasis on the 'two-parent family'. It was important to us to remove the stigma. I penned an article for *One Parent Times* with a picture of Avila on the front cover. She was carrying her ten-month-old baby, Aoife, in a pram, up flights of stairs in Annadale flats, where she had been housed on the third floor. I wondered how the Housing Executive imagined she would manage to get baby and shopping up the flights of stairs at the same time.

A problem specific to Northern Ireland in the Troubles was the high number of women who had husbands in prison. These men were treated by the social security system as being 'on temporary absence', leaving their wives without full entitlement to welfare assistance. As well as becoming single parents, the trauma was compounded by having to manage on a very low household income that had to cover food parcels for their partners and travel to prisons that were often far from home. For respite, I brought these families, as well as other Gingerbread families, to stay at Corrymeela's old-style Dutch house above the sea near Ballycastle, where they could recharge their batteries and spend time together. On finding the kind of peace and tranquillity that they hadn't experienced before, the women began to share their stories. Some of these involved descriptions of partners as 'lean, mean killing machines' who 'boiled over' suddenly and unpredictably. The partners of policemen, soldiers and armed groups had a great deal in common. I saw the frozen watchfulness in the women – a result of the deep personal pain caused by abusive relationships and lives lost to conflict. For women, the trauma was the same on both sides of the religious divide.

The court of public opinion too often decided who was deserving of sympathy. On top of everything else, the wife of a prisoner was unlikely to qualify. It also wasn't easy to be a single parent with an ex in the police or army. There was even a hierarchy for those who were widowed in the Troubles, with those married to the 'culpable' compared unfavourably to those whose partners were deemed 'innocent'. Women needed to get a break from that kind of judgement as well as the turmoil of the Troubles. In the mid-eighties, a group of families in Boyle, County Roscommon, got in touch with Gingerbread to offer the families a holiday. I was the driver once again. When I dropped off our families at each home in Roscommon, I felt like I was leaving them in the middle of nowhere, but when I returned to collect them, the children said they didn't want to leave; they had got a taste of what normal life was like.

Many of our families lived in poor-quality housing in estates with myriad social problems. This led to them being labelled 'problem families', rather than families *with* problems, or, worse, to be thought of as an underclass, a notion that was embraced by Thatcher. Too much of the social policy that I was dealing with used this kind of label rather than responding to them in the way that Gingerbread did. Northern Ireland also had the highest infant mortality rate in Europe, with seventeen out of one thousand babies dying before their first birthday. In addition, the absence of contraception had resulted in one of the highest fertility rates for women, outside of Turkey. Families were caught in a poverty trap, leaving them with no way out.

The absence of sex education in schools – things hadn't changed much since my day – and in many homes was part of the reason why the number of children born to women under the age of twenty was much higher than in Britain. Margo Harkin's film *Hush-a-Bye Baby* showed the difficulties that a teenager in Derry was facing following an unplanned pregnancy in the middle of the Troubles. The stigma surrounding unwanted and unplanned pregnancies was also apparent in the south of Ireland, as the case of Ann Lovett showed. The fifteen-year-old died alone in 1984 while giving birth at a grotto in Granard, County Longford. Also in 1984, I read about the court case of Eileen Flynn that was being heard in Dublin. She was a teacher who had been living with a man who was separated from his wife and by whom she had become pregnant. In her appeal against her dismissal from the school, which was unsuccessful, the judge censored her even further with his remark: 'In other places women are being condemned to death for this sort of offence.'

I had been so shocked by everything I had heard and read and by what the women at Gingerbread were telling me that I was glad of the invitation from the Western Health Board in Northern Ireland to investigate causes of teenage pregnancy, working with two of my university colleagues. We wanted to find out what kind of social policies would best help young women. Since contraceptives weren't available, the girls – and the young men – were taking risks and using alternatives that didn't work. Both were equally ill-informed. One of the health visitors that we spoke to had been warning young people of the danger of using cling film as a contraceptive, not realising that her advice meant that more young men began to use it, having got the idea from her. Cling film was much easier to get than condoms. We concluded that what was needed was information appropriate to the age and needs of each young person. We knew that the problem was that some parents were opposed to 'exposing' their teenagers to sex education, often on religious grounds. It was left to the Belfast Health Trust to pave the way for the provision of accessible contraceptives in the mid-1980s. A rapid decline in teenage pregnancy followed – information and provision had made the difference.

The New Ireland Forum took place in 1983 and 1984. It was established by the taoiseach, Garret FitzGerald, to consult on peace and stability in Ireland. Fitzgerald had wanted the unionist parties to attend but, when they didn't show up, the secretariat was asked to reach out to groups – like the Poverty Lobby – from across civil society, as we were working with both communities. In the submission that we were invited to send to the Forum, we emphasised that the politics of poverty needed to be part of any discussions. We decided to hold our own north–south

Poverty Lobby inquiry, with a two-day hearing at Belfast's Transport House, followed by two days at All Hallows College, Dublin. The organisation of this event was a huge job but worth it when we got buy-in from organisations north and south. It became clear that prejudice on both sides of the border was identical – towards the homeless, single parents, claimants and travellers. The report I wrote focused on how all this affected women, so as to ensure that we considered all the ways to challenge poverty and address the gaps.

There were times when I felt north and south were miles apart on these issues, even though we were on the same island. Some of the groups were also claiming that the Irish welfare system in the mid-1980s was a pale imitation of the British one in the north – we concluded that both systems were failing people. Behind the scenes, unknown to us, the British and Irish governments were working on the constitutional conundrum. We weren't to know the extent to which that would change north–south cooperation. I felt that a key consideration for any constitutional arrangements was that both governments should focus on welfare systems that worked, especially for the most vulnerable in society. I finished writing the report on the north–south inquiry and sent it to the two governments just as Margaret Thatcher and Garret FitzGerald were signing the Anglo-Irish Agreement at Hillsborough Castle.

A decade previously, in 1971, when Margaret Thatcher was the minister for education, she made a decision to abolish free school milk, and that's when she became known as Thatcher the Milk Snatcher. Women from both communities who were furious at her decision came together to form the Mothers of Belfast. They borrowed a cow from the Farmers' Union for their march to Belfast City Council. The council supported the milk campaign, but difficulties arose behind the scenes when some of the unionist councillors told the Protestant women that they shouldn't be involved in an anti-state protest. The same councillors also claimed that because Catholic women had higher numbers of children, the Catholic side were gaining more from free school milk. The Protestant women had little choice but to acquiesce and left the movement just as it was getting on its feet.

Linda Edgerton, who was one of the organisers of the march, began to push for a women's movement to be set up and invited me to join in 1978 when I came home from Michigan. Radical feminists like me were caricatured as the 'flat sandal, roll-your-own cigarette brigade'. I didn't do either. I thought radical meant getting to the root of the problem and, as we said at the time, if we were going to be punished for being 'a bit of a feminist', we might as well stick our necks out and be radical.

Early in the movement's life, there was an issue that was certainly radical and ended up causing a split. In 1978, republican prisoners at Long Kesh went on a dirty protest, smearing their cells with excreta, in support of their demand for special category status to be reinstated. Their female republican counterparts at Armagh Prison were also refusing to accept that they should be treated like ordinary criminals. About this same time, a group of women formed the Relatives Action Committee and held pickets outside the prisons wearing only grey blankets over their naked bodies in solidarity with those inside. In London, members of the Relatives Action Committee came to public attention by chaining themselves to the railings outside Downing Street and then doing the same outside a UN conference at the Hague.

Some within the women's movement took the side of the republican women protesters, while others believed this wasn't the only issue for women in Northern Ireland at the time. Loyalist women with relatives in prison, who might have been sympathetic since they didn't want their men to be labelled as ordinary criminals either, found it impossible to relate to these republican protests. They also didn't want to be seen as 'Green' Protestants since human rights concerns were perceived as the prerogative of nationalists and republicans. There were others who had lost loved ones in the Troubles and who had no sympathy for anyone raising prisoners' rights. The infighting caused by the prison issue led to many of us feeling burned out; transcending these divisions wore me down.

I didn't believe that the conflict over the different approaches needed to be so divisive. Republicans were accused of defining their politics in a way that marginalised other women by turning every issue into support for republican initiatives. I was fed up being repeatedly asked which side I was on. The politics of the conflict was getting in the way of resolving wider women's issues. Even progressively minded men had little sympathy for the disagreements, believing that feminists would make more progress if they were more like-minded. That was a bit of a tall order coming from men who rowed most of the time over politics. It was patronising to expect women to act as a homogenous group. The 'unity' meetings that were held to deal with the disputes were summed up in graffiti on the wall at the Magee campus: 'Women un-free shall never be at peace.'

I was relieved that the campaigns for equal rights from Europe achieved more common ground. Even though the UK had joined the EEC as far back as 1973, these rights were slow to come to Northern Ireland. Politicians told us activists for women's rights to wait until religious discrimination was sorted. Since there were no female representatives from Northern Ireland in the European Parliament or at Westminster, it was left to the male politicians to raise this issue, but most of them weren't that bothered about the Sex Discrimination Act being extended to Northern Ireland.

When Bronagh Hinds became the first female president of Queen's Students' Union in 1975, she organised a women's rights conference that sowed the seeds of the Northern Ireland Women's Rights Movement. I had seen how the movement had taken off in the United States and was delighted to see it make its way across the Atlantic. Like a snowball, the movement gathered momentum, culminating in a march to Stormont to demand that an Equal Opportunities Commission, focusing on equality for women, should be established in Belfast. We were annoyed that the Fair Employment Commission, to deal with religious discrimination, was all we were getting from Westminster. The direct rule minister had originally decreed that we only needed to tackle religious discrimination, but we cheered when the UK government finally responded by extending the legislation, finally recognising in 1976 that equal opportunities for women were just as important.

When the Sex Discrimination Act was introduced, we discovered that the legislation only applied to employment and not to goods and services. This meant, for example, that married women couldn't get a mortgage or a bank loan without their husband's signature, nor could they drink in a bar and were only allowed in if there was a lounge as well. I had direct experience of this – my brother John was working in Belfast and I wanted a lift home. I knew he was in the pub on the Lisburn Road and I went there to meet him – but the bartender told me in no uncertain terms that I had to wait outside. He couldn't have done that after 1979, when Eileen Evason, a fellow women's rights activist, planted herself in McGlades pub and won her sex discrimination case – taken by the EOC – against the bar for putting her out. McGlades argued that admitting women might cause embarrassment but pub licences were being paid from the public purse, so the discrimination was found to be illegal. We paid the same taxes and deserved to be treated as equals. The golf clubs didn't change their rules until they were taken to court on the same grounds – that although they might have been private clubs, their bar licences were issued by the government. I was amused again to read in the newspapers that golfers were complaining that their places of relaxation were being contaminated by women. The old boys networks were being disrupted. The action in the north coincided with the protest in Dublin held by Irishwomen United to assert their right to use the gentlemen-only swimming facilities at the Forty Foot in Sandycove.

While women's rights at work and at leisure were relatively widely supported, the issue of reproductive rights was much more contentious. I agreed with the journalist Nell McCafferty that, 'It is difficult to protest in your town where your mother is watching'. I certainly knew mine was watching closely – her faith made these kinds of issues difficult for her.

The Northern Ireland Women's Rights Movement also produced a Women's Charter that included the rights that women expected as citizens, raising matters as important as childcare. We opened the first women's centre in Donegall Street, Belfast, to offer much-needed information and advice. Our minutes recorded that Mary McMahon was to get wallpaper and paint; Lily Kerr a typewriter; Pat Brown a filing cabinet; Inez McCormack an answering machine; Linda Edgerton a toy library; Jenny Williams a doorbell and Margaret Bruton a tea urn. Bernie had to track down furniture from Community Organisation Northern Ireland as it had gone out of business. Raffle tickets were also on the list, as a Women's International Day concert was being organised, and I was in charge of artists' accommodation. These concerts were big events, as the likes of Peggy Seeger was coming to perform in Belfast. A novel idea was a 'rent-a-crèche' that would be made accessible for women in local communities. To raise awareness that we were up and running, Avila came to interview us for her community radio programme but the opening was repeatedly postponed due to glitches that needed fixing and the 'tyranny of structurelessness' didn't help with the decision-making process. Each meeting seemed endless until Madge Davison insisted on time limits so as to cut out the waffle. It was time to get moving – we were all busy women with day jobs and family commitments – and the revolution couldn't wait.

The centre in Belfast may have been the first, but it wasn't long before women's advice and drop-in centres spread across Northern Ireland. We spent hours discussing fundraising so we could pay our bills. In an old terraced house in Derry, Theresa Kelly lit a fire each morning in the women's centre, but she needed money to pay for the coal. She organised evenings where women were given glasses of wine in return for donations. She chose wine deliberately because she could charge fifty pence per glass. If a hundred women turned up, that would cover the bills for the following month, and we turned up to support her whenever we could. No two women's centres were the same. The one in Derry insisted on political neutrality; the Falls Women's Centre reflected a republican feminist viewpoint; and the one in Ballybeen, a loyalist area in East Belfast, ran up against Castlereagh Borough Council. The unionist councillors found the centre's ethos challenging, describing it as 'radical with trouble-makers and all that sort of thing'. They had thought they were funding a cup of tea and a chat but the women had other ideas. They wanted to observe Castlereagh Council to see how decisions were made but this kind of political activism was to put their funding at risk. After that, the women in the centre had to watch what they said lest they be seen as stepping out of line with their funders. In spite of these kinds of difficulties, the bottom-up women's movement was beginning to take shape.

By the mid-1980s, we had lots of accidental activists – women at grassroots level who were bringing communities together when everything else seemed to be falling apart. Mothers who were trying to keep their youngsters away from joyriding – which was endemic in parts of Belfast – and prevent them from getting into street confrontations, came together to form the Women's Information Day Group. Founder Kathleen Feenan, a tough woman from Twinbrook whom I was very fond of, rotated meetings between single-identity Catholic and Protestant working-class neighbourhoods. Each side took turns to climb on a bus to cross the peace lines every month to meet with each other, building friendships and sharing common experiences as their network grew stronger. When I was invited to speak to the group about welfare reform, Kathleen told me to stay away from the hot potatoes of religion and politics. She didn't want to jeopardise the trust they had started to build – it had been hard won, and they were determined to keep going. One of the women commented at the meeting that there were always tragedies, always catastrophes, and that meant they couldn't stop. Another woman talked about how the men in her loyalist area had noticed her travels and had heard about a talk they'd had. The person giving that talk had clearly had to juggle some hot potatoes explaining the origins of names like 'Fenian' and 'Hun'. A worker from the group heard a UDA man say, 'I hear you've got some interesting history lessons going on.' That told the women in that area that 'the boys' were keeping an eye on them.

The angry unionist reaction to the 1985 Anglo-Irish Agreement had ramifications for the women's movement. Fifteen unionist members of parliament resigned from Westminster in protest and, along with unionist councillors, instigated a boycott of any meetings with British government ministers. They demanded that the women's centres that they were funding should do the same. But even when they threatened to cut the funding, the staff in the centres refused to comply, knowing the impact such a decision would have on their work. The workers from Ballybeen Women's Centre in loyalist east Belfast continued to attend meetings at Stormont, which made them even more unpopular with the councillors. The women's centres then came together to form the Women's Support Network to counter the threats to their funding. The women kept the network running after this threat to their funding had passed – it's still going today.

When Angela Davis was in Northern Ireland in 1986, she came with me to Ballybeen to meet the women. She talked about her experiences, and one point she made stayed with me: that it wasn't good enough to be non-racist; it was better to be anti-racist. I thought the same about sectarianism. We needed to tackle it by changing the mindsets as well as the societal structures.

That same year, the Conservative government introduced the Fowler Review, named after a government minister, which drove a horse and cart through the provision for pensions and social security benefits. I produced a report for the trade union movement to show the impact these changes would have on the livelihoods of thousands who relied on the state as their only form of income. These cuts were going to affect Northern Ireland more than other parts of the UK because of the higher levels of unemployment and larger numbers of one-parent families and prisoners' wives caused by the Troubles. The women's centres rose up again and organised a march to Stormont to protest the cuts. But the irony was not lost on the unionist women when one of them remarked, 'The last time we marched up here was to bring Stormont down.' This time the protest wouldn't make the headlines, in the way the Ulster Workers' Council strike had in 1974. The unionist-elected representatives told the women that they should be content to leave political decisions to them. The direct rule minister, representing the Westminster government in Northern Ireland, did the same, telling the women they should have brought a public representative if they wanted a meeting with him.

The women didn't stop there – nine of them got on a boat and made their way to London to petition at Westminster. They circulated the policy brief I had prepared, but once again they discovered that their own representatives from Northern Ireland weren't interested, so they sought out other MPs from outside Northern Ireland to whom they outlined the serious implications the cuts would have back home. When they heard the MPs use what they had told them in the parliamentary debates later that day, they felt they had been listened to. They came home feeling that those MPs from Northern Ireland representing Protestant working-class communities were not interested in these changes to the welfare system that would be so damaging to their constituents. The beat of the constitutional drum drowned out almost everything else.

Back home, Ian Paisley MP was holding a rally for Ulster Resistance, at which he and his supporters wore red berets, to protest against constitutional changes. He demanded the abolition of the Anglo-Irish Agreement on the grounds that Ulster was being sold out. After this speech, the general secretary of the Presbyterian Church in Ireland remarked that Paisley was up to his old tricks – he was leading the unionist people up the hill, but, at the first sign of trouble, he would lead them down again just as quickly. In 1986, just as the fledgling women's movement was making its mark through small 'p' politics, the larger 'P' politics led to the Northern Ireland Assembly being dissolved. The Women's Support Network remained in place and the Unionist politicians went back to meetings with Margaret Thatcher, despite their complaints that she had hung them out to dry.

I got involved in the Better Life for All campaign that was set up by the trade union movement to create a sense of solidarity among trade unionists from both sides of the community. The campaign adopted an anti-sectarian stance and opposed the use of political violence by advocating that political change would come about only by political means. Betty Sinclair, a leading trade unionist from the Shankill Road and a former leader of the civil rights movement, belonged to the Transport and General Workers' Union and, many years before, had put forward the argument with Sean Morrissey that an anti-sectarian approach was the only way forward. In his role as full time trade union officer, Sean helped to set up the Women's Committee of which May Blood, Eileen Weir, Theresa Kelly, Avila and I became founding members.

May Blood was able to expose the effects of sectarianism by drawing on her earlier experiences. In 1971, during the riots that followed internment, her family had intervened to prevent the eviction of their Catholic neighbours from their home by a Protestant mob. Shortly afterwards May and her family were forced to leave the area. In the linen mill where she worked, she also took a stand against sectarian intimidation and later became a strong advocate for integrated education. She coined the phrase, 'Watch my lips, I'm speaking,' which was her way of making her fellow trade unionists pay attention.

Eileen Weir had also made an interesting journey from the factory floor. She had been a committed loyalist in the early years of the Troubles, and then made a leap into the trade union movement. I had been a passenger in her black taxi – she was one of the few female drivers in Belfast at that time – and she would go on to spearhead the Women's Vision Across the Barricades' project on the interface between Protestant Tiger's Bay and Catholic New Lodge, demanding that women should have more involvement in the way flags and emblems were displayed in their area. Trying to resolve these issues gave us a lot to chew on.

I knew Theresa Kelly from her work in the Derry Women's Centre. Theresa's mother had had to give her up at birth and, although she'd written to the convent in Dublin where Theresa had been left as a baby, Theresa never got the letters. It later turned out that Theresa's holiday cottage in Donegal was almost next door to where her mother had been living all her life, but she only found that out a short time before her mother passed away. I could see that the sensitive way Theresa worked with vulnerable women came from deep inside her soul.

As a result of our work advocating on behalf of women – tackling issues such as equal pay, sex discrimination, childcare and maternity leave – I was elected to the first women's reserve seat on the Northern Ireland Committee of the ICTU in 1986, joining leading feminist Inez McCormack. Shortly afterwards, I was asked to meet the direct rule minister to address the human rights concerns around the strip-searching of women prisoners, which had arisen due to the upcoming move of female prisoners from Armagh to the new prison at Maghaberry. During the Troubles, the right to bodily integrity was fought over. The argument on one side was that women should not be subjected to humiliating strip searches in prison; the opposing view was that women convicted of political offences hadn't considered the bodily integrity of others when they acted in a way that resulted in death and destruction. The language used also caused problems – terrorists and subversives versus combatants and protagonists – and trade unions weren't exempt from the rows.

There was an added dimension to the discussions about strip searching because of Northern Ireland's conservative culture. As a schoolgirl I had been taught to protect my modesty in the changing rooms, where we would undress, often going into contortions to prevent anyone seeing us naked, especially in the shower. When I had gone to pick strawberries as a holiday job, my school friend Jill and I watched in horror as Scandinavian women walked to the bathroom in our shared accommodation without a stitch on. The prison service was arguing that strip searching was a security precaution that prevented the smuggling of weapons and drugs into prison, and that full-body searching – the term they preferred – was necessary. That was not how the women who stood naked in front of prison officers with dogs barking loudly in the background described it. When I met the minister, he argued that since women in prisons in Great Britain were also strip searched, female prisoners in Northern Ireland shouldn't be treated any differently. But republican women claimed that the practice was being used as a form of power and control inside the prison, because they were perceived as the enemy. We could put people on the moon, but we couldn't find the technology to prevent prisoners from being stripped of their clothes. To avoid a mass strip-search during the move from Armagh to Maghaberry, I proposed that leaving one secure setting to go to another negated the need for these searches. They didn't take place on that occasion but it wasn't the end of the practice.

By the late 1980s, community development workers had found creative and innovative ways to deal with the social and economic deprivation caused by the Troubles. My idea was to build on the expertise that women had gained from their important and often difficult work in local communities through a university course that would give them a recognised qualification. I designed a Certificate in Women's Studies, a multidisciplinary programme spanning a range of subject areas. It was one of the first in the UK and Ireland. Women who hadn't been able to avail themselves of further education in their earlier lives craved the opportunity to get a higher-level accreditation and that's what I wanted to give them. Women's and community centres across Northern Ireland provided a rich harvest of talent, and all I had to do was go out and encourage them to sign on the dotted line. They would turn out to be some of the most brilliant and talented students I ever came across.

The sign outside the Chrysalis Women's Centre in Craigavon welcomed budding writers and activists. When I first met Maggie, one of the students I recruited, she was reading Simone de Beauvoir and greedy for more. She had joined a creative writing class with Philomena, who I also recruited. Others were holding poetry readings around the table, and some of the poems reflected the grimness of the place they were living in. Craigavon had been built as a new town in the 1960s – a place I had studied during my planning days. Even back then we had agreed that if Sir Robert Matthew had had a dream when he was designing the new town, he had woken up in the middle of it – the place was a series of poorly designed housing estates, improved only by beacons of light like the well named Chrysalis Centre. I found more recruits among the workers and volunteers of the RATs (Rural Action Teams) and the BATs (Belfast Action Teams), set up to increase social and economic development in areas of disadvantage.

I wanted to counteract the four Cs – culture, cash, childcare and confidence – that had for so long limited women's opportunities, particularly when it came to further education. I managed to get the university to waive the fees for the certificate in Women's Studies and to provide a free space in the crèche for anyone who needed it. That first year, twenty-five women registered, ranging in age from mid-twenties to sixty.

If I wanted the Women's Studies course to carry the same weight as A levels or other degree-entry qualifications, the university insisted that it had to have a mathematics component. This was the first hurdle I had to get over. I was aware that because of the way maths had been taught at school, it filled many of my potential students with fear, so I needed to design a module that they could relate to. Budgeting and balancing household income was something women understood, so I put a component in on basic statistics and managed to get the university panel to agree to that as a substitute. During the planning stage, I also thought about the way we should deliver the course. To avoid formal lectures, I settled on a more conversational style of teaching that would allow plenty of opportunity for questions and discussion.

What I hadn't planned for was the way in which some of the women's partners reacted to them becoming students. A woman whose partner was a teacher had been instructed by him to abandon the course on the grounds that only one of them (meaning himself) needed to have an education. Another man told his wife she was overstepping the mark. He refused to help out with any of the childminding and she had to take her books to the bathroom to avoid upsetting him. One partner complained that women were now trying to take over the world by doing a women's studies course. Other men demanded that their partners fulfil all of the domestic duties before any studying took place at home. A few women recognised the price they would have to pay for becoming better educated than their husband or partner. Some of the students found it difficult to hold their relationships together. When her marriage broke up, one of the women said she couldn't go back to the way she was before, which was the constant demand her husband was making of her. There were times I worried I was the cause of the problem, until one woman said: 'I was a non-person. I was an extension of him. That was then; I've changed now because of this course.'

By the late 1980s, students were hoping for better times, having lived through some of the worst years of the Troubles. It was also because of the conflict that many of them, as so-called ordinary women, were doing extraordinary things. One had helped to set up Lagan College, Northern Ireland's first religiously integrated secondary school in 1981. Another had started a campaign against plastic bullets, following the tragic death of her husband, who had been hit by one of these bullets during a public demonstration in West Belfast in 1984.

What came up again and again on the course was that people's attitudes to victims were often dictated by their own political identity. Some students had difficulty empathising with the sufferings of 'the other side' and there was a tendency to cast aspersions or engage in 'whataboutery'. This didn't mean that discussions on who was a 'genuine' victim and who was the 'terrorist' didn't occur. They did, but we made sure they were carefully facilitated. The norm in most classrooms was not to talk about the political situation as it was seen as too difficult, but I saw how the weight on the students' shoulders lifted as I mediated the discussions.

On the day of the final ceremony, the students were over the moon, and I made sure that each of them had a graduation gown for their photographs. I was worried about the sixty-year-old who had a pacemaker but it didn't make a sound as she walked across the stage to receive her scroll. The pictures of the day show their scrolls being thrown high above their heads and their joy in their university achievements. They presented me with a cake decorated with the feminist symbol. Philomena returned to Craigavon with her diploma and published a book of women's poetry. Maggie entered a degree course later that year and did a Masters degree after that.

It gave me great encouragement that the course had gone so well, and the next step was to extend the programme to Magee in Derry. Magee University College – a beautiful, old, red brick building – had lost out in 1965 when the unionist government had decided to build a new university on a greenfield site in the small market town of Coleraine rather than putting it on the grounds of the historic college in Derry, where Catholics were crying out for jobs and educational opportunities. My father supported the farmers who used their tractors to block workers from coming on to the site at Coleraine. They didn't succeed, but they were still in my mind the first day I drove from the campus at Jordanstown to the one at Magee, which by then had become part of the University of Ulster.

I crawled at a snail's pace across the Glenshane Pass on icy wintry days to teach the course. Patricia Lundy, who was the course director there, and I were determined to give the students in Derry the same opportunities as those on the Belfast campus. One of the students, Mary Doherty, was married to the vice president of Sinn Féin and lived in north Donegal. To avoid being stopped and questioned by the British Army on the checkpoint, she left her car on the other side of the border and caught a bus for the last leg of the journey. My journey across the Glenshane Pass each Friday morning faded into insignificance by comparison. I got to know the women on the course so well and I knew that all of them had made a lot of sacrifices to be there. Like Belfast, Derry had been profoundly affected by the Troubles, and Phil Coulter captured how much the city had changed in his song 'The Town I Loved So Well'. The women told me how their lives had been blighted by unemployment and devastated by violence, but we laughed over the line about men on the dole playing a mother's role – this hadn't been their experience. They had to keep up with all the housework and childcare as well as their jobs in the shirt factories.

Following the success of the university courses in Belfast and Derry, I reached out to regional colleges so that more students could access the course. Hundreds of women took up the offer, and Women's Studies blossomed. Dawn Purvis was one of the students at the Belfast Tech. After she received her qualifications, she progressed to become leader of the Progressive Unionist Party – one of the first women in Northern Ireland to head up a political party.

I linked up with Ailbhe Smyth at University College Dublin, who was running the Women's Education and Resource Centre there. We agreed to get our classes together, with the students spending a day in Dublin, and Ailbhe and her students coming to the north another day. When we had this idea about the exchange, we hadn't anticipated the anxiety the visit would cause among the women from both north and south who'd never crossed the border before. It was particularly difficult for the students from loyalist communities because the Republic of Ireland was perceived as hostile territory. The Dublin students worried that their accents would make them targets in Belfast. By the time we got the logistics sorted, both Ailbhe's head and mine were buzzing. The experiences of living with the conflict in the north were very different from perceptions in the south. It was as if we were living on two different planets. Despite all the hassle, the students loved the exchange, and we agreed we should keep it going, but it petered out due to lack of resources.

Celia Davies became the professor of Women's Studies at the University of Ulster and set up CROW – which was not the best acronym for the Centre for Research on Women. I got on brilliantly with her, and one of our first joint projects was to organise a north–south all-female conference on Women and Religion in Ireland in 1992. We brought together scripture scholars, spiritual directors, theologians, ministers, lay preachers, nuns and community activists to discuss the all-important issue of the impact of religion on women's lives. Lesley Carroll, an ordained Presbyterian minister, addressed the conference and connected with everyone there when she described how hard it had been as a woman to be taken seriously within her church. Whatever else may have divided the different churches, we concluded that the way in which the 'ecumenical patriarchy' operated was a common problem. Hilary Sidwell – friend, Quaker and founding member of Women's Aid in Derry – closed the proceedings with the words of a Women's Friends meeting from 1698: 'All be up and doing, and put your hand to the work and your shoulders to the burden.'

We were all up and doing at the Centre for Research on Women, trawling through unpublished records, newspapers and government files on every aspect of women's lives in Northern Ireland. Eilish Rooney scrutinised class, sexuality, gender, disability, ethnicity and religion, knowing that one impacted on the other. When we designed a Master's degree in Women's Studies, the intersection of these identities became a key focus for us all.

One of the first students to enrol was Bernadette Devlin McAliskey. She introduced herself to her fellow postgraduates saying, 'My name has travelled a lot further than my feet.' I was perhaps the only one there who knew that her feet had walked miles over the Glenshane Pass for civil rights. Some of her classmates might have been daunted by her image in the press but by the time she joined the course, she had spent many years pioneering projects with migrant workers in Dungannon, County Tyrone. The changes in the demographic make-up of Northern Ireland was one of the topics we were covering and Bernadette's experience of working with new communities made an important contribution to our discussions, and to helping to move us beyond the more usual British/Irish binary.

When we designed the Master's degree in Women's Studies, I wanted to fill the vacuum on the history of women's political activism that was missing from the academic literature. I remembered when my friend Margaret Ward, in our days at Queen's, had put forward the idea of researching the role of women in Irish nationalist movements, only to be told by her tutor that women didn't have much to offer to Irish history. Her subsequent career proved how wrong he had been. We needed an anthology for our course but the *Field Day Anthology of Irish Writing*, published in 1989, was of little use to us because of the absence of women. Following our protests, the editors agreed to address the vacuum and it led to a lengthy collaboration among women scholars. Two additional volumes for the anthology were produced but left us asking why we had to keep doing this.

If there were days when it seemed the road to equal rights was a never-ending struggle, there were others that renewed our hope. The trade union movement and women's movement joined forces each 8 March, International Women's Day, to walk together down Royal Avenue in Belfast. By the early 1990s, there were a couple of hundred of us. We held banners as we waved to passers-by and were relieved when they waved back. We sang our women's anthem, 'Bread and Roses', with all our hearts – calling for joy in our lives and food on the table. Surely, the day was coming when our song would be heard far and wide?

> As we go marching, marching
> in the beauty of the day,
> a million darkened kitchens,
> a thousand mill lofts gray
> Are touched with all the radiance
> that a sudden sun discloses.
> For the people hear us singing,
> bread and roses, bread and roses.

5

Bringing It Out in the Open

'They weren't partners in the true sense of that word. It was
the opposite of what being a partner should mean.'

Noelle Collins, Women's Aid staff worker

In 1991 I was delighted, as well as daunted, to be asked by the Department
of Health and Social Services to undertake work on domestic violence.
When I published 'Bringing It Out in the Open' in 1993, it was the first
government-commissioned report on the topic in Northern Ireland and
the culmination of a year's work, during which I went around the country
talking to a hundred women who had been abused as well as to those who
were providing help to them. The help seekers and the help providers
both had important things to tell me. And I realised early on that I was
up against long-held views. One came from English Common Law, which
once held that a man could chastise his wife in moderation. From that
came the belief that a man was permitted to hit his wife with a stick no
thicker than his thumb, hence the 'rule of thumb'. Abusers still thought
they were entitled to hit their wives to show them who was the boss within
the home. Another norm was the perception of domestic violence as a
private issue – not a matter for legislation or public policy. This was linked
to the patriarchal view that an Englishman's home was his castle, and
that the man could behave however he wanted behind closed doors. In
addition, legislators made assumptions about the kinds of men who were
abusers, believing them to be mad men, bad men or 'that lot over there'.
But there is no such thing as a typical abuser, as my study would show.

The law that I was working with in the 1990s, known as the Offences

Against the Person Act, went as far back as 1868, and I set out to change it. It was time we understood how power and control worked – rather than treating offences as one-offs, we needed to recognise a pattern of abuse. I was also determined to extend the protection of the law to all women. It was as late as 1975 before there was any legislation on domestic violence in Northern Ireland, and even then it only protected married women. In the Assembly debate, one of the members who supported the exemption on cohabitees argued that if women chose to live in sin, they would have to reap the consequences.

An important part of domestic violence legislation was the introduction of exclusion orders in the 1980s, which empowered the police to remove offenders from their homes, but ensuring that the courts applied the orders was another matter. One magistrate adjourned a hearing to double-check how the orders worked – that they really meant that a man would be removed from his home. When John McGettrick, a solicitor I worked with who was representing the victim of domestic violence that day, confirmed that was the case, the magistrate said that the orders reminded him of penal times, when men could be put out of their homes. He represented a legal culture that perceived this legislation as an unwarranted interference in family life – an Irishman's home was clearly his castle too. There was more sympathy for the perpetrator than for the victim and that needed to change.

Activists and volunteers had been working on domestic violence in Northern Ireland since the mid-1970s. In 1977, Avila and Cathy Harkin had set up a refuge for the victims of domestic violence in Derry, but to do so they had had to squat in an empty social services building, since there was no other accommodation available for victims fleeing from the abuse of their partners. It was far from plain sailing – they had been told by social services that there was no need for such provision in Derry at the same time as they were being denounced by a local priest for breaking up marriages. The local Ulster Unionist Party MP Willie Ross called for their imprisonment under the Emergency Provisions Act for squatting in a public building. Over that first year, the refuge provided shelter to ninety women and three hundred children. When the building was officially opened, Avila and Cathy invited the direct rule minister for the Labour government, Peter Melchett, to the ceremony. Despite threats beforehand from local republicans objecting to British ministers coming to Derry, the visit went ahead. Avila later mentioned that when Peter Melchett cut the ribbon, he was inadvertently photographed against the backdrop of a poster with the words: 'Women are called birds because of the worms they pick up.' The Northern Ireland Office officials were not amused but Lord Melchett wasn't that bothered.

Women activists in Derry were also supporting rape victims, protesting outside the court hearing of a case in which a local woman had been sexually assaulted by a soldier. Opposed to all forms of violence against women, they also picketed the offices of a Republican group in Derry to object to the tarring and feathering of local women who were dating British soldiers – falling foul of the diktat that there should be no 'fraternising' with the army.

One of the worst cases from the mid-1970s was Noreen Winchester's. She was from Sandy Row in Belfast and had been convicted of murdering her father after suffering years of sexual abuse by him. Women from all sides of the political spectrum came together in 1976 to campaign for her release from jail. Women protesters demanded that the courts quash her conviction and took to the streets again after the Court of Appeal upheld her sentence. The following year a royal pardon freed her.

A few years later, I attended a court case to support a woman who had been gang raped by a group of men. The men, who were from a loyalist paramilitary group, had taken the young woman, who was Catholic, and her Protestant friend to a house on the Shankill. Once they'd forced both women to say the Lord's Prayer, they knew from the ending they used which one was Catholic and her fate was sealed. After she had taken the brave decision to pursue a prosecution against her attackers, she had to go into hiding. A group of women, including Susan McKay, were setting up a Rape Crisis Centre in Belfast, building on Susan's experiences in the Dublin one. It was ground-breaking work, dispelling myths and advocating for women in court. The group put together a rota of volunteers so that one of us would be in court to support the young woman every day.

On the first day of the trial, I turned up at the High Court only to find that the UVF had planted a hoax bomb outside, with the aim of disrupting the hearing, which it did. The trial was moved to the courthouse on the Crumlin Road and I sat there in the gallery, surrounded by men who I soon realised were there to support the perpetrators. It didn't take them long to work out that I was on the side of the victim.

If it was intimidating for me, I knew it must be much harder for the woman in the witness box, seeing the rapists smirking each time she spoke. They joked and laughed throughout the trial but that came to a stop when the judge read out the verdict. He stated that the men's sectarianism was an aggravating factor and handed down lengthy sentences. At least we had that to celebrate when we took to the streets for the Rape Crisis Centre's 'Reclaim the Night' march that year.

It was these women's experiences that were at the forefront of my mind when I set out to do my study into domestic violence. The circumstances in which these crimes were committed all differed, but they were the result of an entrenched set of attitudes that I came across time and time again. I knew that the statistics showing the extent of the problem had to be brought out into the open. While the number of victims of the Troubles was well known, there was barely any information on domestic violence, let alone a figure for the number of families affected. But I also wanted to include the victims' own stories, to show how it feels to experience domestic violence. That meant learning to balance empathy with detachment.

The figures that did exist, I collated at the police station on Montgomery Road in Belfast, and I soon realised that there were lots of gaps. The figures there mostly reflected calls from working-class women, who had few resources to fall back on and so needed the help of the police. Information on ethnicity, disability, age and religion was missing, so they didn't tell the full story. In the course of my interviews with the women affected, I was able to show the prevalence of domestic violence among all these groups and that it was much more frequent than anyone had expected. The domestic violence that was being recorded by the police was only the tip of the iceberg.

Along with the horrors that came out during these interviews, there was hope because these women had survived, and they also talked about that. They hoped that my research would raise awareness and prevent other women from being abused. This was a high bar for me and I felt a huge sense of responsibility. I wanted to channel their feelings into doing whatever I could to effect change.

I began each interview in the same way – asking the woman when she had first experienced abuse and what had happened. I went on to ask about the worst time and then the most recent incident. After every interview I thought I must have heard the worst story until I heard the next, even more terrible one. One woman described how her partner had tried to cut her throat. She was terrified when I met her, as although he had been jailed for the assault, he was just about to be released, and she was scared of what he might do to her. In the course of other interviews I heard about ruptured eardrums, fractured ribs, gouged eyes and broken bones. One man had taken the time to put on his steel-toe boots before assaulting his pregnant wife. Many women I interviewed had contemplated suicide. A significant number also told me about marital rape, even if they didn't use that term. One woman explained, 'I used to let him have his way with me before he went to the pub – to try and stop him from going. But he would go anyway and then he would have his way with me after he came home. I suppose you could say that he raped me but that's very hard to admit.' Unlike rapes in which strangers are involved, intimate-partner rape tends to carry its own unique impact. One woman described how she felt her body was 'occupied territory' because of her partner's sense of entitlement to sex without her consent. Until 1994, the legislation ignored the problem, on the grounds that a married woman couldn't have non-consensual sex with her husband as she had entered into a 'conjugal' relationship. Even after 1994, prosecutions for marital rape remained almost non-existent. It is still no better.

I had heard police officers describe the kinds of incidents that the women told me about as 'just another domestic', but the women wanted me to make everyone understand what it was really like to be in an abusive relationship. Even if their partners seemed like street angels to everyone else, the women knew them as house devils. Some of the abusers were so-called pillars of respectability: church elders and, as some women put it, 'altar lickers', because they attended church so devotedly. But these outwardly respectable and religious men were all too ready to act violently behind closed doors. In the photographs the women showed me, their partners looked like gentlemen, which made it even harder for the women to be believed. As one of them said, 'No one would understand that he was a violent person if they met him. He was so good-hearted, so kind, so happy-go-lucky. He was the life and soul of the party.'

Many of these women were trying to survive in circumstances so awful that they were almost beyond belief. A frequent pattern was that a woman would leave her partner but then return, hoping that he might change. A lack of understanding of this pattern led to the women facing judgement from help providers, rather than belief and support. I learned in the course of my study that each time a woman went back she felt a bit stronger. The women told me that they needed to be able to make their own choices about when to leave, and that's where empowerment came in. Women had all kinds of coping strategies – some stayed because they thought it was best for the children but ended up leaving when they realised how harmful it was for their children to witness the abuse. I also found that most women didn't leave after the worst incident of violence; instead they made the decision to get out for good when they could see that their partner wasn't going to change. They could no longer bear the broken promises. The stories showed that leaving a violent relationship was a process and not an event.

Even after they left, women worried their partners would discover their whereabouts and come after them. One woman felt she would never be free and described how her partner had told her in a singsong voice, 'I've got a big knife waiting for you – c'mon till you see what you're going to get.' She knew he meant those threats and was always looking over her shoulder. Women were forced to go underground, taking desperate measures not to be found. There were even women from the Republic of Ireland who had come to Northern Ireland in the belief that the Troubles would prevent their partners from following them. The segregated communities in Northern Ireland added additional difficulty and meant that victims could find themselves between a rock and a hard place – at home with their abuser, or being forced to flee to a safe house in an area that was anything but safe. A victim of domestic violence that I knew had moved away from her abusive partner and chosen to live in a part of town 'belonging' to the other side. She was trying to build a new life for herself and her children. But she was threatened by paramilitaries, who forced the family to leave the house because they wanted it for 'one of their own'. I helped her to pack up, throwing everything into black bin bags to get them out at speed. A double blow – sectarian abuse on top of everything else she had been through.

For those made homeless as the result of an emergency, there was very little temporary accommodation – most short-stay housing was for men who had been released from prison. I met one woman who was walking the roads with her children to put the day in before they were allowed back at night to their entirely unsuitable guesthouse accommodation. She explained, 'When I moved out, I had to live with three children in one room at the top of the attic. It was freezing and damp, and there were millions of flies, and I had no money. We used to walk around outside, the kids were all foundered and I felt forgotten.' Their 'invisibility' was heartbreaking as it was happening in a country with a welfare state in the last decade of the twentieth century.

The problems didn't magically end once the women had left. Women suffered long after the bruises had healed. They told me they had been emotionally affected through years of watching the steam of their partners' rising tempers, knowing that a beating would come next. Many spent years trying to eliminate the echo of their abuser's insults from inside their heads. They had absorbed what they had been told – that they were ugly or fat or stupid. One woman felt she had been brainwashed, saying, 'He conditioned me to be what he wanted me to be. I was told that nobody else would want me and I believed him.'

I was horrified when I heard that a woman, who lived close to me, had been murdered by her partner when she was five months pregnant; and another woman I knew of through my work with Women's Aid – a mother of six children – was also murdered at around the same time. Too often the men who committed these crimes were being charged with manslaughter rather than murder, on the basis of a lack of intent. A doctor in the City hospital told me of a woman who would be paralysed for life as a result of her husband throwing her down the stairs. In court, the husband claimed it wasn't deliberate. The doctor and I discussed the need to have these crimes properly prosecuted, recognising that the life-changing assaults and murders were the culmination of a pattern of abusive behaviour.

In Northern Ireland, at the time of my studies, political violence took precedence over everything else. Femicides were being overlooked because they were being labelled as ODC (Ordinary Decent Crime) and because the criminal justice system was deluged by all the Troubles-related cases.

As a result of the Troubles 17,500 soldiers and 14,000 police officers had access to personal protection weapons, as did politicians and business people connected to the security sector. The place was awash with weapons, some of which were used by abusers. The number of deaths caused by these 'legally' held guns and their role in domestic violence was a particular concern to me, and came into sharp focus on 4 February 1992. Constable Allen Moore, an off-duty police officer, opened fire with a high velocity weapon on people inside a Sinn Féin advice centre on the Falls Road in Belfast, killing three men. The media reported that his actions were due to the stress of working as a police officer in the Troubles, but I was aware of some of the background that had led up to his actions that day. A police colleague of Moore's had been killed in a domestic violence incident a few days previously. This colleague's wife had a number of exclusion orders against her husband but on the day he died, he had tracked her down and was coming after her with his personal protection weapon. In the altercation that followed, the gun went off, killing him. I knew all this because I was reviewing the 'domestic' violence cases that involved manslaughter in the Public Prosecution Office at the time. It turned out that Moore was a walking time bomb who should not have been allowed to retain his weapons – he had been diagnosed as mentally unwell previous to the Falls Road murders after he was discovered firing shots over the grave of his late colleague. Four people died needlessly – three men in the advice centre and Moore himself, who later died by suicide. These cases highlighted the dangers posed by personal protection weapons, particularly in domestic violence cases, and the police's responsibility to review whether the licensee was fit to hold a gun. I kept raising the issue, in partnership with Women's Aid, until the police agreed to revoke licences when they were presented with evidence that an officer was violent at home.

The issue of having a personal protection weapon in the home had come to public attention before. During a debate in the Northern Ireland Constitutional Convention on 3 March 1976, Ian Paisley had challenged David Trimble about an incident in a rented apartment in Belfast. Trimble's legally held gun had fallen off a table, causing a bullet to be discharged near his partner. It was an accident, but Paisley wasn't going to miss the opportunity to raise the matter in a public forum. It was another example of the harm that could be caused when guns that are kept in the home are accidentally discharged.

Paramilitaries may not have kept guns at home because of the risk of police searches, but they had access to them. A case that stood out for me was the wife of a paramilitary member who had experienced domestic violence. She explained, 'He would put a gun to my head playing Russian roulette – and I didn't know if there was a real bullet inside. He did it so often that I didn't care if I lived or died.' One of the workers at Women's Aid told me of another woman who had circular bruises on her neck that had been inflicted by the muzzle of a gun. This was the kind of thing that was going on in Northern Ireland. I was able to show that women were in more danger because of the availability of guns, irrespective of which 'side' they were on.

Because of the Troubles, if a woman was being assaulted and called the police, they would first have to verify that the call was genuine. Concern over possible paramilitary attack meant that on occasions it could take the police up to six hours to respond to a domestic violence call. I had experienced this problem myself when I phoned the police after a car accident in Ardoyne. The officer on duty asked that I call back after ten minutes to give them time to check out the call as it had been made from a 'troubled' area. It was a long ten minutes, and it gave me some sense of how victims must have felt, waiting for help to arrive. Women living in predominantly republican areas in the countryside had the longest wait. I visited a woman who had lived on a farm in County Tyrone and had called the police after an attack. Just as I had been asked to call back, she was asked to do the same, but before she could, her husband had smashed the phone. She had run across the fields to a neighbour to make the second call. The police finally arrived by helicopter, and the woman's young daughter described the scene to me, saying, 'The policemen took my daddy up into the sky.' This wasn't El Salvador; it was Northern Ireland in 1992. Even if the police could come by road, they would arrive in a convoy of heavily armoured vehicles, with their army escorts holding sub-machine guns. These visits were anything but discreet – the neighbours could see the police coming from a mile off, and that added to the caller's distress. Women told me how humiliating it was climbing into the back of an armoured Land Rover to be brought to safety.

These no-go areas also meant that exclusion orders were either not served or not properly enforced. Getting a protection order in the first place was an ordeal. Brave women had faced their partners in court only to find that the protection orders weren't worth the paper they were printed on. The men who were the subjects of these orders knew that, and continually breached them. This was the case for a woman I interviewed in south Derry. While I was there, her husband walked in, despite a court order being in place to exclude him from the family home. It was terrifying. As he asked what I was doing talking to his wife, I kicked the tape recorder under the chair to make it look as though we were just having a chat. I knew how serious the consequences would be if he realised that she was telling me what he had put her through. He left when he had decided I wasn't a threat. The experience brought home how dangerous it was for women whose abusive partners could act with such impunity.

Some women were also angry that their abusers were evading the police when even 'the dogs in the street know where to find them'. They alleged that collusion was the reason – that these men were being enticed by the police to act as informers, to pass on intelligence on 'local terrorists' in lieu of being arrested for their domestic violence offences. In many instances, this lack of enforcement led to women being grievously injured and even murdered. To combat this problem, I campaigned to have a legal reform introduced, which resulted in breaches of protection orders being treated as criminal offences rather than civil matters, so the police could no longer ignore them. The Domestic Proceedings (Northern Ireland) Order came into force in Northern Ireland in 1980, and when it did we celebrated the fact that we were now ahead of the rest of the UK. It was quite an achievement for a small group of determined activists.

I was aware that there were also women who couldn't seek help from the police. They were mostly from republican and loyalist working-class areas where the paramilitaries were in control. When the police questioned women, they tended to ask more questions about the husband's political activities than the domestic violence. Ultimately nothing ever came of the domestic abuse incident. What I heard often, from both sides, was, 'In this area, you don't go to the police.' In these no-go areas, the armed groups acted as judge and jury, deciding on how the perpetrators of rapes and sexual assaults should be punished. The penalty often involved ordering the abuser to leave the area, thus displacing the problem and putting other women and girls at risk. The issue came to the fore when perpetrators who had been put out of their local areas were found to be working in youth clubs and centres in other communities, where they continued their serial sexual abuse. The groups also handed out punishment beatings – also known as paramilitary-style attacks – but tended to go easier on members of their own organisations. In fact, there were incidences when men who were known to be abusing their partners were still seen as heroes. This applied to paramilitaries as well as to men in the police and army. The link between militarism and toxic masculinity was apparent for all to see. As a result, women with abusive partners who couldn't turn to the police also hesitated to ask the paramilitaries for help. Some were afraid that their partners would be permanently disabled if they were subjected to punishment shootings or beatings; others feared that the paramilitaries would ask them for something in return – to hide weapons or to provide a safe house.

In the predominantly macho culture of 1990s Northern Ireland, heavy drinking was par for the course. From an early age, I had learned to walk on eggshells around anyone who was intoxicated, aware of how excessive drinking could change an otherwise mild-mannered man. Often men who drank too much used it as an excuse for their abusive behaviour. The courts no longer permitted the excuse of being drunk as a way out of a dangerous driving charge; they needed to stop allowing it as a mitigating factor in domestic violence cases.

The churches also played a role in perpetuating abuse, especially when clergy told victims that they should put up with it, or offer it up as a sacrifice – that their reward would come in heaven. One minister I was told about went as far as telling a woman that she was living in sin by leaving her husband and seeking refuge with Women's Aid. He had told her that God was making all these things happen to her and was punishing her for a reason. Rather than insisting that families should stay together at all costs, clergymen like him should have been much more aware that the price for that could be too high. A deeply religious woman who had left her husband explained the impact that her church's thinking had on her: 'I felt as if I was standing naked in Belfast. That I was completely stripped to the bone – because it had all fallen down around me, everybody could see into my soul.' Like so many other women, she'd also heard the expression, 'You've made your bed, you have to lie in it.'

I had an opportunity to tackle this thinking when my cousin Paddy asked me to 'preach' in his church in Poleglass, West Belfast, in 1988 – one of the most nerve-wracking invitations I have ever received. By the time that Sunday came around, I was even more nervous, and anxious to do a good job. It was my opportunity to share the women's experiences, and to make the points that emotional abuse could be just as damaging as physical assaults and that they both stemmed from patriarchal attitudes. I spoke from the heart but, as I looked across the packed church, it was hard to gauge how I was coming across. So, it was a relief to hear members of the congregation say afterwards that it was time the issue was brought out into the open. Afterwards Father Paddy distributed our Women's Aid leaflet, 'When Home Is Where the Hurt Is', so that women knew what to do if they needed help. We hoped that since the pamphlet was freely available to them, other clergy would do the same.

Traveller women were also having a hard time. Refuges for women had a rule against taking boys over the age of fifteen. This meant that any woman with older sons could not bring them when they left an abusive partner to go to a refuge. That tended especially to be a problem for Traveller women, who often had large families. In addition, Travellers have a highly developed communication network and codes of honour specific to their culture. These make it difficult for women to keep their place of refuge secret from other women in their own community as well as from their partner. There was a lack of safe houses for women who needed extra security measures because of the risk of their partner trying to abduct their children. I sat with my mouth open as a woman told me the story of how she had escaped to a Traveller site in England but had to flee again when she saw her husband's car at the gate. Word had spread about where she was staying and it was the police who managed to 'rescue' her. They brought her to Heathrow airport and, when they saw that a group of men was following the family, they arranged for the airline to get her and her eight children on the next flight to Belfast. When the family landed, the police in England had arranged for their colleagues in Northern Ireland to take the family straight to Women's Aid. She explained to me that, within her community, a woman was never allowed to leave her husband: 'We have a very strict life with the one husband. When we get married, it's for life and it's not easy to separate.' Migrant women and refugees were particularly vulnerable when trapped in abusive relationships because their visas so often depended on them staying married.

As part of my research for the report, I was also recording the journey of abuse investigations through the criminal justice system: the number of initial reports and referrals to the Public Prosecution Service; how many went through the different stages of the court process; how many repeat offences were recorded; the number of prosecutions; and the sentences handed down.

Kate's story is one I will never forget. She was working in the university library when I first interviewed her as part of my study. She was one of the kindest, most gentle people I had ever met, and I came to know her as the most devoted of mothers. She told me about her husband, a prison officer, at whose hands she had suffered years of abuse. He had access to a personal protection weapon that he used to threaten her and her children. One night she reported him to the police, who removed his gun but returned it the next day. That was a major mistake – Kate's husband was enraged that she had been in touch with the police and threatened to kill her. He stalked her and one morning he attacked her and her daughter with a knife in the university car park. Kate was taken by ambulance to A&E, where her husband – who'd been slightly injured when the daughter had fought back – was waiting. He was in the next cubicle and pulled back the curtain, with the words, 'I didn't get you this time but I'll get you the next.' I stayed in touch with Kate and asked Women's Aid to support her through the court case, as I knew her life was in danger. Even though the charge against him was downgraded from attempted murder to wounding with intent, and he pleaded guilty to the lesser charge, we knew that he would continue to pose a threat once he got out of prison. Kate and her children were put into the witness protection programme – this was a first for a domestic violence case, usually reserved for Troubles-related cases.

Kate's story didn't end there – her husband demanded access to his children, and a judge ordered that she return for the custody hearing. This was nothing but a ploy by Kate's husband to cause her and the children further trauma and, as soon as the police explained the cost of interrupting the witness protection programme that Kate was in, the judge dismissed the case. Kate was safe, but her husband carried on threatening anyone whom he perceived as having prevented him from seeing 'his' wife and 'his' children, including me. This sense of ownership led him to believe that he could do what he liked to Kate's friends and family. With her new identity, Kate had gone to live in England. I really missed her. She had got her freedom and her life had undoubtedly been saved, but it was a strange freedom. She and her children had to start a completely new life, away from everything they'd ever known.

Another story that has always stayed with me is Sharon's. Her case fitted the pattern I had found among women subjected to domestic violence who had killed their male partners. I had met Sharon in prison on a few occasions after she had been convicted of murder and sentenced to thirteen years. She had explained to the court that her partner had attacked her with a knife and that she had managed to get it off him. She was holding the knife when he came at her again, and claimed that he had been fatally wounded as she tried to defend herself. When she appealed her conviction, on the grounds that she was suffering from 'battered woman syndrome', I wanted to know what her defence team would say. They argued that because of years of domestic violence Sharon was suffering from a depressive illness. I didn't like the use of battered woman syndrome to explain what she had done, and it didn't work for Sharon. Her original conviction was upheld. It was my belief that a stronger argument for diminished responsibility should have been made in the first place, given the evidence of serial abuse. When she was first remanded in custody, the officers told me that she'd had multiple stab wounds to her body and was covered in blood from head to toe.

The women I have met over the years who have killed their partners are tortured by the fact that no one understands why they did what they did. They have almost always experienced prior trauma, whether as children or adults, and I have long felt that those experiences need to be taken more seriously by the criminal justice system. I think of these women as having been subjected to 'intimate terrorism', the same as if they had been held hostage or kidnapped. Victimhood was mostly being measured in terms of broken bones and physical injuries when we needed to understand what women experience from living under a tyrannical regime of abuse and what we now call coercive control. Violence, perpetrated by partners, was more akin to long-term deprivation of liberty rather than a series of unconnected violent episodes. If a hostage killed her captor, she could plead self-defence to a charge of murder. For a victim of domestic abuse, deprivation of liberty did not constitute a legal argument. Instead, the courts focused on the psychiatric one. The limitations in the criminal justice system's understanding of intimate-partner violence meant that women like Sharon were forced to argue mental illness as their key defence.

I was lucky to have Joan McKiernan, Lynda Spence and Jessica Doyle work alongside me at different times as my research assistants. We all shared a sensitivity towards victims of domestic violence and a commitment to drive forward change. We stood together, and over the years we published a series of reports. I was encouraged when the findings of my first study resulted in the first UK government policy that provided a new approach, as well as services, for victims and their children. I couldn't have been more delighted since so many research studies end up gathering dust on official shelves.

After each publication, we were approached by a range of organisations working with medics, midwives, social workers, the court service and the police to see if we would come and provide training. Using the findings, I helped to draft the Public Prosecution Service's guidelines on domestic violence. In the training with police officers, I heard some of them say that they had joined the force to fight terrorism and not to split up families. The training I delivered tackled this kind of thinking. I also worked with probation officers to introduce the first-ever programmes to tackle the behaviour of abusers. The efficacy of these programmes has improved as the years have gone on. The outcomes differ – if the perpetrator has not become a serial abuser, they have a chance of working and being effective. The best result comes from abusers taking responsibility for their behaviour and changing it, and from probation officers checking back with partners to ensure that this is, in fact, the case.

While I could see the positive impact that the training was having, there were still gaps in the system, as I saw for myself when I became involved in Debbie's case. I discovered some of the reasons why only a minimal number of rapes reported to police got to the point of conviction when I accompanied Debbie, a young woman with cerebral palsy, through a rape trial in 2001. Her mother had asked for my support after the Public Prosecution Service had dropped the case of rape against her former partner, who had been for a time Debbie's stepfather. I wrote to them on Debbie's behalf to ask why, and was told that they believed she wouldn't be a competent witness because of her cerebral palsy. They hadn't even interviewed her. They agreed to reconsider and, after meeting Debbie, they informed the alleged abuser that the case was going to trial. Once the stepfather discovered – in information received from the Prosecution Service – that I was supporting Debbie and her mother, I began to receive anonymous phone calls at home. I couldn't prove any of them were coming from him, but on the first day of the trial, when I saw him outside the courthouse, I watched his reaction carefully as I said to him, 'If you jump out from behind a hedge, I now know what you look like.' He walked away like a coward and that was the end of the phone calls.

The trial was held in Antrim courthouse, and I was shocked at the way the proceedings unfolded. The judge insisted that the jury shouldn't see Debbie in her wheelchair, which meant that she had to be in the witness box before the jury entered the court, so she had an even longer time in the eyeline of her stepfather. During her cross-examination, Debbie had an epileptic seizure and had to be taken to hospital. When it resumed later that day, the defence barrister told the jury that he thought Debbie's 'performance' had been for their benefit, describing her as 'a bit of a drama queen'. Debbie said later that she felt as though she was the one on trial.

In other rape cases, I had heard lawyers say that 'the witness is only as good as her evidence'. Debbie did have compelling evidence that she wanted to give – that she and her mother had spent time in a Women's Aid refuge to escape her stepfather's violence, and that her cousin had also been sexually abused by him during the same period – but she wasn't permitted to give it as this wasn't considered to be 'similar fact evidence'. After everything they had been through, it was devastating for Debbie and her mother when he was found not guilty. I was appalled by the verdict, and felt it showed the jury's lack of understanding of the behaviour of sexual abusers. When Debbie's cousin later bravely gave evidence in a separate trial against the same man, he was convicted. It became public knowledge that he was an abuser who targeted single mothers to get access to the children.

When I later wrote a report for the Department of Justice recommending a raft of changes across the criminal justice system, from the police, prosecution and defence lawyers to the court service staff, I had Debbie's experiences in mind. The system had to provide more support for witnesses so that justice could be served. There was more work to be done to ensure public confidence in rape trials.

It took almost thirty years from when I first raised the reality of coercive control for it to become part of domestic violence legislation. When Avila and I talk about how far we still have to go, we cheer ourselves up by remembering how far we have come, especially when we cast our minds back to what it was like in the 1970s, going into the pubs in Derry to raise money for Women's Aid. Avila's poem says it all:

Maintain the smile
Rattle of expectant tin –
With bated breath
Waiting the hit or miss
Of search through pockets.
Congenial gaiety
At comments such as –
'The more they get the better!' –
Abandoned to their pint
We struggle out.
Sigh of relief –
Think of oil bills,
Annie's fractured skull,
Milkmen to be paid –
No church collection for Women's Aid,

No government grant,
As with scant respite
We count the coppers;
Track the change
To make the change –
Holding our her-esies tight.

6

Starting a Family in the Midst of it All

'Three things are important in this world: good health,
peace with one's neighbours and friendship with all.'

African proverb

In 1980, I moved to the Holylands, an area of south Belfast near Queen's University built by a developer who had visited Cairo, Damascus and Jerusalem and named the streets after the places he had been. The first of my friends to buy a house in the area – although in the less exotically named Rugby Avenue – was Maura Lavery, who lived at Number 21. Mary Ryder acquired Number 19, and Eileen, Chris and I became her lodgers. A year later, I bought Number 17 and soon after Chris bought the house across the street. The houses cost next to nothing because the area had become run-down, but we loved living there. We formed a commune for meals on special occasions, with starters at 21, dinner at 19, pudding at 17 and the end of the night across the street with Chris. Three of us had April birthdays, a day apart, and we celebrated for what seemed like forever. But it wasn't all fun and games, as even the most street-smart women in Belfast were far from safe at the time. Assaults as a result of spiked drinks were a common occurrence, so we stuck together like glue. I always remembered what had happened to my friend in the States when her attacker separated her from us. Maura, Mary, Eileen, Chris and I watched out for each other. It was like having a solid rock to lean on through some of the worst years of the Troubles.

The area was considered safe but that wasn't the case on 2 February 1980 when a UVF gunman targeted a man as he was walking home past our house. The man escaped but his friend, William McAteer, who was standing beside him was shot dead. One of the bullets came through our front window, ricocheted off the sofa and got lodged in the fireplace. I wasn't in the house at the time but Mary was, and she was called to court to give evidence. In the end she didn't have to testify because the accused pleaded guilty. She'd been on tenderhooks for weeks for fear of intimidation, which was frequent enough in those days and the cause of many trials collapsing. Not long after, a student was murdered on his way home from the pub just around the corner from our house. I'd heard students singing 'James Connolly', a song that marked them out to the loyalist gunmen who were lying in wait for an easy target. The songs you chose could put your life at risk, and I was concerned for the students who passed by my window at night, singing at the tops of their voices. On the day of the young man's funeral, we stopped classes for a minute's silence as a mark of respect.

During the spring and summer of 1981, the news was dominated by the hunger strike. Margaret Thatcher refused to concede 'special category status' to prisoners with conflict-related convictions. The prisoners refused to accept this decision; both republicans and loyalists regarded themselves as combatants and not criminals. The fight over whether the conflict was a war or whether it was terrorism went on for years, but, in the case of the republicans during the hunger strike, it was literally fought to the finish. Ten republican prisoners began their hunger strike on 1 March 1981 in protest; Bobby Sands was the first to die on 5 May. Twenty-three-year-old Thomas McIlwee was the ninth, and in the weeks leading up to his death and after the strike ended my mother watched his mother's heart break during the charismatic prayer meetings in Portglenone monastery that they both attended.

Along with everyone else in Northern Ireland, and many others across the world, I had watched as Bobby Sands was elected MP for Fermanagh and South Tyrone on 9 April 1981. His victory resulted in the British government introducing legislation to make sure sentenced prisoners couldn't ever again stand for election. It also resulted in Sinn Féin entering the political fray, which they had boycotted until then. Party organiser

Danny Morrison's remark that Sinn Féin would have a ballot box in one hand and an Armalite in the other became part of the party's new lexicon. I was all for Sinn Féin joining mainstream politics, but I asked myself how long a party looking for votes in a democratic society would be able to balance a rifle and a franchise: these two things were polar opposites.

The violence was never-ending and the IRA's definition of 'legitimate targets' seemed to become broader and broader. Even attending Mass was dangerous – Judge William Doyle was killed as he sat in his car after Mass at our local chapel in Derryvolgie, and the seventy-two-year-old woman sitting beside him was seriously wounded. The following year, Mary Travers, the daughter of a local magistrate, was also killed after Mass outside the same church during an IRA attempt on her father's life. When I later interviewed him as part of my work on domestic violence (he was the magistrate in the family court), he described to me the empathy he felt for the victims because of the feeling of powerlessness he'd had the day his daughter was murdered. The university wasn't exempt either – on 7 December 1983, Edgar Graham, a law lecturer at Queen's and a member of the Ulster Unionist Party, was murdered by the IRA close to the university library. The murder brought back memories of my friend Michael Mallon, who had studied with me in the same library just before he was killed by loyalists in 1974.

A few months later, on 12 April 1984, Peggy Whyte was murdered one street over in University Avenue by a bomb at her home. The Whytes were one of the few remaining Catholic families in the area. The bomb, planted by loyalist paramilitaries, killed both Mrs Whyte and the Protestant policeman who had responded to her phone call after she became suspicious of the bag that had been left at the front of the house. I heard her son Jude speaking afterwards about the problem of sectarianism, making the point that when bombs go off, they 'don't discriminate between Protestants and Catholics'.

As well as the violence all around us, I lost two good friends to cancer in the mid-1980s. When Madge Davison and Cathy Harkin were both diagnosed, I wondered if their illness had been caused by the CS gas that they had both been exposed to when they were on the front line of the civil right marches. Madge was living near me, on Agincourt Avenue, and was studying law as well as teaching classes on my women's studies courses. When I brought her home in the evening, she used to swig from a bottle of medicine to ease her 'bad stomach' and I begged her to go to the doctor to find out what was causing it. By the time she went, the cancer was too advanced, and she died not long afterwards. When Cathy, the founder of Women's Aid in Derry, died in 1985, she too left a hole in my heart. These two brave women had planted the seeds first for civil rights in Northern Ireland and then for women's rights, and I had worked closely with both of them. I didn't want either of them to be forgotten. I was glad when the annual memorial lecture for Madge at the West Belfast Festival was announced and also to see the plaque for Cathy at the Women's Aid refuge in Derry.

I first met Brian in 1980 – like me, he was a member of the Belfast Campaign for Nuclear Disarmament (CND) group and a campaigner against apartheid. Brian had studied furniture design at art college and had joined the civil service by the time I met him. We were friends for a couple of years before we got together at Avila and Brian Gormally's wedding in 1983. Brian was encouraging and supportive of my independent life, and I treasured that greatly. I'd always said I'd never get married – so my friends had the last laugh when I asked them to keep a date in April 1984 free. I wasn't sure the time would ever be right to settle down and have children, so it was a big decision for me. I worried about the difference marriage would make to my life but, as it turned out, it wasn't marriage that was the big change, but children.

On the day of my wedding, my father – renowned for his punctuality – walked me up the aisle ten minutes early in Drumagarner chapel, outside my home town of Kilrea. The early pace of the day didn't continue when we were held up by a protest on the way to the reception in Portstewart. The Orange Order was blocking the road in Coleraine because it was angry that Londonderry City Council's name was changing to Derry City Council – dropping the 'London' that Doire (the city's Irish name, meaning 'oak grove') was given during the seventeenth-century plantation. Waiting for the bandsmen to disperse, our driver became anxious. He told us that he'd been driving hunger striker Francis Hughes's coffin three years before when he took a route via loyalist Sandy Row, and found himself surrounded by a protest. He'd had to put the car keys in his mouth to keep them from the protesters – and had only made it out with a police escort. As he told the story, I watched him getting paler and paler. The two Brians (groom and best man) got out of the car to ask the police to let us through, but to no avail. After waiting another half hour, I got out of the car in my wedding dress to make the same request. The police officer told me there was nothing she could do and that it was up to the bandsmen, and one of them finally decided to let us pass. We arrived at the reception over an hour late, only to find that most of the guests had taken the bypass around Coleraine and were wondering what had happened to us.

My family and Brian's were like chalk and cheese – the folks from rural Kilrea meeting the city dwellers from West Belfast, but they all enjoyed the day. I made a speech and was glad of the chance to say the things that are usually left to the men to say after dinner – that I was grateful to my parents and valued the independence that they had given me all my life. We had our wedding pictures taken just as the sun was setting at the water's edge in Portstewart.

I felt thankful that, unlike previous generations of women, I wouldn't be expected to go home and shut the door once I was married. The staff in human resources wanted to know not just my new address but my new name. I told them that I wasn't Mrs B. Smart and that I was still living at the same address.

Brian – Mr B. Smart – had been brought up on the Falls Road in the Beechmount bungalows. His family's home was meant to have been replaced many years before as it had been built after the war to temporarily house families in West Belfast. Belfast City Council, however, took twenty years to make a decision on redevelopment. When the families were eventually rehoused, farmers removed the bungalows to turn them into cattle sheds, which signalled how little the council cared about the state of the accommodation people were forced to live in. When the children were still young, Brian's father had an accident in the shipyard, so his mother became the breadwinner, working the 'granny shift' from four to eight in the mill. After the bungalows were demolished, the family moved to Springhill, Ballymurphy, and that's where Brian spent his teenage years during the Troubles.

Brian grew up fast and furious. When the army first arrived in Northern Ireland, local children thought it was exciting and asked to play with the soldiers' guns, but their guns weren't for playing with. Soldiers out on patrol once lost a machine gun after it fell from the open door at the back of their jeep. The commanding officer sent a soldier to ask the local headmaster, Sammy McKeown, to help him recover it. Sammy obliged: he told the boys in the school that his office would be open that afternoon if the gun happened to make its way there. When it turned up, it was handed back to the army, minus a piece so that it couldn't be used again, and no one was asked any questions. But the longer the soldiers remained in the area the more the hostility towards them increased, especially because of the regular stop and searches of the young men in the district. Brian was frequently spreadeagled against a wall and subjected to 'p' (personal) searches, with strikes from butts and lead coshes to the head if he didn't respond sharply enough. He remembered his college books getting torn up as he was thrown into an armoured truck and driven around the area. He was dumped out on a street and, as the soldiers drove off, he heard them shout 'Fenian'. He thought he had been put out on the Shankill Road, where anyone identified as a 'Fenian' would have been far from welcome. That was what he was supposed to think, as it was part of their sick game – he was, in fact, quite close to home. The soldiers didn't win the hearts and minds of local women because of their conduct – mothers were so anxious that they would wait on corners for the buses to arrive back from college. The soldiers would shout 'mummy's boys' as their sons got off, and the women would shake their heads in anger and despair. Little did anyone know that the army would be there for decades.

Eighteen months after the wedding, we were delighted to find out that I was pregnant. At the antenatal appointments, it turned out that keeping my 'own' name was a bit of a problem for the midwife. When she learned that my surname was McWilliams but that the baby's would be Smart, she insisted that I would have to take my husband's name too. She also told me that because I was an 'older' mother (at the age of thirty-two!) she had been trained to call me Mrs, even though I asked her to call me by my first name. When they called for 'Mrs Smart' at clinics, it took a few moments for me to realise that I was the person they were looking for. The system bothered me because it must have been especially hard on single mothers, and it would have cost nothing to treat us all equally by using our preferred names. I thought it couldn't get any worse until she asked, 'What do you drink?' I didn't realise that she had to ask the pregnant women she saw how much they were drinking, and so I replied that I could drink anything. She wrote, 'Mrs Smart doesn't smoke but drinks anything.' I deleted the last three words when I found them in my notes at the next appointment.

I was looking forward to the birth of the baby but was on the receiving end of plenty of anxiety-inducing advice. I was told not to eat eggs any more because of the risk of listeria and also felt obliged to moderate my consumption of milk as reports were circulating that the Chernobyl nuclear explosion could be contaminating it. Mother Earth was in deep trouble from the chemicals that were permeating our lives.

On 13 June 1986, two weeks beyond his due date, and after twenty-six hours of hard labour, Gavin came into the world. He needed a lot of oxygen, and then, when he became jaundiced, Brian and I looked at him curled like a ball of cotton wool in an incubator for a second time. So it went on, one hurdle after another. The next was getting mastitis – having grown up on a farm this was something that I thought only cows could get. There were no medals for breastfeeding through that. When I returned to the ward for medical attention to fix the complications caused by the birth, the other patients and I chatted about what we were in for. Some were there to be sterilised because they couldn't afford to have any more children or because their health was at risk if they did. When the chaplain appeared on the ward, there was a rush to the bathroom as the women didn't want him to hear why they were in – most of their husbands were in the dark. I was certain he wouldn't want the details of why I had been admitted. There was a warm atmosphere on the ward with everyone supporting each other and joking that the RC (Roman Catholic) or P (Protestant) marked on the files at the bottom of our beds was to show what we wanted for breakfast – rice crispies or porridge.

The maternity leave permitted a short twelve weeks and it ended at the start of the autumn term. It wasn't the best way to plan a family, as my leave ran through the summer break. I was still getting used to the idea of having a little person to look after, and this one was trying my patience. I walked the floors night after night as Gavin had colic and I knew nothing about lactose intolerance. He refused to take my expressed milk from a bottle and had to be fed from a spoon in the university nursery where he was cared for during the working day. In the first month he had endless ear and throat infections. It took its toll on Brian and me. None of us got much sleep. I was trying to bring my best self to work and my best self back home again, trying to be mother, wife, daughter, sister and colleague. I had fought hard for all women, including mothers, to be accepted in the workplace, to chair meetings, to get elected, to fulfil their potential. Being a full-time mother and worker was tough, even with a very supportive partner.

Childcare suddenly became our biggest monthly outgoing; being able to remain in paid work depended on it. The government was spending billions on defence and tiny sums on helping parents achieve a work-life balance. The issue wasn't in any of the manifestos I saw. The business case for childcare was straightforward and clear, so I joined up with my friends, Marie Abbott and Liz McShane, to campaign for subsidised community nurseries – if Sweden could do it, why couldn't Northern Ireland? We figured our kids would be adults by the time it happened but we persevered anyway.

Because Gavin was getting sick so frequently, after six months we took him out of the university nursery that we could barely afford and looked for a childminder. Breid Aiken was the first to come into our lives and she was an immediate success. When Breid decided to take a college course, Brian's mother offered to look after Gavin for that day each week at her house. On the first morning of this new arrangement, I forgot to take Gavin to his granny's, and I arrived at the university with the baby in the back seat of the car. On days like that, the division between work and family became more porous, and there was sometimes no point in pretending that there was a wall between the two.

That was especially the case when meetings were called at weekends – I had to bring Gavin with me if Brian was away for work. Regular Saturday trade union gatherings were held in Transport House, where the ATGWU Regional Secretary, John Freeman, organised a 'crush'. I taught him how to say crèche, as it didn't sound right when he said that the children were happy in the crush. Two years before, I had addressed the TUC conference in Blackpool about the rising number of women in the workforce and the need for more flexible contracts to accommodate them. I reversed the nursery rhyme 'Clap hands for Daddy', in which the child is waiting for its father to come home with sweets in his pocket, saying that it was time to 'Clap hands for Mammy', who was now also working outside the home, and needed to be recognised in her own right. When I was there, I'd been told that a Blackpool pub had installed baby-changing facilities in the men's toilets – more evidence of the change in traditional roles. Back in Belfast, at the Irish Congress of Trade Unions (ICTU) conference in the King's Hall in 1986, Gavin slept in his cot under the table and much better than he ever did at home. When we left, I discovered that his pram was rattling with coins – I loved the Irish tradition of giving money to a newborn.

Now that I had a young baby, I kept asking myself what kind of world he would grow up in. I was concerned about the possibility of a nuclear war, whether by design or blunder, and I didn't want the world to sleepwalk its way into another disaster. It was the fortieth anniversary of Hiroshima and Nagasaki, and that's what was on all our minds when Ellen Diederich and Fasia Jansen came to Belfast with their CND group from Germany. They stayed with us on Rugby Avenue and we became friends.

In August 1986, Ellen and Fasia invited me to speak at a CND meeting in Oberhausen as part of a festival they had organised. Our neighbour, Ian Knox, agreed to bring me to the airport, but the journey ended up being like one of his cartoons in the *Irish News*. He'd checked his oil before the journey, but had forgotten to put the cap back on the tank, so the car overheated outside Dundalk and he couldn't take me any further. I asked a school bus driver who happened to be parked nearby to take me the rest of the way, and promised to pay him when I returned. The bus driver bid me farewell by saying I had a lot on my plate – he was right. I ran like lightning to get to the gate, carrying a cot, a backpack and a ten-week-old baby.

No one had warned me that there would be a firework display the first night in Oberhausen. When the firecrackers exploded, I dived under the bed with Gavin in my arms. Having spent a few weeks in Belfast, Fasia understood why I'd thought it was gunshots. It was that same night I learned that Fasia had been in a concentration camp as a young girl – detained by the fascist regime because she was Black. The marks that had left must have been on the inside because all I saw was the love she

School days were happy days – me, aged eighteen, in
my final year at Loreto Convent, Coleraine.

My sons, Gavin and Rowen – the joys of my life.

Family gatherings at home in Kilrea, County Derry.

showed towards my little boy as she held him. I took a picture to remind me of how well she was able to soothe Gavin, and on the plane back to Belfast, as he slept in my arms, I began to think about her past and what Gavin's future might hold if our conflict didn't come to an end. Fasia had shown me how she hadn't allowed hate to take over her life. It was something I never forgot.

But Belfast felt full of hate. On the night of 17 February 1987, we got a call from Brian's brother Kevin, who was at their parents' house in Ballymurphy. Members of the Irish People's Liberation Organisation (IPLO) had taken over the house earlier that evening, holding the family hostage while they set up an attack on a local man. The IPLO had chosen Brian's parents' home because it had a telephone, which the gunmen needed to alert the shooter when their target was approaching. While they were waiting, the family were made to watch *The Deer Hunter*; the gunmen knew it was going to be on the television that night. It was torture for them to be in the same room as these armed men who, later that night, shot Michael Kearney. During the phone call from Kevin, Brian could hear his mother crying and saying that they were all very shaken and needed him to come over to be with them.

Michael Kearney had been on the IPLO's death list as a result of an internal feud. Another republican paramilitary group, the Irish National Liberation Army (INLA), was involved in this murderous infighting as well. The murders, as well as the tactic of severing the fingers and ear lobes of their victims resulted in Cardinal Ó Fiach pleading, 'Is there no one among the relations and friends of those responsible who can convince them of the madness of what is going on? In God's name let them cry out with me today, "Stop it. Stop it. Stop it for good."'

I remember standing at the kitchen sink and hearing Gordon Wilson on the radio after the Enniskillen bombing on Remembrance Sunday on 8 November 1987. He talked about what his daughter Marie had said to him as she lay dying in the rubble. The tears were running down my face as he pleaded for no retaliation.

A year later, in 1988, our friend Brian Gormally attended the funeral of Mairéad Farrell; her brother Niall was a close friend of his. She was one of three IRA volunteers who had been shot by the SAS at Gibraltar and all three were being buried together at Milltown Cemetery. What happened that day was caught on the world's cameras. Michael Stone, a UDA member, threw grenades and fired shots into the crowd, killing three of the mourners and injuring dozens of others. Brian said afterwards that it was a dreadful experience: three people were being buried and three more were lying dead nearby. He had gone out of respect to Niall, and came home shocked to his core.

More deaths followed three days later, and they were to leave a mark on West Belfast. Two off-duty soldiers in a car drove towards the funeral procession of one of the three who had been killed at Milltown. When they were spotted reversing rapidly, the crowd assumed that another loyalist attack was unfolding. The two men were dragged from the car, brutally assaulted and then shot dead. And it didn't end there. I later heard that an off-duty policeman, serving in an ice cream shop on the Lisburn Road that I used to go to, had been killed with a gun that had been taken from the soldiers that day.

Once Gavin got up on his feet, he never stopped running. I wasn't there to see his first steps but I learned that little things like that would have to be sacrificed if I was going to be a working mother. Mothers had told me that it was when the second child came along that life got really busy and I knew what they meant after Rowen was born in February 1989. Busy it may have been, but the two boys have always been my greatest joy. Any time I had to leave them I felt guilt, but later they would tell me that they were glad that I did what I did. It also helped that I had found another incredible childminder, Pat Lavery, who came to us when Breid left to do her social work course. Pat became the boys' surrogate mother while I rushed from pillar to post, from home to work and back again. Too many meetings took up too many Saturday mornings. Luckily, Brian was free to go and watch the boys' matches; when I couldn't do that at the weekends, guilt piled on top of guilt.

Shortly before Rowen was born, I heard the news that Geraldine Finucane's husband Pat had been shot dead at their home. I knew Geraldine through Avila and Brian, and we became good friends. Geraldine had met Pat at Trinity College Dublin; theirs was a mixed marriage – she was an East Belfast Protestant and he was a West Belfast Catholic. I watched her cope with great dignity during all the setbacks, as she tried to get to the truth about Pat's murder. Geraldine and I often spoke about what life might have been like had she not been widowed so early. We used to go to a place near to where she took her summer holidays, and as the years went on, it made my heart break to hear her say, 'This should have been the time for Pat and myself but I have to just get on with it.'

In 1989, while we were refurbishing our new home to get ready for our second child, we went to live with Brian's family in Ballymurphy for six weeks. This was the area where the Parachute Regiment had killed eleven people, including a mother of eight children and a local priest, in August 1971. It was still bedlam when we stayed there, with soldiers on duck patrol, marching one after the other down the streets. Not long after we arrived, a gun battle broke out between the army and the IRA. Gavin was playing outside the house, and I was able to grab him just in time. I kept him indoors after that. It turned out to be a long six weeks. Each night when I read him a story, the light from an army helicopter glared through the bedroom window. We couldn't get to sleep until the soldiers returned to the barracks and the local dogs finally stopped barking – usually after midnight.

By the time we returned to our own house that summer, effigies of Gerry Adams were being placed on a bonfire around the corner for the annual Twelfth of July events. As our boys got older, they knew that their friends who played with them during the year might not want to play with them in the weeks coming up to the Twelfth. In spite of the enormous bonfire that was a danger to the houses nearby – it was later moved elsewhere – we loved living there and we loved it even more when our best friends Avila and Brian moved into a house on the opposite side of the street. It was Avila who covered over the 'No Taigs here' graffiti on the corner with a few brushstrokes of white paint. An elderly resident who was passing by commented approvingly, not because of the sectarian tone of the graffiti but because she was worried that its presence would bring down the value of her house.

The toxic politics and sectarian strife continued to permeate our lives – not just in Belfast but also in the small town of Kilrea. Tommy Gibson was a part-time ambulance driver for the Territorial Army when the IRA shot him on 9 October 1989 outside the bank on the Diamond. On the day of his funeral, the shops closed as a mark of respect.

Brian and I, with the two boys, went to stay with my parents in Kilrea as often as we could in the summer, joking as we set off in the car that everywhere else in the world people got to enjoy their summers, but in Belfast that was rarely the case. On one of those hot summer days, Brian, our two boys, three of their young cousins and I were sitting in my father's fishing boat when a tour boat, the *Maid of Antrim*, came steaming down the river. When the children screamed at the surge it was causing, which threw us from side to side in our small boat, I remembered my father's words, 'You have to be careful with those currents on the Bann.' For months, I had nightmares thinking of what might have happened had Brian not been able to steer the boat back to the riverbank.

Coming home to my family was the highlight of our boys' young lives. My father had been such a hard-working man when we were children that his time with his grandchildren was very precious to him. The tradition each Christmas was for the cousins to cuddle up together after a night of fun jumping between the mattresses laid out on the attic floor in front of a roaring fire. Each summer, the cousins would gather up and it didn't matter if it was hail or sunshine, we would set off in a convoy for a day on Portstewart strand. The little ones would take to the dunes while we sat on the sand, or more often in the car, reading the Sunday papers. Rows over sandcastles would frequently be followed by my mother saying, 'Isn't God a wonderful wee man?', wanting us to see the bigger picture. She taught us how to appreciate the beauty of the place with her calm presence and peace of mind. Being in her company always helped to recharge my batteries.

In the spring of 1989, Brian and I walked down Royal Avenue with our boys in their prams for the ICTU May Day Parade in Belfast. It was another joyful occasion, and my sons' little faces brought the words of 'Bread and Roses' back to me:

As we go marching, marching, we battle too for men.
For they are women's children and we mother them again.
Our lives shall not be sweetened from birth until life closes.
Hearts starve as well as bodies, give us bread, but give us roses.

In November 1990, the new secretary of state, Peter Brooke, said that Britain had 'no selfish strategic or economic interest in Northern Ireland'. I felt this was a sign that the political landscape was changing. I also sensed unionists would say that they were being 'sold out' and that this was another concession to Sinn Féin. Republicans would also be trying to figure out what this new approach from the British government meant, having justified the war as one against 'the British forces of occupation'. Choices were going to be demanded of all of the parties – a choice between adhering to old dogmas or choosing to think differently. We had seen the Cold War coming to an end, with the Iron Curtain rolled up and the Berlin Wall coming down. I wondered if we could shift the stalemate at home by replacing the well-worn language of division with some glimmer of hope.

But there was little to be hopeful about in the early 1990s. On 24 October 1990, the IRA carried out a series of proxy-bomb attacks, which killed six soldiers and Patsy Gillespie, a man who lived in Derry who worked as a cook in an army base. He had been forced to drive one of the bombs to a border checkpoint while his family was held at gunpoint. The bomb exploded when he opened his door to warn the soldiers what was happening.

Back home in Kilrea, on 1 December 1990, Hubert Gilmore, a former UDR man, was killed at the bottom of our street. He was viewing the site where he and his wife were planning to build their new bungalow. She had been sitting beside him in the car and was so seriously injured in the attack that she was unable to attend her husband's funeral. What made it even harder for her was the IRA statement saying her injuries were 'regrettable'.

Almost a year later, in August 1991, Sinn Féin's Gerry Adams was in Drumagarner chapel for Tommy Donaghy's funeral, which coincided with Sunday Mass. During the prayer for peace, I turned to make the sign of peace with the person seated behind me, who turned out to be Gerry Adams. It was the first time I had seen him in person. There is no monopoly on suffering when a loved one or friend is murdered and that was the case for Tommy Donaghy. A memorial was placed on the spot where he was shot. Shortly after his death, the Ulster Freedom Fighters (UFF) issued a statement saying that 'while the Protestant genocide continues, the republican movement will pay a heavy price'. It was hard to explain to my children what all this meant as they stared at the IRA memorial on the site near the river.

In 1992, the UFF were active again in Kilrea when they killed Danny Cassidy, whom I knew because his sisters had been at our primary school. My sister Mary raised funds for the Cassidy children who had been close by on the day he was murdered. Danny Cassidy's picture had been part of a montage sent to the *Antrim Guardian* newspaper that included the personal information and addresses of twenty local men that had been taken from police files and had got into the hands of the UFF. At the funeral, Bishop Daly said, 'The constant cruel harassment and humiliation of Danny Cassidy by some police units was a factor in his murder.' Friends started to ask questions about collusion between rogue police officers and loyalist paramilitaries. The police called for an inquiry following confirmation that an official security document had been leaked but said they didn't know who was responsible. Parliamentary elections were taking place the following week, and an *Irish Times* journalist asked a young man outside Kilrea polling station about the effect of the recent killings on elections. He told her, 'This town is too small for the scale of killings. It's really just a wee village. At the end of the day, it doesn't matter who gets in because it won't stop the murders.' The issue of collusion remained unanswered and became a running sore.

The situation was no better in Belfast. On 5 February 1992, two UFF gunmen attacked Sean Graham's betting shop on the Ormeau Road, not far from where we lived. Five people were shot dead and many others lay injured on the floor. The UFF said it was in retaliation for the IRA killing of eight Protestant construction workers at Teebane Crossroads. My son's best friend, Peter Duffin, lost his grandfather that day and often spoke about it. A plaque and plastic flowers still mark the spot. The gunmen that day shouted 'Remember Teebane' as if the revenge killings were justified by what had happened there. A widow of one of the Teebane workers wrote to say that the Ormeau Road attack hadn't been carried out in her name. I read that a twenty-three-year-old who was found guilty had said in court that he had joined the UFF because 'everyone was doing it'. Families were grieving and young men were getting locked up – it was a pattern I had become used to.

I was celebrating my birthday on 28 April 1992 when I heard the news that Philomena Hanna had been shot dead in a chemist's shop in West Belfast close to the peace line at Lanark Way. Philomena lived near Brian's family and was at work when the killer came past on a motorbike. He fired a shot, did a U-turn, and immediately sped back towards the Shankill, having succeeded in his random sectarian attack. Cars couldn't get through the security barrier in Lanark Way, but this attacker was able to bypass it on his motorbike. Philomena often crossed the peace line, bringing prescriptions to families living on the Shankill. The UDA/UFF, which claimed the murder, was proscribed as an illegal organisation four months later on 10 August 1992. How had the UDA been a legal organisation for decades? It was a shock to realise that membership of this paramilitary group had been permitted until then.

The violence at the interfaces spurred local women on both sides of the peace line to act as an early warning system, to try to stop any trouble before it got out of hand. They were struggling to keep their children safe and to prevent them from being recruited into paramilitary organisations. The women asked IRA and UVF ex-prisoners to tell the young people not to be idolising the 'combatants' and to make clear the realities of prison life. Young boys were driving stolen vehicles and making younger girls and boys act as sandbags in the back windows of cars to prevent soldiers firing at the drivers. All too often, the misnamed 'joy riders' became death riders. Shootings, kneecapping and serious assaults were meted out as 'punishments' by paramilitaries from both sides. Mothers called it child abuse when their children ended up permanently disabled. Both men and women in the local communities set up projects to help their disaffected teenagers from getting caught up in what became known as 'anti-social' behaviour.

The long-established Women's Information Day Group, whose members and organisers I'd known over the years, brought women from divided communities together on a monthly basis to tackle these issues. It was also good to see staff from the women's centres on opposite sides of the divide coming together to address real needs and produce real benefits. The work that the wider women's movement had undertaken throughout the 1980s was starting to pay off. More support and development on an inter-community basis came from the Women's Resource and Development Agency (WRDA), an organisation I tried to help in any way I could.

On 2 February 1992, I joined the thousands who had walked to Belfast City Hall where the Irish Congress of Trade Unions had organised a rally. Its demand was 'the right to live free from intimidation and violence.' Our banners flapped overhead, stating 'enough is enough', reflecting our outrage at the recent sectarian murders, including those in the workplace, across Northern Ireland. The following year a new initiative, Counteract, was set up by the trade unions to create alliances across the factory floors. It was a clear indication, if one was needed, that the trade union movement had shifted from a 'non-sectarian' approach to an 'anti-sectarian' one.

I had been attending events like the 'Beyond Hate' conference in Derry city in 1992, where Sinn Féin's Jim Gibney shared what a Protestant had told him – 'that unionists couldn't hear what Sinn Féin had to say because of the deadly sound of their gunfire'. Sinn Féin had recently published 'Towards a Lasting Peace', and, although the title was encouraging, I wanted to see what Jim meant when he said, 'We now have a realistic programme for peace in our time.' If Sinn Féin had a strategy, it had been a long time coming. In 1992, the Opsahl Citizens' Inquiry took place, inviting contributions about the way forward for Northern Ireland. Thousands of submissions came from far and near and it held public sessions, which I attended. When the loyalist parties gave evidence on how they could envisage a new constitutional future, I realised the importance of including voices that were normally excluded. There was also a notable absence of women.

The church leaders were also at work in the early 1990s. Two Redemptorist priests from Clonard monastery, Father Alec Reid and Father Gerry Reynolds, were working on a cross-community basis with Presbyterian minister Ken Newell. I first met Ken when he asked me to speak about my work on domestic violence one Sunday night at Fitzroy church. I wasn't aware at the time that he and the priests had opened up a back channel to Sinn Féin. Archbishop Robin Eames from the Church of Ireland, Methodist minister Harold Good, Presbyterian minister Roy Magee and Chris Hudson, who later became a Non-Subscribing

Presbyterian minister, rolled up their sleeves to engage with loyalist leaders. Paul Arthur, my colleague in the university, summed up the need for understanding political nuance: 'It's not just about going out and throwing holy water or giving hugs, it's about good interpretation.' It was difficult to work out whether Sinn Féin's position on 'national self-determination' for the island of Ireland and the loyalist position on 'responsibility sharing' inside Northern Ireland could ever meet, but through intermediaries they had started to move from a position of estrangement to one of engagement.

At the same time, Taoiseach Albert Reynolds and Prime Minister John Major were also in talks, with the government process feeding into the ground-level talks and vice versa, even though the very existence of the back channels was being denied in the most indignant terms at official levels. As these initiatives were taking place, a series of incidents occurred that had the potential to blow all this apart.

On 20 March 1993, two children, Johnathan Ball and Tim Parry, were killed and many were injured in IRA bomb attacks in the English town of Warrington. Eight months later, on 23 October, an IRA bomb exploded prematurely in Frizzell's fish shop on the Shankill Road. The blast killed nine civilians and injured many others. One of the two IRA men who had planted the bomb was also killed; the other was badly injured. When the casualties arrived at the hospital, Sandra Peake, a nurse who would later become a friend of mine, told me that on that day the staff did what nurses and doctors are trained to do – they didn't ask who were the victims and who was the perpetrator. She would go on to become director of WAVE, an organisation for victims and survivors of the conflict, and recruited me as a volunteer. It was there that I met Alan McBride whose young wife Sharon had been working in the shop alongside her father, the owner of Frizzells. Both of them had died in the bombing. Alan talked about his two-year-old daughter and how she lost her mother: 'Zoe and Sharon were inseparable. It was just lovely to watch the two of them. I think one of the biggest losses for me is not just losing Sharon but losing the love that Sharon had for Zoe. Seeing that up close and personal was a really beautiful thing.' He made it his life's work to show that behind each tragedy, there's a family left to suffer.

The funerals took place day after day, and on one of the days, two of the cortèges passed each other by accident; one was the funeral of a victim of the bombing; the other was one of the bombers. When the two groups of mourners encountered each other, the anger on their faces was clear to see and I wondered how we would ever be able to come together again after such an atrocity. When Avila gave birth to her baby in the Royal Maternity Hospital two nights after the Shankill bomb, I ran the gauntlet of army checkpoints to get there. The centre of town was deserted, people were indoors, and the soldiers were the only ones on the street. It felt as if a curfew had fallen over the city. As I held baby Conor in my arms, I despaired at the world he was coming into. Avila later reflected on that night – by then the IRA had declared a ceasefire.

> My son was born on the cusp
> Of summer and winter time,
> The nurse mistimed him.
> A siren's scream away
> The Shankill bled with pain –
> So many dead.
> As I counted his toes
> I counted the years
> That might deign him
> Victim
> Or perpetrator –
> In bomb blast,
> Drive past,
> Tit for tat –
> So fine a line.
> In the after haze
> Of gas and air
> I query the sparseness of the choice.
> Conception to birth –
> Dirt to dirt –
> Cortèged banshees wail.
> One year later
> My baby boy celebrates the fragility of peace
> With first steps.

Before that ceasefire would come, however, there were many more lives lost. The UDA warned that nationalists would pay a heavy price for the IRA attack in the Shankill. It was like the Trojan war: 'Do terrible things and terrible things will be done to you.' The UDA retaliated in an attack at the Rising Sun bar in Greysteel on Hallowe'en night. Gunmen in boiler suits wearing balaclavas walked in shouting 'trick or treat'. The revellers thought they were carrying make-believe guns and wearing costumes, but the woman who told them, 'That's not funny' was the first to die when the gunmen opened fire. At the end of the onslaught, out of the two hundred enjoying themselves in the bar, the UDA had killed eight and wounded thirteen more. Like those on the Shankill, the dead included the elderly, the middle-aged and the young. In the space of one week, there were twenty-three funerals.

More tragic news was to come on 18 June 1994 as I sat at home on a Saturday evening watching the Ireland vs Italy World Cup match. Amid the excitement, there was a news flash – there had been a devastating attack on the customers of a pub in Loughinisland. They had been watching the match when the UVF blasted the place with gunfire, killing six customers and seriously wounding five others. The INLA had shot dead three men two days before; the UVF said this was their retaliation. When I went to Sunday Mass at St Bernadette's Church the next day, heavily armed policemen were guarding the entrance. The priest asked us not to congregate outside once the Mass had ended. This had never happened before, and it seemed like we had come to a precipice. A neighbour even remarked to me that it was time to call in UN peacekeepers. I started looking out of the window to see who was there before answering the door; it was hard to explain that to the boys.

While the public despaired, contacts and talks continued to take place behind the scenes, which eventually led to the IRA ceasefire on 31 August 1994. I felt a cloud lifting as the IRA declared 'the complete cessation of military operations' in order to 'enhance the democratic process'. The *Belfast Telegraph* headline that evening was 'It's Over'. There were pictures on the front page that showed the suffering at the Abercorn, where Jennifer McNern had lost her leg, and a picture of Gina Murray weeping at the loss of her child in the Shankill bomb. I also watched the TV news showing a cavalcade of cars, draped in Irish tricolours, blasting their horns as they drove around West Belfast. Some of them who were interviewed said that they were relieved they could now hang up their bulletproof vests and would no longer need locked gates at the bottom of their stairs or reinforced security doors.

But leaders on the unionist side were the opposite of joyful, with dire warnings of impending turmoil and the leader of the Ulster Unionist Party, Jim Molyneaux, describing the ceasefire as 'destabilising' for unionism. It baffled me how anyone could think like this. The loyalist paramilitaries ignored him and also refused to take any notice of Ian Paisley's negativity. Two months later, the Ulster Defence Association, the Ulster Volunteer Force and the Red Hand Commando announced their ceasefire. David Ervine, Plum (William) Smith, Gary McMichael and Gusty Spence sat together under the umbrella of the Combined Loyalist Military Command to make their statement. Gusty Spence expressed 'abject and true remorse' for the suffering on the group's behalf.

Not long after the ceasefires, I was invited, because of my work, to an event at the Europa Hotel as part of the 'Justice in Times of Transition' project. Organiser Tim Phillips, from Boston, had brought Nobel Peace Prize winner, and former president of Costa Rica, Óscar Arias to talk about his experiences of negotiating a transition from conflict. His words had a profound effect on me: 'You have marched, denounced, demanded, divided, slayed, bombed and even starved yourselves to death at times … You say it is difficult to achieve peace here? Perhaps it is. But it was not easy in South Africa. It was not easy in El Salvador. And yet it is happening. And if it can happen there, why not here?' I also listened to another speaker, Jan Urban, whose Charter 77 demands and Civic Forum in Czechoslovakia had led to new democratic institutions. His words also left their mark: 'When you spend most of your time as a victim, or believing yourself to be a victim, there's no responsibility attached.' He advised us not to leave it to the establishment to make all the decisions; groups from civil society also needed to be involved. Cyril Ramaphosa and Roelf Meyer came from opposite sides of the political divide in South Africa. That night they shared how they had been transformed by coming together to draft South Africa's new constitution. When Roelf was asked about leadership, his answer was, 'Don't look for a Mandela. Do what is required yourselves.' I went home that night wondering how, as someone already active in civil society, I could become more active in the fledgling peace process.

Champions at home as well as those from abroad kept pushing the process forward. President Clinton unlocked another door when he issued Gerry Adams with a forty-eight-hour visa, ignoring the advice coming from the FBI, CIA, State Department, the British government and even some in the Irish parliament. He followed through on a promise he had made when he arrived in the White House that he would try to find a solution to the 'Irish' problem, and, in response, hundreds of thousands turned out to welcome the first American president to visit Northern Ireland when he landed in Belfast just before Christmas in 1995 with First Lady Hillary Clinton.

While the president was visiting Mackies factory, the Falls Road and East Belfast, Hillary Clinton was meeting community activist Joyce McCartan in the Mornington Project café in the Lower Ormeau. Joyce, who I knew to be a formidable woman, had lost thirteen members of her extended family during the Troubles, including her seventeen-year-old son, Gary. I often heard her remark, 'You can't fry a flag in a frying pan.' Hillary Clinton was presented with a Belleek china plate, decorated with doves and shamrocks from women on both sides of the community, and Joyce gave her a teapot that she treasured. Everyone who was there that day remembers her saying, 'I want a chance to listen to each of you. What you have done in the last twenty-five years is important for Northern Ireland and the world. Perhaps it is because we have children that we have a link with the future that gives us hope and energy to try to make things better. Wherever I have gone in the world and met with women it is a common theme that they want to make the world a better place for their own children. And there is a lot the world can learn from what you have done here.' The following day Hillary Clinton talked about the visit: 'The women I spoke with yesterday are not high-level diplomats or professional negotiators. They have not yet been elected to office. But they are women, Catholic and Protestant alike, whose lives and families have been affected by the violence. Their grief became their and our call to action.'

I walked into the city centre with my sons to watch Bill and Hillary Clinton switch on the Christmas tree lights. For eight-year-old Gavin and six-year-old Rowen it was a magical night, sitting on security barriers and looking at the lights reflect on to the podium's bulletproof glass. The *Irish News* described it as Belfast's 'biggest-ever street party', with a hundred thousand people from all parts of the city coming together. It was a sight to behold. Van Morrison sang 'Days Like This', and we hummed the tune all the way home. I hoped that the political parties would use the momentum that was building to make a real breakthrough.

7

Changes to the Political Landscape

'Peace isn't going to be made on our backs again.'

Annie Campbell

The British government had been reluctant to internationalise the Northern Ireland conflict, preferring it to be seen as a domestic skirmish, but the need for the neutrality of outside representatives in the negotiations became unavoidable when the question of decommissioning reared its head. In February 1995, Secretary of State Patrick Mayhew had declared that some arms would have to be handed over before the representatives of armed groups were allowed to attend peace talks. Unionists put forward the argument that decommissioning was a test of the commitment of the political parties affiliated to armed groups. But the parties aligned both to the IRA and to the Combined Loyalist Military Command argued that it should not be made a precondition to entering negotiations. I felt at the time that having a ceasefire was the key to finding a way forward, but if disarmament were to be demanded in advance, the armed groups would interpret that as a call to surrender.

It came as a relief when both governments appointed Senator George Mitchell, the former majority leader in the US Congress; Canadian General John de Chastelain; and former Finnish prime minister, Harri Holkeri to lead an international body on arms decommissioning. They recommended, in their report of 23 January 1996, that decommissioning should take place in parallel with the peace talks, and that parties involved would have to sign up to six principles – later known as the Mitchell Principles – one of which was a commitment to democracy and non-violence. For the first time since the ceasefires, there seemed to be a way through the impasse.

As the report hit the headlines, my life came to a standstill when my mother rang to tell me that Mary had been in a serious car accident. I went to collect my younger sister Noeleen to drive home to Kilrea, but when we got there, everyone had gone to the hospital. Dr McGurk, our GP and neighbour, appeared in the kitchen and told us that the man driving the other car involved had died at the scene, and that Mary was in a very bad state. When I asked if my parents were all right, worrying that one of them might have a heart attack because of the shock, he gave me some memorable advice. He said that people of their generation had experienced tragedy in their lives and were better at coping with shock, and told me to steel myself for what I was about to walk into. When I got to the hospital in Coleraine, I walked past Mary's bed in the intensive care unit. The trauma had turned her hair white and I didn't recognise my own sister. She was being stabilised before being transferred to the Royal in Belfast where the world-leading orthopaedic surgeons who had honed their skills in the conflict would do their best to save her life.

When I got to the Royal and asked where I'd find Mary, she hadn't arrived. I feared the worst but it turned out that the ambulance had broken down and she'd had to be transferred to another one outside Antrim Hospital. I noticed that at the entrance to the ICU, workers were removing the security doors, no longer needed because of the ceasefires. There were sparks flying, so I went over and told them to hold off because my sister would soon be coming through, attached to an oxygen tank on a trolley. They stopped just in time. I was then asked to sign organ donation forms as Mary's blood was failing to clot and she wasn't expected to survive the night. Both lungs had been punctured; seven of her ribs were shattered; and her right leg and both kneecaps were broken as well as bones in her foot and face. I sat at the bottom of her bed going over and over that list in my mind and willing her to hold on.

For three days, the longest of my life, she remained unconscious and I knew her life hung in the balance. Her condition was stable, though, and the surgeons finally made a decision to go ahead with the operation that was needed to repair the broken bones. She was on a ventilator, and every day for twelve days I prayed that I would be able to speak to her soon.

My mother came often and prayed by her bedside, but my father couldn't bear to see her like that. When she could finally breathe by herself, she asked what had happened. I said what I had to say to so many victims: 'Some day we might find out.' It was later proved that Mary wasn't at fault – that the other driver had been on the wrong side of the road.

During the second week at the hospital, I went home one night to discover our hamster had died. There was sorrow as Brian buried our family pet in the garden. The boys thought I was fonder of their hamster than they had realised when I started to let out the tears that I had held back for so long. After Mary had been moved to the high dependency unit, I took the boys, then aged nine and seven, to see their beloved aunt. They climbed in beside her and gently hugged her and stroked her face. Mary said that their touch helped her to bear the hardness of the plaster of Paris that encased her, and eased the discomfort of all the tubes. Their love was just as healing as any hospital treatment. I was learning at first hand how a person comes to cope with trauma and shock. The importance of care, the need for love and support – these were vital for healing whether a tragedy was accidental or inflicted. The truth could wait but she needed to hear that as well. She never did get the full truth, though, as she had only been given a partial account of that night, and we never got to the bottom of why the other car was on the wrong side of the road.

As soon as the plaster of Paris was removed, Mary had to go through months of excruciatingly painful rehabilitation. She put every ounce of her energy into that, never once complaining about the chronic pain, and determined not to spend the rest of her life in a wheelchair. A year later, she took her first steps by the river Bann and I could see she was on the road to recovery.

On the evening of 9 February 1996, while I had been sitting at Mary's bedside willing her to survive, the IRA rocked London with a huge bomb that killed two people, injured a hundred and caused property damage that would cost millions of pounds to repair. The IRA ceasefire was over. I hadn't seen it coming, and I didn't think anyone else had either. A few weeks later, the two governments announced that they would convene all-party negotiations on 10 June and said that Sinn Féin could join if the IRA reinstated its ceasefire. The British government set a date for the election of parties to the peace talks of 30 May 1996.

I had published a journal article the previous year showing how the political system in Northern Ireland was devoid of women – at the time, there were no women MPs from Northern Ireland at Westminster and none in the European Parliament either. I was determined that women would be involved when it came to something as important as negotiating peace. In the article I had written that, 'when men and women finally sit down to design a new constitution (if there will ever be such a thing) then women will have a right to be at the table.' The women's movement had been active in community politics and the time had come for us to claim a new role.

A group of us had already started laying the groundwork after the publication of the British and Irish governments' Joint Framework Document the previous year. The Framework Document, as the name indicated, had been painstakingly negotiated by the two governments to provide a pathway to the peace talks. Its publication prompted Baroness Jean Denton, junior minister of state, and Lady Jean Mayhew, to invite Kate Kelly, a civil servant well known to many women's groups, and me to Hillsborough Castle to discuss how women activists could respond to it. Like us, they too had observed the absence of women from Northern Ireland politics. The document promoted the importance of parity of esteem, pluralism, respect and inclusive relationships, no doubt thinking of unionism and nationalism, but we believed they equally needed to be applied to men and women. I left the meeting having agreed to find out if there was an appetite for a cross-community women's conference at which we could create a response to the Joint Framework Document. The Derry Women's Centre issued a press release, saying, 'In a nutshell. Put gender on the agenda.'

That would have made a good title for the conference, but I went for 'Women, Politics and the Way Forward'. The organisation wasn't plain sailing. An initial problem was that Baroness Denton and Lady Mayhew represented the establishment so, at the suggestion of women from both sides, I was left with the unenviable task of writing to them to suggest that it might be better if they didn't attend. Lady Mayhew replied to my letter saying, 'I understand completely why you didn't think it would be appropriate for me to attend. It is extremely important that all women are encouraged to speak as freely as possible.'

I was relieved, given the mediation I had undertaken to make it all happen, when hundreds of women from across Northern Ireland turned up at Draperstown's Rural College on a beautiful June weekend. It was the first time I could remember such a diverse range of women converging in one place to talk about political peace-building on an inter-community basis. To accommodate the overflow, we broadcast the proceedings into an adjacent room. We left nothing to chance, providing childcare, food and transport to enable those with children to travel long distances to participate. Long-time women's activist Annie Campbell introduced the proceedings by saying: 'Peace isn't going to be made on our backs again.' May Blood reinforced the message when she said:

> You might not put yourself forward for election, but you are involved in community politics. We can't leave it to the existing politicians. The people who were elected to look after us aren't really looking after us. We have to form our own group if we're ever going to make a difference and it has to be through politics.

Co-organiser Liz Porter and I wrote the conference report, with the key conclusion that if the government's commitment to improve the status of women in politics was genuine, then specific mechanisms to involve women in the anticipated constitutional talks were vital. Avila floated the idea of a women's political association, involving women from all the parties, and, seven months later, following the announcement of multi-party peace talks, we sat down with a glass of wine in a cafe on the Lisburn Road to work out how to make it happen. The ideas flowed with each glass and we arrived at the notion that we could form our own women's political party to run in the election.

Our plan to change the world wasn't just pie in the sky – Avila had worked out that the new electoral system for the peace talks gave us a remarkable opportunity. The system had been deliberately designed to ensure that the two smaller loyalist parties – the Progressive Unionist Party (PUP), aligned with the UVF and the Red Hand Commando, and the Ulster Democratic Party (UDP), aligned with the UDA – would be elected. Since the system allowed for ten parties to be at the talks, we worked out that night that a women's party might be able to reach the threshold for admission if it won enough votes from across Northern Ireland.

We floated the idea to the Women's European Platform; its chair Bronagh Hinds immediately came on board and agreed to circulate the idea of a 'women's caucus' or a 'women's network' to women's groups across Northern Ireland. To give the political parties the opportunity to do something about their lack of female candidates, Bronagh wrote to them and referred to the Joint Framework Document saying, 'While we approve of attempts to achieve parity of esteem and parity of representation we wish this to be applied to women.' She asked them to gender-proof their list of candidates but, when the majority of parties didn't reply, it became clear that this was a non-issue for most of them. Irked, the Derry Women's Centre issued a press release stating that 'further change is needed to broaden the base and allow independent women, community leaders and trade unionists who are anxious to engage in solution-focused talks to take part.' Bronagh also gave the British government the chance to make things fairer when she asked if it intended to make a childcare allowance available to participants in the multi-party negotiations. The credibility of the government's parameters on equality and inclusion was being tested in ways it had never imagined.

When the government published the list of parties that would be participating in the election, it had made the assumption that there would be no new parties entering the fray. Eileen Calder, who worked in the Rape Crisis Centre, pointed out how she used to spoil her vote at each election as that was the only way she could express her disapproval of the existing parties. Like most of us, she felt politically homeless.

Bronagh contacted a Northern Ireland Office official to enquire what the position would be if a new party wished to stand. Stunned silence at the other end of the telephone was followed by the question, 'What party?' Bronagh responded, 'A women's party.' The official promised to check with his superiors and some time later he rang back to ask, 'What is the name of this party?' Bronagh requested time to consult. A round of frantic phone calls to women activists confirmed that the will was there to form a party, especially since none of the main parties had bothered to reply to our letters. The Women's Coalition was the obvious name – 'coalition' rather than 'party' allowed women who were members of other political parties to join us – but we put Northern Ireland in front not just to get higher up the ballot sheet, but to avoid having WC as an acronym. Bronagh phoned the NIO official to confirm the name. Now we had a party and we were on the all-important list – but we had no office, no staff, no structure, no telephones ... and only six weeks to go to the election.

Using our pre-existing networks, we invited women to attend an open meeting at the Ulster People's College in South Belfast, and well over a hundred turned up – it was standing room only. Bronagh explained what we had done and asked for responses. What came back reflected the diversity among us: some women were already committed to specific political parties and weren't going to change; others felt that it would be impossible to set up an organisation in such a short time. But enough thought the idea was worth a try and, at the very least, we hoped we'd make the other parties sit up and take notice. We arranged another meeting for the following week, at which we sketched out what the Women's Coalition might look like. Naturally we wanted women to have a strong voice in the peace talks, but we wanted more than that. We wanted a process reflective of, and fit for, a divided society in which women – unionist and nationalist, loyalist and republican, or neither – could see themselves. We intended to be cross-class, all-age and to be able to identify and put forward issues that would otherwise be overlooked in the forthcoming talks. In short, we did not want to be just another party composed of political professionals. Our supporters agreed the registration of the party on the basis of three principles – inclusion, human rights and equality. These were to be the values that would underpin all our work.

After that, we started putting ideas into action. Determined to be one of the ten parties with the most votes, we needed to get as many women as possible to put their names forward to run. It was the cumulative vote across the country that would allow two representatives of the Women's Coalition to be at the table. We also wanted to prove the existing parties wrong – they'd said publicly so many times, 'We'd love to put forward more female candidates, but women just don't want to stand!' May Blood came up with an idea. She offered to pay for a newspaper advertisement that said, 'If you subscribe to the principles of inclusion, equality and human rights and are happy to stand for the Coalition, then get in touch.

If you want this opportunity to put women into the mix, this is it.'

The pace was hectic, and women like me with young children found it hard going. It was even harder for those who lived in Derry and Enniskillen or further afield and faced a four-hour round trip to every meeting. But energy and excitement drove us on. We held weekly meetings to discuss the position papers that had been drafted and to organise ourselves. A breakthrough came when Kate Fearon, a key player in the Coalition, asked political scientist Sydney Elliott to address one of our meetings. Kate asked him, 'How many votes do you need to get two representatives to the talks?' When he replied, 'Somewhere around eight to ten thousand votes,' Kate stuck her neck out, saying, 'But that's just easy.' We needed one hundred women across Northern Ireland to get one hundred votes each, so we came up with the idea of a kitchen-table campaign to demystify the process and reassure women that they could do a lot of the work from home. Lots of women who were keen to stand were concerned about their safety, as well as about press scrutiny, and found it reassuring to know that any publicity would focus on the party and not on the individual candidate, as it was only two or three representatives that would go to the talks table.

Meeting by meeting, the number of women agreeing to let their names go forward crept up. When women said, 'Oh, I couldn't possibly run,' Bronagh would remind them, 'Look, you're not going to get elected but we want you to run. We have to gather up votes from each constituency.' Another stalwart, Felicity Huston, helped the cause by referring to one of the Belfast City councillors: 'Just take a look at him, for goodness' sake. If he can do it, you can too.' Such entreaties were often answered by women with their hands up, saying, 'I'm in.'

The next issue on the agenda was leadership. Staying true to the principle of doing politics differently we decided on a co-leadership arrangement: one from a Protestant/Unionist/Loyalist background and the other from the Catholic/Nationalist/Republican community. As it happened I had agreed to speak at an international conference in Australia so I missed the meeting about leadership. When I got back, between hugs at the airport, Brian told me that I'd been proposed and accepted as one of the leaders. The phones hadn't stopped ringing with journalists asking to speak to me and calling him 'Mr McWilliams'.

We were so structure-less at that point that no one had even asked me if I wanted the role. I wondered how I'd juggle everything, but I was honoured to be chosen, particularly as I knew that if we won enough votes, I would be going to the peace talks. My next step was to see the vice chancellor as my job as a lecturer might be in jeopardy. Reporters were showing up on the campus looking for interviews. My luck was in when my boss, Trevor Smith, told me that he had run as a candidate himself, years before, for the Liberal Party. He said I had done the right thing, and that it was important for academics to get involved in the process, but predicted it might be tough for a woman to break through the machismo of local politics. He was right about that.

May had proposed Pearl Sagar, a community activist from East Belfast, as co-leader on the basis that she wouldn't take any nonsense from anyone. Pearl agreed to be nominated and later said, 'A lot of people were frightened to stand up and speak out. And who can blame them? You'd need to have been mad to put yourself forward in the Women's Coalition. I think I was mad enough to do that.'

Meanwhile, women were volunteering for a number of roles. Avila started fundraising, submitting applications for support to the Global Fund for Women and the Joseph Rowntree Reform Trust. May took on the role of treasurer and Bronagh got together a drafting team, working on a leaflet to outline our policies. We used the acronym WOMEN to get across our points: Working for a solution; Offering inclusion; Making women heard; Equity for all; and New thinking. Our strapline was: 'The Coalition is a genuine cross-community initiative to shatter the mould of politics in Northern Ireland. We are Catholic and Protestant, Unionist and Nationalist, Republican and Loyalist.' We tested every decision and action we took against those words. Pearl and I, for example, came from different cultural traditions, and our intention was to build on that cross-community ethos. Agreeing to work with and across our differences was part of the process and was one of the reasons we had formed the party in the first place.

Time was marching on and we were under pressure to finalise our list of candidates. I thought about what Jane Wilde had said: 'It will take a lot of courage, a lot of determination, a lot of having to expose your own identity in this society where identity is so closely linked with trouble, with violence and with danger.' With some trepidation, we pinned up sheets of paper on which we would list the names of the women who agreed to stand. It was like being at an evangelical meeting as I stood at the front of the room declaring, 'Tonight I need to have names against each of the areas.' Those women who stepped forward nudged others and you could hear the murmur in the room, 'If I can do it, so can you.' With cajoling and persuasion, we ended up with seventy names on the sheets of paper. In line with our core ethos, we had asked each woman to identify her background to ensure that each tradition was fairly represented among our candidates. Our backgrounds were as different as our ages, and when we looked at the final list it was like a mosaic: there were women from all classes and every part of Northern Ireland, rural as well as urban. We came from Catholic, republican, nationalist traditions as well as Protestant, loyalist and unionist backgrounds. Some didn't fit precisely into any of these and some hovered between the different traditions. The candidates worked in the home, in business, in trade unions, in all tiers of education and in public service. This was the kind of diversity we wanted to bring to the negotiating table.

The next step was registering our candidates for the election. We hadn't realised how long it would take to fill in the details of the candidates and their constituencies, and we were on our hands and knees on the floor writing down the addresses when I realised the time. It was an hour before the deadline for lodging the papers at the electoral office, and we had to get from the Ulster People's College to the city centre. Our car came to a standstill outside the Europa Hotel – I wasn't sure whether it was a traffic jam or a bomb scare but either way I knew I had to get out of that car and start running. I took off in the direction of Royal Avenue, forms in hand and surprised at how fast I could still run when I had to, even though I wasn't entirely sure of the exact location of the office. I was thinking of what I was going to say to the candidates because I had let the whole thing go down the tubes by not keeping an eye on the clock. One of our younger members was running beside me, shouting directions to Cathedral Square, so I kept going until I spotted May Blood pacing up and down outside the electoral office. As I turned the corner, May gestured to me to slow down. I could see the television cameras and slowed to a walk at the office door. She was telling reporters that we had left it to the last minute on purpose; she whispered to me that she was ready to kill me. I handed the papers to the security guard, and hoped the press didn't heard him say, 'Don't be giving those to me, love. You need to get yourself upstairs.' We took those stairs two at a time, lodging the papers a minute before five o'clock. Anything was possible after that.

With our candidates registered, we got to work on a campaign launch. We needed a slogan that would get our message across and wake people up. As I stood at the front of the room in the Ulster People's College during discussions on the manifesto, I heard a voice cry out, 'Let's wave goodbye to the dinosaurs.' And that was it. We couldn't afford to go to a professional designer for posters; but someone said that a neighbour had a computer with desktop publishing capability. He didn't know me from Adam, but that didn't stop me knocking on his door. He laughed when I explained that I urgently needed him to design and print a graphic of dinosaurs wearing ties with a slogan alongside, using the suffragette colours of green, white and violet, the first letters of which I had only just learnt stood for 'Give Women the Vote'. He did a great job then and there, but when I told him that his artwork would be on walls across Northern Ireland during the election, he begged me not to tell anyone he had designed it because he was fed up with politics. I thanked him and never saw him again.

As we anticipated, the long-standing parties weren't impressed with our slogan. When any politician said what a cheek it was for us to call them dinosaurs, we politely explained that we hadn't called them a dinosaur and their name wasn't on the poster. We would often add, 'If you are going to self-identify as one, please don't let us stand in your way.' A journalist wrote that when she was passing the Coalition office she heard people laughing and joking at a political meeting. This was clearly not something she was accustomed to.

We needed to make it work without losing the fun – along with the enthusiasm, experience and expertise, there was always a lot of laughter. For our first press conference, we decorated the room with balloons in our colours, and we sat in a row with a makeshift banner behind us. Although we had a new logo, we'd only been able to produce it in felt tip, so it didn't look very professional. The media was more used to having one party leader to whom they could put their questions, so we created a stir when we took it in turns. The journalists found it hard to get their heads around the fact that we didn't have a top dog. We shared the roles to help build women's confidence, 'sharing in' as well as 'sharing out' the decisions. We also surprised journalists by applauding every time we heard something being said that we liked, making it feel more like a public meeting than a press conference. When Jane Morrice pointed out that the Coalition represented a microcosm of Northern Ireland and therefore should give us a better chance of finding new ways forward, that brought another round of applause. We were either very brave or very foolish to be sticking our necks out like this. But, as Anne Carr said, 'The traditional politicians wouldn't know where to start. So why would you ever have peace talks without women at the table?'

The BBC's political correspondent, Martina Purdy, interviewed me after the press conference. I was anxious because I sensed from the media that the party was thought of as a novelty, but the interview turned out better than expected. She said that we had a serious message, that our politics was the struggle for new ideas, and she outlined how we intended to put these into action. The *New York Times* covered the story along with dozens of other international outlets. I reminded the candidates that we shouldn't forget about the importance of the local media, quoting Tip O'Neill's famous remark, 'All politics is local.'

As much as we tried to work with the media, we were up against it at times. I couldn't figure out why journalist Suzanne Breen questioned our stance in an article in the *Belfast Telegraph*, asking: 'Where Is the Fighting Spirit of Our Grannies?' She contrasted our campaign with that of the suffragists a hundred years before, who had broken the windows at their own Ulster Unionist Party headquarters in Glengall Street in Belfast. *An Phoblacht* (Republican News) commentator Rita O'Reilly dismissed us, saying we had failed to address the key issues of national liberation and partition. We were more shocked to hear a member of the Workers' Party claiming that because we were a Women's Coalition, we wouldn't be hard-nosed enough to make difficult decisions. The Social Democratic and Labour Party (SDLP) deputy leader, Seamus Mallon, suggested we were a cult factor that 'would grow in on itself and kill itself off'. When Peter Robinson, the deputy leader of the DUP, was asked about us by the press, he said:

> The Ulster woman in the past has seen herself very much as being in support of her man. As far as those individuals that I have seen in the Women's Coalition, they haven't been at the forefront of the battle when shots were being fired or when the constitution of Northern Ireland was in peril. They are not representative of the decent Ulster women that I speak to. Women should leave politics and leadership alone.

It was a relief when the US Consul General Kathleen Stephens showed that she understood what we were trying to do: 'In the negotiations the Coalition would be addressing the disconnection between the very insular world of politicians and the lives of everyone in the community.'

To build confidence among the candidates, we developed a war chest of responses for the questions we knew we'd be asked.

Q: 'What's your position on the constitutional status of Northern Ireland?'
A: 'We will be solution focused, putting forward workable options to achieve an accommodation on the various interests.'

Q: 'Why are you competing with women in other parties?'
A: 'Our actions complement the work of women already involved in politics.'

Q: 'Are men excluded from membership of the Women's Coalition?'
A: 'We have men in the party who support our positions, and we are not a separatist anti-men party. We have taken advice from the Equal Opportunities Commission who have confirmed that what we are doing is perfectly legitimate. Every citizen has the right to stand in an election.'

And this was only the start.

In writing our manifesto, we tried to be as inclusive and consultative as possible. Because of our diversity – one of our great strengths – it took hours to reach a consensus, but this turned out to be time well spent. Despite all the differences between us, we managed to get agreement on some of the most difficult issues in Northern Ireland, including a bill of rights; reforms to policing and the criminal justice system; reparations for victims of the conflict; devolution of power with proportional representation; social and economic development; and transfers from English to Northern Irish prisons for those with conflict-related convictions, to facilitate family visits. We also proposed in our manifesto that an independent commission be established to mediate on the parades disputes that were causing so much tension year after year. It buried the notion that we were a single-issue party and proved to be a solid foundation for what lay ahead.

The test of how we could put our principle of inclusion into practice came early in the election campaign. The government intended to exclude Sinn Féin representatives from the multi-party talks because of the breach of the IRA ceasefire with the Canary Wharf bomb in London on 9 February. We argued that they should be included, applying the logic that 'if they were going to be on the table (that is, discussed), then they needed to be at the table.' But we also called on the IRA to reinstate its ceasefire, since the continuing use of violence was unjustifiable. The gun had to be taken out of politics.

There was a danger that we would be ostracised for adopting this stance, so we expanded on this point in our paper, 'Including All Voices', in which we argued that one of the reasons that previous talks had failed was that the parties that were part of the problem had not been given the opportunity to become part of the solution. Loyalists and republicans would have to be at the table and the biggest parties (the UUP and SDLP) – who were accustomed to negotiating with the governments in London or Dublin – would have to engage with them and extend their frame of reference. To make peace, constitutional parties would have to sit down with members of armed groups and we emphasised that civil society representatives should not be relegated to the sidelines of the negotiations.

Our temporary HQ was above the Downtown Women's Centre in Belfast's Donegall Street. Ann McCann volunteered to run the office –

she was the oil in the Coalition's engine. After her brother was murdered by UFF loyalist paramilitaries in 1974 on his way home from his job in the shipyard, Ann had spent years working for the Peace People, and she now became invaluable to the Coalition. Like all of us, Ann was hoping against hope that things were about to change. She was our bookkeeper, and made sure that every last purchase was accounted for, especially in the run-up to the election. For her sake, I kept a meticulous record of what was going out and what was coming in, just as I had for my father's cattle-dealing books.

Everyone was given a job on the rota, volunteering in the office or at home, addressing and stuffing envelopes, making rosettes or running up banners on sewing machines. Although we were fortunate that everyone was working for free, we had to pay rent for the office, the phone and the fax machine, as well as paying for publicity materials, so we needed to do some serious fundraising. A great boost came on the back of an article in which *Irish Times* journalist Mary Cummins wrote:

> Just to get an idea of the exhilarating buzz of women busy with the business of politics, go North. If you want to feel the burn of women shedding their invisibility and standing against the powerful, established, and male-dominated parties, dig deep in your pockets and send your money North ... Even if the men agree to sit facing each other, there will probably be more stop starts while they decide the shape/colour/height of the table. If you want an end ... to the intimidation and threats which have passed for politics in the North, support the Women's Coalition.

An election campaign was expensive – unlike the longer-established parties, we had no funds to draw on. I wrote to anyone we could think of who might be able to give us a few pounds. Some responded generously; others replied saying they'd never given a penny to a political party and didn't intend to start now – it hurt that they couldn't see that we were trying to change that kind of thinking. I always thought of them as 'The Coasters' that John Hewitt writes about in his poem:

You showed a sense of responsibility
with subscriptions to worthwhile causes
and service in voluntary organisations;
and, anyhow, this did the business no harm
no harm, at all...
You even had a friend or two, of the other sort,
Coasting too: your lives ran parallel...
You always voted but never
put a sticker on the car;
a card in the window
would not have been seen from the street.
...You coasted along...
You coasted too long.

But the time for coasting was over.

Our posters had to be hung high on the lampposts to stop the vandals from getting at them. This didn't always work, and when they were pulled down, we got out the next day and put them back up. We glued them to whatever bits of cardboard we could find in skips and supermarkets, covered them in cling film, punched holes and tied them to the poles with baling twine or string. We looked on enviously as the other parties hired cherry-pickers to hang their professionally produced posters in all the best spots. It was a case of 'first up, best dressed', so we were out at dawn every morning to try to get some of these for ourselves. We had to get our name out as we were a new party, but I often questioned whether this was the best use of our time. One afternoon, as I stood on my kitchen ladder hanging a poster on a lamppost, a passer-by remarked that it was good to see a candidate who could 'walk the walk' as well as 'talk the talk'. Gavin approved as well – his teacher had seen me up a ladder and she'd told the class about it. I'd worried that he'd be embarrassed, but when he said he was proud of me, I floated off on the strength of that. Rowen thought I was doing a great job as well but for a different reason. When we went out in the car to canvass, he was in charge of the loud hailer and used it to shout, 'Vote for my mum. She keeps her promises,' and would often add, 'Don't you, Mum?' I just laughed, as he was enjoying the fun of it all. But it was a busy time at home – Gavin was preparing to transfer to secondary school, and Rowen, aged seven, needed help with his homework. I couldn't have done what I was doing if Brian hadn't been doing most of the heavy lifting at home.

When I had time between university teaching commitments, I gave as much support as I could to the candidates, making trips to Derry and Enniskillen at weekends. I was full of admiration for the hours the women were putting in and the sacrifices they were making. Mary Catney, who was standing in West Belfast, knew that she didn't stand a chance of winning a seat, but that every vote counted in our bid to get into the peace talks. Like all of our candidates, Mary was multi-tasking: working as a youth worker; looking after her five-year-old; and canvassing every other moment for the Women's Coalition. I heard her say that talking to the media was like cutting your toenails – not very glamorous but it had to be done. When she was asked about the colours on her rosette, she told the interviewer we chose them because of the suffragettes, but that the difference between them and us was that we were knocking on doors to bring out the vote rather than having to chain ourselves to railings.

We were thinking all the time about how to reach new voters, particularly women and young people who might have been put off by the adversarial nature of politics. From early morning to late at night, we canvassed outside shopping centres, leisure centres, post offices and schools, explaining what was meant by our byline 'Women In Talks; Women For Talks'. It was great to see young men wearing our T-shirts with 'X-press yourself, Vote for the Women's Coalition' printed across the front. It was an even bigger novelty that our younger members were handing the T-shirts out to concert-goers. We were telling anyone who hadn't voted before that this election would be different. Parties would have to talk to each other, instead of talking over each other. At least that was the expectation.

Going around the country, I heard some men say that they were glad to see a new party entering the political scene with a very different message. But all too often when we asked them to vote for us, we got the reply, 'The wife is giving you a vote but I am voting in the usual way.' When I knocked a door one evening and asked the woman who answered if she would give us her vote, she replied, 'I have to ask my husband; he tells me how to vote.' Another man in Belfast who said as he walked past us on Royal Avenue, 'I wouldn't vote for a woman. Never have and never will.' He sounded like one of the dinosaurs.

Our politics meant that we canvassed in all areas, unlike most other parties, who stuck 'to their own side'. As a result, we had twice the ground to cover, and it wasn't all plain sailing. As we were canvassing in a loyalist area of Belfast one evening, a supporter recognised a man at the door of one of the houses. He was the same man who had, unsuccessfully, years before, tried to kill our supporter as he had been coming out of his work. The gunman had missed and escaped on his motorbike. Luckily, he hadn't recognised our canvasser, but it was a close call and we didn't knock on any more doors that evening.

The nearer election day got, the more positive I felt. We'd worked out the number of votes we'd need to get into the talks, and I believed we could do it. We'd stood up well to our detractors and were punching well above our weight, encouraged by the numbers who said they were going to vote for us.

On the day of the vote, 30 May 1996, I went from polling station to polling station and back to the office for more leaflets and refreshments in between rounds. Two of our dedicated activists – Sister Anna, a partially blind eighty-three-year-old Anglican nun, and her companion and carer, Rosaleen Hillock – were given one of our new mobile phones to keep in contact with the office while they sat in deckchairs outside a polling station at a Presbyterian parish hall in South Belfast. As I was getting ready to leave the office, I could hear Sister Anna, in her impeccable English accent, shouting down the mobile to Ann McCann, 'We are up here, and many, many people are voting, and we need bodies here, send bodies up here, we need them right away.' Ann McCann turned to me and said, 'She thinks she's in a war zone.' Sister Anna had arrived in Belfast as an interface worker in the early years of the Troubles and was known to ride her bike through crossfire, holding up a black umbrella and declaring in ringing tones that she was coming through, having placed all her trust in God to keep her safe from the bullets.

After the polls closed that night, I collapsed into bed but immediately started to think about the count that was to take place the next day. I spent what was left of the night tossing and turning, worrying how I was going to cope if we won the places at the peace negotiations. Mary was still recovering from her car accident, and the boys were young and needed their mother. I had spent six weeks juggling my academic work, canvassing and campaigning, as well as doing my bit at home. It had been the busiest time of my life. Politics and life had become intertwined, a perfect example of how one didn't take account of the other. That night, I kept asking, over and over, was it the right time? Would there ever be a right time? But I still wanted us to win.

The next morning I went to the BBC for an early morning interview and braced myself for any commentators who were going to write us off. I had to believe in the true friends I'd made in the Women's Coalition and in myself. Afterwards, I headed to the City Hall where the count was taking place, carrying in my pocket the two press releases that we had prepared: one if we won, the other if we lost.

By the time I arrived, the first results were starting to come in from the towns around my homeplace in Derry. Our vote was high, thanks in part to my large extended family, who had all turned out to vote for us. If the votes in the other areas were as high, I knew we were in with a chance. Just as things were getting exciting, I had to leave to buy shoes for Rowen's First Communion, as otherwise he'd be going in his trainers. I rushed out to collect the boys to take them to a shop on the Cregagh Road where Rowen told anyone who would listen that he couldn't see the point in buying shoes that would only be worn on his Holy Communion day. It was a bit of a rarity to hear a Catholic child talk like that on the Cregagh Road and the silence from the customers seemed deafening. When we went to leave one of them wished me good luck, but I wasn't sure whether she was referring to my chances of getting Rowen into the shoes or the election. Either way, I took her words as a good luck charm, and, when I rang Bronagh to find out how we were getting on, the news was positive. I rushed to get back, calling Brian at his work to tell him that we were close. I could barely wait to get to the count centre, though I was drenched from getting caught in the rain while running to the car, to home, to the shops and home again before I finally made it back.

When I got there, our supporters were still phoning in from across Northern Ireland so that Bronagh could record the tallies on her sheet. When I took their calls I told them to hold their nerve, even if our votes were in the hundreds while the larger parties were counting theirs in the thousands. I told the press that we had gone out and claimed a space in this election – and it looked like we'd finally got our foot in the door. Around us stood men who were talking anxiously about percentages and topping the poll.

As it came close to the final call, David Ervine made a statement, saying that the 'fringe' loyalist parties, the PUP and UDP, were no longer on the fringes – they were now home and dry in seventh and eighth places, and added, 'We can't break the mould in one fell swoop but we are certainly on the way to doing it.' Ulster Unionist councillor Jim Rodgers was telling reporters that the public needed to be warned against 'a conspiracy of rogues' made up of republican and loyalist extremists. Gerry Adams was congratulating the Sinn Féin candidates and also applauding candidates from rival parties. I thought it was a nice touch, but as his entourage was making its way through the scrum in the hall, a young DUP supporter, sporting a red, white and blue rosette, hissed, 'Murderer', to the approval of his senior colleagues. I was taking all this in as I stood on the sidelines, nervously waiting for the last two places to be confirmed.

The declaration came shortly afterwards, putting us in ninth place with just under eight thousand votes. It was enough to send two delegates to the peace talks, and some achievement for a party that had only been formed six weeks before. When people started to congratulate us, saying that they couldn't believe we'd done it, I replied, 'You've no idea of the team we have behind us, working day and night to make it happen.' We were overjoyed. Now we knew that the parties entering the peace talks were UUP (181,829 votes), SDLP (160,786), DUP (141,413), SF (116,377), Alliance (49,176), UKUP (27,774), PUP (26,082), UDP (16,715), NIWC (7,731) and Labour (6,425).

I went home to celebrate with Brian and the boys. I was glad it was over but I knew there would be no let-up in the work. The BBC asked me to participate in a panel the next day. I was apprehensive but also glad to have been invited, as one of the Coalition's aims was to increase the representation of women in political debates. I arrived at Broadcasting House to find that the other participants included John Taylor (deputy leader of the UUP), John Hume (leader of the SDLP) and John Alderdice (leader of the Alliance Party). When John Taylor said live on air that 'the women' wouldn't have much of a contribution to make, I reminded him that the country was made up of different people, men and women, nationalists and unionists, and that 'he better listen to that'. The producer wrote to me afterwards, saying she was looking forward to having more women on her panels in the future.

That same day, the *Belfast Telegraph* carried an illustration of how the negotiating table would look, showing ten men in shirts and ties to represent the ten elected parties. I rang the editor to tell him that since the Women's Coalition would be present at the table, one of the figures should not be wearing a tie! By the evening edition the editor had corrected the error and the new illustration showed a woman with an open-necked shirt seated with the men around the table. Journalist Mark Simpson blamed the sub editor for the *Belfast Telegraph*'s headline: 'Hens' Party Leaves The Nest In Style'; he compensated by writing, 'The Women's Coalition had the last laugh at the polls. They edged out more established parties like the Ulster Tories, the Workers' Party and Democratic Left. Not bad for an organisation which was formed only six weeks ago.'

8

The Forum Debates and Time Out of Northern Ireland

'When we speak we are afraid
our words will not be heard
nor welcomed
but when we are silent
we are still afraid
So, it is better to speak.'

Audre Lorde, 'A Litany for Survival'

As the dust settled after the election, a letter arrived from Secretary of State Patrick Mayhew. It stated that both governments were inviting the Women's Coalition to participate in the forthcoming multi-party peace negotiations that would meet from Monday to Wednesday each week, starting on 10 June, and in a Forum for Dialogue and Understanding that would meet each week on a Friday. The letter said that the British and Irish governments would cover the delegates expenses at the negotiations; it always struck me that there was no word of complaint from Ian Paisley about this, even though he was on record saying that he would have nothing to do with the Irish government.

The Forum had been set up by the British government to give the unionist parties a political platform, it was a separate process even if it was to run in parallel with the negotiations. It had been one of David Trimble's preconditions for entering the negotiations. His Ulster Unionist Party wanted an opportunity to air its views on the process in public, which it couldn't do in the closed sessions of the peace negotiations. Nationalists had no interest in the Forum since it had no executive powers – the SDLP's

Mark Durkan described it as a Fisher-Price parliament, and Sinn Féin declined to participate, not wishing to give legitimacy to a body set up by the British government. It was also angry about its exclusion – on the basis that the IRA's ceasefire hadn't been restored – from the peace talks. The talks would be held in Castle Buildings at Stormont and the Forum in the Interpoint Building in Belfast city centre.

The reallocation of Sinn Féin's seats to other elected members was the first problem in the Forum. It took me just one day in attendance to rename it the Forum for Monologue and Misunderstanding after rows broke out over the new seating arrangements. John Gorman, a former army major and member of the UUP, had been appointed chairperson of the meetings. At the very first meeting, on Friday 14 June 1996, the chair lost control of the proceedings. He informed the press that afternoon, 'It wasn't an easy business chairing a meeting of a hundred politicians.'

The Alliance Party was the first to complain, insisting it was a party of the centre, which entitled it to be seated in the centre. PUP's David Ervine was as frustrated as I was when he told reporters that people were showing off and letting their egos get in the way. When the rows spilled over to the following Friday, the *News Letter* included a send-up of events so far: 'It was like a day at the circus when the ringmaster is stoned. The clowns did what they pleased and the lions were loose without their tamers.' The UKUP's Bob McCartney derided the entire proceedings: 'If that is what David Trimble called for then he has created not so much Frankenstein's monster, as Dopey the dwarf.' Due to complaints that the bottles of drinking water came from Tipperary, they were replaced with a brand from Northern Ireland.

As we were moved from seat to seat, I was able to exchange a few pleasantries with my neighbours, first the DUP's Rev. William McCrea and then the UUP's John Taylor. I noticed others doing the same, introducing themselves to people they'd never met before. When I got to my feet to speak, the chairperson said he had forgotten my name, so I said clearly: 'I am Monica McWilliams of the Northern Ireland Women's Coalition. There are not too many of us here.' Given that the room was full of men, I thought the least he could do was remember the names of the handful of women who were present. I proposed that he leave the Sinn Féin seats empty and move on. He remembered my name after that.

Just as the Forum was getting off the ground, however contentiously, the IRA exploded a bomb in Manchester on 15 June 1996. It made me question what the IRA's intentions were at a time when Sinn Féin said they were serious about entering the peace talks.

In one of the early weeks, the already volatile assembly became even more fraught when Ian Paisley proposed that a rule be inserted that the Union flag should be flown over the building. This was a heated debate, during which an SDLP member shouted, 'If we could agree on a flag to fly over the building, there would be no need for a Forum or peace talks.' I made the point that the Coalition included women from various traditions in Northern Ireland, and our members took the view that, irrespective of how anyone felt about the Union, there were regulations, for reasons of equality, about the flying of a Union flag over a privately rented building. I could hear shouts of 'Shame!' and 'Disgrace!' from the unionist benches so I asked the chairperson to impose order, requesting that the members show me the same courtesy as I had shown them. When I added that it was against the Forum regulations to have a rule inserted that didn't have cross-community support, again there were shouts of disagreement and comments like 'Make her sit down' and 'You silly woman'.

During one morning of debate about the flag, there were roars of 'Traitor!' when Pearl put forward the Coalition's point of view. That afternoon, she asked the chairperson to check whether the comments made about her were on the record, as the chair often said he hadn't heard anything. They were. She told him, 'It's a pity you didn't hear the word "traitor" being used this morning. I certainly did. I happen to be a Protestant and I object to anybody in this room calling my Protestantism into question.' As she spoke there were loud shouts of 'Out of Order. Out of Order', with the UUP's Jim Rodgers yelling, 'Sit down and shut up.' I was thinking of Pearl's safety – she had just been singled out as a traitor. Unlike some Forum members who had their own personal security, Pearl had none.

After the debate I encountered John Taylor walking down the corridor with three trainee lawyers. I repeated to him what David Trimble had said to me when I'd met him at a US consul event the night before – that the rules on flying the flag should be appropriately applied. Taylor hardly acknowledged me, and the baby barristers (a title bestowed on them by a sharp-witted politician) quickstepping alongside him conveyed to me what an important man he was, as much as to put me in my place.

I found a side room and phoned May Blood to tell her that it was time for the Women's Coalition to decide whether we should stay or go. She reasoned that we should remain since the Forum was the only place for the public as well as the press to witness the way women in the Coalition were being treated. Because the talks at Castle Buildings in the early part of the week were held in private, the more public Forum was where we got to meet people, including the visitors in the public gallery. I could see how members of the unionist parties at the Forum were using these Fridays as a kind of therapy session – a place to vent their frustrations at the exchanges at the peace talks in the early part of the week.

The biggest rows were between the Ulster Unionists, who were in favour of the talks, and the DUP, who were attending the talks but seemingly hating every day they were there. John Taylor challenged Ian Paisley about telling the public that he'd never speak to the Irish government but was now talking to them every week in the negotiations, concluding, 'Let us have no more of this double talk and humbug from the leader of the DUP.' Before he sat down, John Taylor had it recorded that a DUP member had flicked him the two-finger sign from the opposite benches. I was on the receiving end of a lot worse.

It wasn't long before we had another major setback – the public disorder that followed the RUC chief constable's announcement that the Orange Order would be banned from the Garvaghy Road in Portadown. The conflict over parades was centuries old, and its current iteration in 1996 had the potential to derail the peace process.

Thousands of men had gone to Drumcree, and there were pictures on TV showing a bulldozer that had been brought there by loyalist protesters to demolish the police barricades. Once again we were on the edge of a precipice – even the BBC's Kate Adie had turned up. Journalist Susan McKay's interviews in the newspapers with those involved were such a revelation that I began to wonder if menace would defeat the rule of law. In the Forum, Rev. McCrea was describing what was happening as the 'Siege of Ulster', while his DUP colleague Ian Paisley Jnr told members that the two governments, along with the SDLP and Sinn Féin, had awakened 'a sleeping giant ... and who can tell what actions it will take in defence of itself and in defiance of republicanism?'

I anticipated that the debate would be hot and heavy in the Forum that day, and it was. First, members of the unionist parties denigrated the Chief Constable Hugh Annesley for deciding to reroute the parade away from the nationalist community on the Garvaghy Road. Then they claimed that IRA/Sinn Féin – which was how they referred to republicans – had orchestrated the community opposition.

As I got on my feet, I said that the Orange Order and the local residents needed to sit down and talk – it was the only way to find a solution. Mediation Network, a group I knew well, had made their best efforts the previous year. Even though what had been agreed had fallen apart – with nationalists perceiving Paisley and Trimble to be rubbing their faces in it after the two men joined arms to parade triumphantly into Portadown – I still believed that mediation was needed. In its absence, we had the standard zero-sum game – either one side or the other would have to blink first.

There were a few other Forum members who were also disturbed by the turn of events. One of them was the Alliance Party's leader, John Alderdice. I could hear the emotion in his voice when he said, 'I love Northern Ireland. I want the place to survive ... Attacking the police and smashing policemen's heads has put this whole community at risk.' A saving grace during these troubled days were the comments from Presbyterian Church leaders calling on the right to parade to be exercised with sensitivity and apologising to Catholics for any hurt caused.

On 11 July, the chief constable reversed his decision. The residents' group had not been given any advance notice of the change, and rioting broke out as police in armoured vehicles poured into the area and corralled the residents to allow the marchers to pass. Near where I lived in South Belfast, hundreds of residents were forced to stay in their homes to allow the Apprentice Boys to march down the Ormeau Road. I could hear them shouting their outrage from their houses. The British secretary of state used the analogy of a volcano erupting with terrifying ferocity to describe what was happening across Northern Ireland. Strange as it might seem, all of this only made it clearer that we needed the peace talks.

On 7 July, loyalist paramilitaries murdered Michael McGoldrick. He had been singled out as a Catholic while working as a taxi driver to support his family following his university graduation a few weeks before. It was heartbreaking that his wife was expecting their second child. His father made a powerful plea on the day of the funeral: 'As I bury my son … bury your pride with my boy.'

At the first Forum meeting after the funeral, I spoke of Michael McGoldrick's death, and quoted a verse from Eavan Boland's poem, 'Child of Our Time', on the death of a child in the early years of the Troubles. She wrote of how we must:

> … find for your sake whose life our idle
> Talk has cost, a new language. Child
> Of our time, our times have robbed your cradle.
> Sleep in a world your final sleep has woken.

The country was at a standstill, with loyalist blockades in many areas. I was stopped at one of them late at night, coming home from Dublin, where the Women's Coalition had been holding a meeting with Taoiseach John Bruton. A loyalist group had diverted the traffic at Newry away from the A1, the main route to Belfast, so we ended up on a side road, where a group of hooded men wielding baseball bats and wearing balaclavas were blocking our way. Avila was driving and both her daughter Sinead and Kate Fearon were in the car with us. When they asked Avila the purpose of our journey, she simply said that we were on our way home, and they waved us through. On the other side of the road block, police jeeps were parked up, and officers were standing chatting. I got Avila to pull over, so I could ask the officer in charge why these men had been allowed to block our path. He claimed that there was nothing he could do. Kate tried to phone Newry police station from her mobile to report what was happening, but got no response. Police reforms were long overdue. The SDLP left the Forum after 12 July and never came back, saying that it was a talking shop for unionists.

During the summer of 1996, someone had the great idea of taking politicians from all ten parties in the talks out of the confines of our political situation for a week. That someone was Tim Phillips, from the

Project for Justice in Times of Transition, who had brought international leaders to speak in Belfast the previous year. I was one of those invited, and I was looking forward to participating in the workshop 'Managing Change in a Diverse Society' at the Kennedy School of Government at Harvard University.

On our way from Logan Airport to Cambridge, Massachusetts, police outriders with sirens blaring accompanied our bus. Initially, I thought some VIP must be on the highway, but then I realised the security was for us. As one of the few people on the trip who was speaking to all the other participants, I counted us on and off the bus each day. By the end of the week, I was on first name terms with the head of security.

As part of the itinerary, and probably to help us to get to know each other better, we went to a Boston Red Sox baseball game. The bus escorting us to the venue came with outriders again and they stopped the rush-hour traffic so we could go through at speed. We arrived at the stadium, where people were shouting, 'Stand back and let the celebrities pass.' I was first off the bus and heard a passer-by remark on the tattoos clearly visible on some arms: 'They're not celebrities; they must be inmates out of jail for the game.' It had been the same at the airport in Shannon a few days before when the immigration officer checked the exemptions on some of the visas – you needed an exemption if you had been in prison for a criminal offence – and then asked, 'Are you really the representatives of political parties from Northern Ireland?'

At the stadium, because of the unionist position that it was not speaking to republicans, its delegation refused to sit with the two Sinn Féin representatives in their allocated seats. The organisers had to buy additional tickets so that individuals who didn't understand the first thing about baseball could watch the game separately in peaceful ignorance.

Later that week, we went to Martha's Vineyard, where human rights activist Rose Styron had invited us to her home. When we went swimming in the sea in front of the Styrons' house, I told the DUP's Jim Wells that he could now say that we'd crossed stormy waters together. David Ervine had scars on his back, which he told us had been caused when he was accidentally put into a bath of scalding water as a baby, putting paid to the assumption that the injuries were Troubles-related. Some people on the trip had never exchanged a word before and these kinds of personal exchanges helped to break the ice. That evening, the DUP's Paul Berry was singing a gospel song in the garden while I was being introduced to Katherine Graham, the owner of the *Washington Post*, and broadcasters Walter Cronkite and Mike Wallace. It was a night full of incongruities.

During Louis 'Skip' Gates's talk on identity and ethnicity you could have heard a pin drop. His insights were as applicable in Northern Ireland as the USA. Although the formal programme was at the centre of our learning, I gained just as much from the time we spent in people's homes, in conversation with hospitable hosts as well as with each other. In the group photos, members of the two main unionist parties refused to be pictured with Dodie McGuinness and Seán MacManus from Sinn Féin. Resolving the problem of standing alongside each other would take another decade.

The workshop had been well titled – 'Managing Change in a Diverse Society' – but we weren't doing much of that back in Northern Ireland as tension was still building and violence continued in the streets. In the early hours of 9 September 1996, members of the UDA firebombed the Windsor Women's Centre. The President of Ireland, Mary Robinson, had visited the day before, to cut the ribbon on a new baby unit and to talk to women from diverse ethnic backgrounds – and her visit had also sparked a very contentious debate in the Forum. My friends Eleanor Jordan and Joy Poots, who managed the centre, were alarmed when they saw the extent of the damage and by the fact that the UDA attack was being seen locally as a warning to women not to use the centre. When they got in touch with me, I said I would be happy to help in any way I could. I knew that these two courageous women, like everyone else who helped to run the centre, worked tirelessly for the benefit of the local community. Windsor Women's Centre got back on its feet, cleaned away the smell of smoke, replaced the computers that had been destroyed and won an award for its good work on training and employment. No one was going to stop these women from providing opportunities in a low-income, working-class area of Belfast.

The following month, on 4 October 1996, I was stopped in my tracks again during a debate at the Forum when Ian Paisley said, 'You might as well have a discussion with Hitler about better terms for the annihilation of Jews as discuss with Southern Ireland the way forward for Northern

Ireland.' In response, I asked, 'Is it not objectionable to compare Hitler and Fascism with the government of the Republic of Ireland?' only to get the reply, 'I do not know where the lady has been living. In some cuckoo land of her own.' It was a lonely few minutes as no one else was challenging what he had just said. But I got up again and stuck at it. I argued that responsible political leadership should acknowledge that change was coming, and engaging in shaping it was better than standing like King Canute trying to hold back the tide. Presbyterian minister Ruth Patterson's letter to me the next day gave some comfort: 'I have heard the exchanges which took place in the Forum. I find Ian Paisley's remarks offensive and want to assure you that I most strongly support the stand that you are taking.' I made a note to thank her and reminded myself to encourage anyone who felt pushed into a corner not to be afraid to speak out.

In yet another contentious debate in the aftermath of the Dunblane tragedy, when a man went into a primary school and shot dead sixteen children and their teacher, I noted that the British government had introduced a ban on handguns. Because of Northern Ireland's unique circumstances, this law did not apply to us, even though the country was awash with licensed and unlicensed weapons, so I proposed a motion to have the legislation extended to Northern Ireland on the grounds of parity. The unionists objected, with Ian Paisley Jnr expressing amazement at 'the mentality of the Women's Coalition'. Another of his party colleagues declared, 'Let us ban sex because some people are getting raped.'

The DUP's Jack McKee said in the Forum that the 'hatred of unionism and loyalism had been bred into people like the Peace People, the Women's Coalition and the like.' I pointed out that it wasn't worthy of Protestantism to preach a gospel of hate and enmity towards those who differed in religion and politics but I couldn't appeal to his better nature. In response to a speech I made one Friday, in which I had neither threatened the Union nor promoted terrorism, Rev. McCrea replied, 'Many of the women in Northern Ireland are good, loyal citizens. They will stand by all the men of Ulster to see that this country of ours is preserved from terrorism. Let us not insult the ladies by suggesting that the ladies will follow hook, line and sinker the line that is taken by the Women's Coalition.' In our seats, Pearl and I hummed the tune of 'Stand By Your Man'. Rather than fight fire with fire, we responded with good humour, but we still found the remarks infuriating.

During one of my speeches, I heard Ian Paisley Jnr holler, 'Moo, Moo, Moo'. As we walked out of the chamber, he asked me if I had enjoyed the craic. The visitors who were in the gallery that day later approached me to say that they couldn't believe their ears. Eleanor and Jerry Dunfey from the Global Citizens Circle in Boston had come to observe the proceedings and I could only imagine what they were thinking.

If Pearl and I chose to stay quiet in order to listen, we were accused of having nothing to say, but when we asserted ourselves, we were told to stop preaching. It all seemed so ridiculous, but I couldn't let it get under my skin – there was a lot at stake in the peace talks. Instead, I covered myself with a coat of armour each Friday morning.

The Coalition was in two minds about whether to remain in the Forum. We consulted our members, who agreed that we needed to stick with a 'politics of presence', an idea that originated from the belief within the feminist movement that it was worth trying to make changes from inside as well as outside the system. We decided to stay but issued a press statement that said:

Far from fulfilling its objectives of promoting dialogue and understanding, the Forum has provided a platform for some of the most sectarian commentary to reign. There is much made of fair play in Northern Ireland, but there is no fair play when politicians behave like bullies. There is a culture of unacceptable political behaviour that is a major part of our problem. It has been exemplified by members of political parties here and it has been allowed to pass by others … The sexist remarks in particular have been commented upon widely and have helped to expose the antiquated patriarchal attitudes that still exist.

Our election platform had been one of 'Including All Voices' but I began to wonder if we had been over optimistic. Rather than acting in a manner that could have inspired confidence in the wider community, the Forum showed the importance of checks and balances in a political institution.

Back at home, Gavin and Rowen were my reality check. I was worried that they might be upset by reports of the Forum on TV. One bright summer evening, as I was reading Rowen a bedtime story, he looked at me and said, 'Those men shouldn't be calling you a silly woman but you are a bit silly expecting me to go to sleep when it's still bright outside.' The boys seemed to be taking it all in their stride. I was lucky to have two support teams: Brian and the boys at home, and my friends in the Coalition.

Recognising how hard things were at the Forum, a team came each Friday to support Pearl and me, providing the kindness and sanity we needed to counter all the unpleasantness. They were also volunteering their expertise to the Forum's committees, only to be labelled 'time wasters' and 'whingers'. Jane Wilde, who had taken leave from her job as director of the Institute of Public Health, acted as a comfort blanket, reminding us, 'Maybe they are not used to intelligent women standing up and saying things that are obvious and sensible. That is why it is worth fighting for – just ask yourself why anybody should put up with this absolute rubbish?'

While we believed in the value of public political participation, we were also active in the community. For months, a group of loyalist men – angry at a ban on the Orange Order's parade through the predominantly Catholic village of Dunloy, County Antrim – had been protesting at the Catholic church at Harryville on the outskirts of Ballymena. On 8 March 1997, which was both International Women's Day and International Day of Prayer, Avila and I went with other members of the Coalition to hold a silent vigil outside the church as an expression of our solidarity with local parishioners, who had to run the gauntlet of the protest in order to attend Mass. While I was handing out white roses at the door of the church I suddenly heard pings on its corrugated roof. Assuming these to be gunshots, I stepped forward to shield an older parishioner and got hit on the side of the head with a rock. It had been thrown by one of the loyalist mob on the opposite side of the road. Television cameras recorded the moment, so when reporters asked me live on air if I was okay, I simply answered, 'The rocks they have in their heads are as big as the ones in their hands.'

Although I hadn't been badly injured we still had to get back to the car, carrying the banner under our coats and without being spotted by the wall of protesters. The *New York Times* ran a subsequent headline: 'Ulster Women's Party Tackles Sectarians', which summed up why I had joined the Women's Coalition in the first place.

Each year for the St Patrick's Day events at the White House, Pearl and I headed off to Washington DC with the other parties. At one of the American Ireland Fund dinners, Ian Paisley Jnr began heckling the taoiseach, who was about to deliver his speech. The people at the back of the room turned around to see Paisley Jnr unfurling a banner on which the Union Jack was prominently displayed. The former Finn Gael general secretary, Ivan Doherty, moved forward to have a word with him and then left it to the FBI to sort it out. The episode caused quite a stir from where I was sitting but the people up front didn't seem to notice. During the traditional Capitol Hill lunch, Vice President Al Gore joked that he was only a kneecap away from the presidency – he was holding the fort for President Clinton who was recovering from knee surgery. When no one from Northern Ireland laughed, I wondered who would tell him that kneecapping was something that paramilitaries did, using baseball bats to batter young people accused of anti-social behaviour.

At the line up in the White House that evening, President Clinton enquired how things were working out, just before Derry's Phil Coulter played 'The Town I Loved So Well'. Clinton then asked John Hume to sing 'Danny Boy', saying it was the best love song ever written. On Capitol Hill, we came across Ted Kennedy again – we had met him earlier that year at the US Consul's house in Belfast, where he had proudly presented us with a copy of his Senate speech on the Ulster-Scots in America. His interest pleased the unionist parties since the widely held perception was that Irish Americans like Kennedy were only interested in their Irish heritage and 'the greening of America'. On the way down from Capitol Hill, I took a photo of Gary McMichael and David Ervine pointing the way – to the Catholic University.

There were jokes about what the British were up to – they were hosting a St Patrick's Day lunch at the ambassador's residence the next day. When a cab driver asked us if it was true that Saint Patrick had banished all the snakes from Ireland, David Ervine replied, quick as a flash, 'He left an awful lot of two-legged ones behind.'

The leaders of the parties had been invited to meet President Clinton in the Oval Office, but there had been an oversight and the Women's Coalition hadn't been put on the list. A National Security Council official apologised and asked if we would meet with the First Lady, Hillary Clinton, instead. It felt a bit like the women meeting the women while the men met the men, but we didn't see Hillary as second best. When he called her chief of staff, Melanne Verveer, he said that the meeting with the Women's Coalition should only take a few minutes. In fact, we chatted with Hillary Clinton for over an hour – she had been well briefed about the negotiations and the way women were being treated. When she asked how we were coping, we told her that what was happening said more about them than it did about us. It was in some ways a surreal experience – exchanging coping strategies with Hillary Clinton in the White House. She knew, and we knew, what it felt like to be on the receiving end of hostile commentary. Melanne Verveer enquired if they could do anything to help, so I recalled Hillary's famous statement that 'women's rights are human rights' and proposed that she might say a few words at the reception that evening, to which hundreds had been invited. I thought the political parties from Northern Ireland might benefit from hearing something along those lines.

When she introduced the president, Hillary Clinton first paid tribute to the women in the peace process, in the north and south of Ireland. Her words received thunderous applause from White House guests. The men from Northern Ireland also applauded and then turned to look at Pearl and me to see if we looked surprised. We were hoping that after her intervention there would be a change in behaviour and there was a notable difference. What women who are made to feel isolated at high-level events need are more champions and we found them in Hillary Clinton and Melanne Verveer. We learned later from Melanne that Hillary called her after our meeting, and said, 'We need to help them', and added, 'We should hold a woman's conference in Belfast.' They would go on to deliver on this, and more, in the coming years.

In May 1997, with the agreement of President Mandela, Padraig

O'Malley organised for the parties from Northern Ireland to go to South Africa. The National Democratic Institute in Washington DC, Chuck Feeney's Atlantic Philanthropies, the American Ireland Fund and the Dunfey family from New Hampshire sponsored the visit because they probably believed as I did, that one divided society can learn from another. We left on 28 May – most of us fell asleep on the last leg of the journey and only woke when we landed at the Denel Overberg military camp. We were taken by bus to a place on the southernmost tip of South Africa. Sinn Féin members came on a different plane, via Paris, since unionists had been given an assurance that they wouldn't have to mix with them at any point. That meant two planes and two buses, and even our meals had to be taken in rooms where potted plants had been strategically placed to make sure that the parties on either side wouldn't even catch sight of each other. I didn't have access to a phone, so it wasn't going to be possible to speak to Gavin and Rowen. I was going to miss them but I was also looking forward to meeting Mandela.

Pearl and I shared a bungalow with the ANC's Baleka Mbete-Kgositsile, deputy speaker of the South African Assembly, and Patricia De Lille, a leading member of the Pan Africanist Congress. We talked about how some South African men felt emasculated because they perceived that women were taking over and displacing them from their jobs. The cessation of political hostilities hadn't led to a cessation of gender-based violence, with South Africa becoming notorious for the high number of criminal assaults on women and girls. Paying attention to private, domestic relationships was becoming an important issue in South Africa, and something I was already aware of in Northern Ireland.

President Mandela came to talk to us and joked that we had brought apartheid back to South Africa since 'two of everything' had to be provided at the conference centre. To stay within the agreement, Mandela even had to give his talk twice. But they couldn't plan for everything. Sinn Féin's Rita O'Hare was at a reception on the first night of the gathering. She was the party's representative in the USA, a matter of considerable annoyance to unionists, who believed she should have been extradited to face charges in a UK court for having absconded during bail proceedings in Northern Ireland in 1972. It took some time for the DUP's Gregory Campbell and Edwin Poots to realise that she was the woman they were chatting to that night. They finally clicked when Gregory read Francesca O'Hare on the name badge attached to her lapel and then moved as fast as he could to tell Peter Robinson to get out of the way before any photographs were taken.

The Troubles in Northern Ireland were put into proportion when compared with what the South Africans had been through. The ANC were represented by ministers Mac Maharaj and Kader Asmal, and Deputy Speaker Baleka Mbete-Kgositsile. Mpumalanga Premier Mathews Phosa was also there, as was Cyril Ramaphosa. De Klerk's National Party was represented by Roelf Meyer and others present included the former head of the South African Defence Forces, General W.G. Kritzinger, and former MK commander A.M.L. Masondo. The Freedom Front's General Constand Viljoen also came as did Peter Smith from Buthelezi's Inkatha party, Patricia de Lille from the Pan Africanist Congress and Colin Eglin from the Democratic Alliance. In all, nineteen South Africans were present. Each of them outlined their role in the transition while we got the chance to ask whether they were for or against the changes. I had often heard my friend Kader Asmal, who had spent his time in exile as a law professor in Dublin and was now a minister in the South African government, cite author L.P. Hartley's famous opening lines: 'The past is a foreign country.' Cyril Ramaphosa and Roelf Meyer elaborated on that theme by explaining how they had come from opposite sides to negotiate a new constitution for South Africa. I had met both of them before at the meeting in Belfast in 1995 but had no idea at the time that they would become important interlocutors in our own process. During the four days at the De Hoop Nature Reserve, Unionists linked up with Roelf Meyer while other parties spent time with Cyril Ramaphosa. South Africa was providing space for reflection on what we were about to embark on ourselves.

Mandela added his own remarks: 'You are all white, you all speak English, you are supposedly Christian but you seem to hate each other.' He would have known the reason why since it was he who recited Yeats: 'Too long a sacrifice/ Can make a stone of the heart'. I liked that he said human relations were key to building trust and creating the conditions for peace. It was a reminder to us – as if we needed any reminding – that 'you make peace with your enemies and not just your friends'.

The South Africans were acutely aware of some of the difficult issues that were stalling our talks and they spoke to us at length about these. They had not allowed decommissioning to become a red line since weapons were still readily available in neighbouring countries. Mandela's message to us was clear – we had to decouple the two demands of the need for a ceasefire and the need for decommissioning.

In front of us, the former head of the South African Defence Forces was sitting beside the former head of the military wing of the ANC, an example of how enemies had become friends. The two generals made an important point; that it would be the soldiers on the front line, and not the politicians, who would be the first to die if the agreement to end the conflict was not upheld. As is the case in all conflicts, casualties among the civilian population would also have been high. Hearing these lessons from South Africans was to stand us in good stead.

After these discussions, the loyalists agreed to meet with the republicans. David Ervine and Billy Hutchinson felt confident in arguing the loyalist point of view in the meeting. I gave them the keys of my bungalow and went off for a walk while the two parties met in private for the first time.

After I had explained to the DUP the night before that Mandela had never been a member of the Communist Party, I thought it was a nice touch that they changed into their best suits to have their picture taken with him. I hadn't time to change into better clothes for the photo that would take pride of place in my home, along with those I had taken of Graca Machel with President Mandela. They looked so happy together. Mandela wrote a short note to each delegation. Mine said, 'To the Irish Women's Coalition, best wishes to an organization of outstanding ladies.' I hadn't the heart to tell him our correct name or that we didn't refer to ourselves as 'ladies'.

The frostiness between parties started to melt one evening during a sing song. The South Africans thought they could beat us but we had David Ervine doing his version of 'My Way' and Bríd Rodgers singing in Irish. Davy Adams stole the show, changing the words of 'American Pie' to send up the parties in the room. The South Africans said we should get together more often.

If South Africans could settle their differences, I wondered if we would be able to do the same. On the last day, I asked Martin McGuinness if he thought the visit had been productive. He replied that it had been a memorable one. I had taken on board the importance of having a ceasefire before peace negotiations could take place; I wondered if he had as well. I got to know Martin during this time and could see his sensitive side when he gave me a poem as we went our separate ways to head home. I also got to know Peter Robinson better – he was very quick witted – and I was hoping that we could continue to work in the way we had in South Africa.

When we got back to Belfast on 2 June, we discovered that the *Belfast Telegraph* had heard about the cross-party sing songs. The SDLP's Mark Durkan dismissed the reports that we had been on a jolly as tittle-tattle, saying his lasting memory was of the important things we had learned. What we had come away with had less to do with the mingling in the bar and more about finding some humanity in our political opponents.

Back at the Forum, the debates and disputes on parades hadn't changed. In January 1997 the North Committee, established to consider the parading issue, had made changes to the way over three thousand marches would be conducted and policed in Northern Ireland. It recommended the transfer of police powers on the re-routing of marches to the arbitration of an independent Parades Commission. Nine out of ten parades were organised by the Orange Order and it was unhappy at the suggestion that a commission be established to deal with disputes. At the Forum, the DUP's Sammy Wilson had this to say about the committee's chair: 'I do not care if Dr North is consigned to the icy wastes of the north Atlantic or if he is consigned back to the darkness of Dublin,' implying that the Irish government had influenced the recommendations. The words of his colleague Jack McKee in the Forum were more worrying: 'There is, if people are not careful, going to be violence in Northern Ireland. The blood of Ulster people will run red in the streets if our traditions and culture are interfered with ... They ain't seen nothing yet.'

I wrote to Dr North, commending his proposal for a Parades Commission. During my postgraduate studies on town and country planning, I was taught about planning control and the need for restrictions on development rights, based on the impact on local neighbourhoods. I always thought that taking independent expert advice was a good idea. The Parades Commission would ask for applications in advance of parades, marches or protests; restrictions would be imposed if necessary; and the gatherings would be monitored, with penalties for not adhering to decisions. In the vast majority of cases, parades could go ahead unless their route went through a contested area. To take the decisions on parades out of police hands was the only way forward since the issue was a cause of alienation between citizens of all traditions and the RUC.

The usual English solution to a Northern Irish problem was to hold another round of consultations. The Women's Coalition commissioned Tom Hadden, a lawyer at Queen's, to draw up a legislative draft, similar to an Order in Council, which we sent to John Holmes, the prime minister's private secretary. He wrote to thank us and then left it to sit on a shelf in Downing Street. In response our press statement noted, 'It is not the government who does not have enough time; it is the people of Northern Ireland. We are only seven weeks away from the first contested parade of the year. A solution should have emerged by now and this is it.' Mo Mowlam, then shadow secretary of state for Northern Ireland, took the same view: 'If the Women's Coalition can produce draft legislation with such speed and very little administrative back-up, why can't the government?' The *Guardian* called it another coup for our party.

But by the time the Labour Party entered government in May 1997 and Mo Mowlam was appointed secretary of state, the parades season was upon us. It was too late to introduce legislation, so the police once again had to advise her as the new secretary of state on whether the Drumcree Orange parade should proceed. It was groundhog day, and we were staring into another abyss. Mo Mowlam banned the march and then reversed the decision following the chief constable's warning of widespread violence and public disorder. There followed a series of turbulent meetings. The SDLP met her before we did – its representatives objected to their constituents being corralled into their homes on the Garvaghy Road in Portadown and on the Lower Ormeau in Belfast. When we met her in Stormont Castle, we told her that the decision to allow the march had been based on threats – who could create the most disorder – without considering the implications for the people who lived in these areas. I argued that we couldn't go on living like this – left watching and waiting while the country burned down. Mo Mowlam threatened to resign, but that was the last thing we wanted and most of the other parties felt the same.

In October 1997, at a sensitive time during the negotiations, First Lady Hillary Clinton returned to Belfast, where she paid tribute to the role of women and young people in the peace process during the Joyce McCartan Memorial lecture at the Jordanstown Campus where I had taught. When she spoke, she held up the teapot that Joyce had given to her and said:

> This teapot stands for all those conversations around those thousands of kitchen tables where mothers and fathers look at one another with despair because they cannot imagine the future will be any better for their children. But this teapot also is on the kitchen table where mothers and fathers look at one another and say, 'We have to do better. We cannot permit this to go on. We have to take a stand for our children.'

The Forum limped on for another year until April 1998 when the British government stood it down. I was relieved when it came to an end – it had served its purpose as somewhere for unionists to vent. It didn't help that Sinn Féin had refused to take its seats and that the SDLP had walked out after the Drumcree and Lower Ormeau parade disputes in July 1996. That left only a small cohort of parties that included the Women's Coalition to demand that instead of tearing Northern Ireland apart we try to put it back on its feet. The Forum didn't assist in that process – it was politics at its most raw, and the sectarianism and sexism on display only made things worse.

Out of the country, we seemed to be able to leave the toxic atmosphere of the Forum behind. We were able to get a better and more positive sense of each other and of what might be possible. If we could harness that at the multi-party peace talks, I hoped we might produce a better outcome.

9

The Peace Talks

'If we want peace, we don't have the luxury of who we speak to.'

Pearl Sagar

The week before the peace negotiations began, I couldn't help thinking of what W.B. Yeats had written about the intractable problem of Irish politics:

Out of Ireland have we come.
Great hatred, little room,
Maimed us at the start.

The 'little room' we had been allocated was in Castle Buildings next to Stormont House, where British ministers had resided from the time of direct rule. Despite its grand name, it was no castle – it was a concrete block from which the civil servants had been decanted to make room for the ten parties elected to the talks.

On 9 June 1996, the day before the talks began, Bronagh, Pearl and I met with the British minister Michael Ancram in the Northern Ireland Office. The proposed voting mechanism for the peace talks was a procedure known as a sufficiency of consensus – previously used by the South African parties in their negotiations – and we were there to try to adapt it and make it a better fit for the process in which we were about to engage. The procedure as proposed by the British and Irish governments would have meant that if the two biggest parties (UUP and SDLP), along with the two governments, reached consensus on an issue, it would pass, and no one else's point of view would be taken into consideration. But the Woman's Coalition had other ideas – we felt that reaching consensus like that wasn't sufficiently inclusive. Bronagh proposed that consensus should not be just confined to the two largest parties; that it would be much better to have more parties around the table included, since that would help to achieve a genuine sufficiency of consensus. This would mean that each time a vote was taken, the larger parties on either side would have to work on building a consensus with the other parties, ensuring a much stronger sense of ownership for all involved. We also proposed that while a party could lodge a disagreement to any decision, it wouldn't be allowed to exercise a veto.

A few days later we were delighted to hear from a senior civil servant, Chris Maccabe, that the two governments had redefined the term 'sufficiency' and that the new voting procedure now required that a majority of the parties declare their support for the tabled proposals. This new procedure was to prove crucial throughout the process.

Before I entered the negotiations, I'd done my homework. There had been scarcely any opportunity to meet any of the negotiators from the other parties but I knew some of them from my past. I had seen David Trimble teaching (in my class at Queen's), Ian Paisley preaching (outside the City Hall) and John Hume marching (for civil rights). The people I wanted to get to know were David Ervine and Billy Hutchinson as the PUP was, like us, one of the smaller parties at the talks, so I invited both men to my home. Each of us as parties had a distinct political agenda but I wanted us to work together whenever we could. We were smaller than the other parties so we formed a Group of Four, with the PUP, the UDP and the newly formed Northern Ireland Labour party, which gave us more clout when we needed it.

The night before the talks opened, Avila, Bronagh and I had worked late into the night preparing our opening statement at my kitchen table. Drafting papers in this way for the following day became a ritual all the way through the talks. But often we never got to deliver what we were preparing because of the ongoing rows. The talks were more civilised than the Forum but the tension was still there – and not just between the opposite sides but just as frequently between the unionist parties. We were to find that out, even on the first day.

On 10 June 1996, the day that the talks opened, Pearl, May, Annie, Kate and I met in the Stormont Hotel. Our intention was to travel in one car and to walk into Castle Buildings together. But we didn't get very far – our car conked out on the Prince of Wales Avenue, leading up to Parliament Buildings, and we had to ask a passing driver to give us a lift in his van. The driver couldn't believe he was helping a group of women to get to the peace talks on time. He pleaded with us not to stop talking until we reached a resolution.

Things felt a bit surreal that morning – just eight weeks ago the party hadn't even existed and now we were about to participate in groundbreaking peace negotiations. We had been issued with identity cards to show we were bonafide delegates and allowed inside the highly secure building. Mine was a red one and I waved it at the scrum of reporters standing outside Castle Buildings, joking that I was being sent off the pitch before I'd even got started.

Pearl and I got to the room where the talks would take place, and took our places at the table with Annie, Kate and May seated directly behind us. The parties had been placed around a rectangular table in alphabetical order. Ian Paisley's party, the DUP, was using a different name – Ulster Democratic Unionist Party – which meant that all the unionist parties were clustered together on the same side. I was hoping the alphabetical seating plan would lead to more mixing of the participants, but it didn't work out that way. Pearl and I were seated directly opposite the unionist parties. The British and Irish governments were at the head of the table with their officials seated behind them. Among the sixty or so people in the room, we were the only two women. Pearl was thinking the same as me when she whispered in my ear, 'It's just the two of us at this table.'

There were big personalities from the three main parties in that room, including John Hume, Seamus Mallon, David Trimble, John Taylor, Ian Paisley and Peter Robinson. After all the rounds of failed talks over the previous years, there was no love lost between any of them. There were two conspicuous absences – Gerry Adams and Martin McGuinness. Sinn Féin had not been permitted to participate because of the collapse of the IRA ceasefire. Gerry Adams was standing outside the gates of Stormont that first day telling reporters that he was entitled to take his seat with the rest of us because of his party's electoral mandate. Pearl and I had co-signed a letter to him, saying that the breakdown in the IRA ceasefire had stunted the process and it was time for the bombings, the shootings and the violent beatings to stop. We reiterated our support for Sinn Féin's inclusion and said we would work hard inside the room if Sinn Féin would work as hard to create the conditions to come in.

That day was the first opportunity in over seventy-five years for the British and Irish governments, and the political parties, to map out a different future. It was a historic moment when Prime Minister John Major and Taoiseach John Bruton sat down together to make their opening remarks. John Major went first, saying:

> Today, we launch a new opportunity to reach lasting peace in Northern Ireland ... the hopes and expectations of the people of Northern Ireland rest on your shoulders. The ultimate say in the negotiations belongs to you. Only you can resolve the issues. Only you can agree an outcome.

John Bruton had come straight to the talks from the funeral of Garda Jerry McCabe who had been shot three days earlier by the IRA. He began by reading out the names of elected representatives who had been murdered during the Troubles, one of whom had been a close friend of his. He went on to say:

> Those who thirst for peace and for a better future will not understand if we allow the opening of the negotiations to get bogged down in recriminations or in arguments over procedure.

As he spoke, I thought of the people close to me who had died in the Troubles. Others must have been doing the same. John Taylor had survived a murder attack during which the Official IRA had pumped seven bullets into him. Malachi Curran in the Northern Ireland Labour Party was the owner of a pub in which a young man had been shot dead. Peter Robinson had lost a friend, murdered by the IRA at the age of twenty-three. Gary McMichael's father had been murdered when the IRA exploded a booby-trap bomb under his car. John White (UDP) had served a life sentence for murdering Paddy Wilson, SDLP member, and

Irene Andrews. It had been described as one of the most vicious killings in the Troubles and I was wondering how Seamus Mallon was feeling about having to sit beside the man who had murdered his close friend. John White was in the UDA in 1974, at the time my good friend Michael Mallon was shot dead. Others at the table had also been involved in the 1974 Ulster Workers' Strike at the time Michael was killed. There were wall-to-wall bad memories in that room, but by necessity they remained unspoken. The reason I was there was to make sure we never went back to those times.

I was supposed to be at Gavin's school sports day but it was Mary who took pictures of him holding up his medal while I sat listening to unionist parties objecting to the appointment of Senator Mitchell as chairperson of the talks. I'd explained to Gavin that I couldn't watch him run his race because I had to do something important that day, but as time ticked on, that felt less and less like the truth. The arguments continued into the next day and there was little I could do but wait it out. Participants retired to the coffee bar where some of them asked for strong liquor to deal with the frustration. I found a space to mark exam papers as the rows went on until after midnight.

The unionist side of the table was tearing strips off each other, with the DUP accusing the Ulster Unionists of surrendering Ulster. Earlier that day I had been walking outside when David Trimble got into a spat with Rev. McCrea – it wasn't pleasant to watch at such an early point in the talks, especially when they were nominally on the same pro-Union side. Ian Paisley Snr told the media, 'This is a battle for the soul of this province. I will dedicate my life as never before to overturning the dastardly deed.' John Taylor told the press that appointing Senator Mitchell as chairperson was the equivalent of an American Serb presiding over talks on the future of Croatia. Senator Mitchell then went out to tell the press, 'Let's nail one thing on the head. I'm not an Irish American Catholic, I'm a Lebanese Maronite.' He assured everyone within hearing distance that he had not come with a pre-drafted American agreement and said that if there were to be an agreement, it would have to come from the parties around the table. David Ervine was right when he pointed to the ludicrous position of the unionist parties, saying, 'Those who adore the Mitchell Principles seem now to be opposing Mitchell.'

Eventually, Senator Mitchell was confirmed as the chairperson, along with co-chairs General John de Chastelain and former prime minister of Finland, Hari Holkeri. The DUP and UKUP were not in agreement, but there was a majority of parties in favour, which meant the dissenters couldn't exercise a veto. More drama followed after Secretary of State Patrick Mayhew vacated his place as chairperson for Senator Mitchell to take over. Anticipating that someone might occupy the seat in protest, a government official made to sit in it. I could see the UKUP's Cedric Wilson advancing on the seat from the front and shouted, 'Stop that man!' The official got there just in time. Paisley was yelling 'No, no, no, no' as Senator Mitchell finally took his appointed seat. It was 12.32 on Wednesday morning and we were all exhausted. Paisley challenged the governments for imposing Senator Mitchell as chair, and shouted at him, 'We don't accept you. We object in the strongest possible terms.' He then left the room with his party, followed by the UKUP. The rest of us gave Senator Mitchell a standing ovation.

After a 'tour de table', we were asked in turn to affirm that we accepted the Mitchell Principles. I declared that, on behalf of the Women's Coalition, we did, and the other parties present gave the same undertaking. As we expected, the DUP and UKUP returned the next day. They were allowed to accept the Mitchell Principles in Mitchell's room, but once they were back at the table their big talkers made speeches that went on for hours.

All the representatives at the talks were issued with a little grey book, titled *Substantive All-Party Negotiations*. It was useful for checking to see how the three strands of the talks had been set out. The first strand was the relationships in Northern Ireland in respect of a power-sharing government; the second was the all-Ireland relationship, dealing with cooperation on the island of Ireland; and the third was the relationship between the British and Irish governments. When I read the proposed rules of procedure included in the book, I never imagined that they would take so long to agree. The book was in my hand most of that time.

Our success at the ballot box confirmed our right to be in the room – it had put us on a level playing field, with the same speaking rights as everyone else. But at times we got the sense we were thought of as 'the girls' – the 'little women' who lacked experience – and that it wasn't worth having us in the loop. Some of the meetings with the governments were confined to the larger parties, from which we were deliberately excluded. We would find out about these exchanges from Pearl who smoked herself half to death picking up snippets of information wherever the smokers congregated. Information is power but we also believed in building relationships – it was a key part of coalition building.

The relations between the parties were far from cordial and the plenary sessions became more and more wearying. When Senator Mitchell suggested we should try to build trust with one another, delegates raised their eyes to heaven. We didn't belong to a class of professional politicians and because of that we regularly heard remarks like, 'So you are for peace? Typical little housewives', or 'The only table you should be at is the one you are going to polish.' It was as if being for peace was something to be ashamed of. For some, we were part of the pan-nationalist front – 'Sinn Féin in skirts'; for others, were in league with the Progressive Unionist Party – 'PUPs in wolves' clothing'. To be called 'the Greek chorus of women' was the most laughable, the implication being that we were in the British government's pocket, because we knew too much.

But we weren't the only ones getting grief – the PUP was getting it as well. In response to remarks about his past, Billy Hutchinson said, 'These were the same people who spoke to loyalists out of the sides of their mouths and gave them encouragement.' When David Ervine backed up Billy's comments, it led to bitter exchanges on the pro-Union side of the table. I also saw the toll the process was taking on John Hume, who was being excoriated by the same unionist parties for having engaged in talks with Gerry Adams. He had been constantly travelling between the talks in Belfast to London, Brussels and Washington DC. He looked exhausted as well as fed up with all the filibustering.

At the Forum, language had become a political football and the same was true at the peace talks – delegates were arguing over 'may' or 'shall'. On and on it went for months. It was farcical and, as far as I could see, a political settlement was nowhere in sight. Each time John Hume asked the unionists to stop dragging their feet over nothing, the UUP's Dermot Nesbitt retorted that 'the devil is in the detail'. Adjournment after adjournment was called to deal with the tension in the room. One of the delegates was overheard describing the plenary sessions as 'caucus interruptus', which was as good a description as any. There was so little rapport between the parties that during those first few months we wondered if the talks would be able to continue. The standing joke between the Coalition members at the end of each week was, 'Have a nice weekend. Don't know if I'll see you on Monday.'

By September 1996, four months after the process started, it was touch and go whether all of the parties would sit around the table again. The events of that violent summer had bled into the Forum debates and they also had the potential to derail the peace talks. Two of the unionist parties, the DUP and UKUP, issued indictments against the two loyalist parties, the PUP and the UDP, and Alliance accused the UUP, the DUP, the PUP and the UDP of violating their pledge to the Mitchell Principles. When the accusation of non-compliance to the principles was referred to the two governments, London and Dublin said they were obliged to consider the views of all of the participants around the table. The DUP and UKUP were alleging that the PUP and the UDP had threatened violence as a result of an internal loyalist feud. The unionist parties wanted the Loyalist Command Council, of which the UDP and PUP were members, to lift its threat of issuing 'summary justice' against Billy Wright, aka King Rat, who was in charge of the renegade Loyalist Volunteer Force (LVF). Hughie Smyth denied that any PUP members had been involved and said that if it had not been for the restraint of parties like his during the parade season 'this city would have been burned to the ground'.

The Alliance Party accused the DUP of breaching the Mitchell Principles, citing Rev. McCrea's sharing of a platform in Portadown with anti-peace process agitator Billy Wright on 4 September, at which McCrea had made a provocative speech. I agreed with John Alderdice when he said at the table that the violence of the tongue can be as dangerous as the violence of the gun. That was especially the case when it created space and justification for sectarianism. Ian Paisley Snr waved the book containing the ground rules for the negotiations asking, 'Is this the Pope? Is this infallible?' I said his remarks would appal as many Protestants as Catholics in Northern Ireland. Senator Mitchell had to call for order several times.

As part of the Women's Coalition's commitment to the principle of inclusion, we discussed making contact with Sinn Féin. There was widespread support from our members from a unionist background. Annie Campbell's mantra became: 'We have got to talk to the people who allowed the ceasefire to collapse, instead of using it as an excuse to do nothing.' So I wrote to Dodie McGuinness on 8 October 1996 to say that the Coalition wanted to meet Sinn Féin. At Castle Buildings, the ghost of Sinn Féin was decidedly rattling around the table. Dodie replied, saying that she and party member Siobhán O'Hanlon would meet us. The meetings with Sinn Féin were frustrating at times. We realised that its members were more used to talking to others in the 'republican family' rather than to people who had a different perspective. However, the informal chats did turn out to be informative.

When we met Sinn Féin representatives, we said that support for the IRA's military action was self-contradictory and self-defeating if the party wanted to win majority support in the North for a united Ireland. Their position was aggravating tension, especially for the loyalist parties that we were also talking to. We told them that Sinn Féin was not helping the situation by being seen to treat the loyalist parties as some kind of unreconstructed dupes, as if sectarianism was all one-sided. We also didn't like that Sinn Féin was prioritising its relationships with the British and Irish governments, seeing them as being more important than the rest of us. In doing so, the local unionist parties felt that Sinn Féin was failing to acknowledge the deep fears and hurt of the local unionist community.

Some of our initial meetings with Sinn Féin ended up being held in unconventional places. On one occasion, when Dodie McGuinness and Siobhán O'Hanlon got locked out of Conway Mill, we met in my car. The *Sunday Times* reported the story. We never knew where that leak came from, but it certainly landed us in hot water with some of the other parties. Just as John Hume had been criticised for meeting with Sinn Féin, we too faced accusations of 'messing up the pitch'. Anne Carr summed up our rationale when she said, we needed to create a place 'where people weren't feeling so driven into a corner that they have to lift a gun to shoot somebody. Change was needed. Peace is people choosing to live differently and we are going to talk to them.'

As someone also from a unionist background, Pearl admitted that she struggled at these first meetings with Sinn Féin: 'Nobody wanted Sinn

Féin at the table, the IRA was still killing people. Who wants killers sitting at a table?' She had talked it over with her husband, who was supportive, and he had told her that if she wanted everyone involved, everybody had to be involved; that there were always going to be people she didn't like in the world but she would still have to work with them.

Years later, she described how she'd felt at the meeting:

> I sat down in this room with people that I hated, and I mean hated. I hated them because my husband was in the British army that they hated. I also had a cousin who was a police officer, who was gunned down in front of his children. They were representing the people who killed them and I remember sitting in that room, and I'm not even sure what they were saying that day because all that I could hear was my heartbeat, in my eardrums, and it was horrible.

Martha Pope was Senator Mitchell's chief of staff – a constant presence and the eyes and ears of the talks, liaising with each of the parties as well as the British and Irish governments. She spent time beyond the confines of Stormont, to get a feel for the local communities in some of the areas that had borne the brunt of the violence. In November 1996, the press carried reports that she was having an affair with Sinn Féin's Gerry Kelly, who had served time for IRA offences. They ran the story without first checking if Martha had even met Gerry Kelly, which she hadn't. I wondered if the allegations had been deliberately planted to damage the standing of the US talks secretariat, and suspected, if that was the case, that whoever had planted them had singled out Martha because she was an easier target. The news crossed the Atlantic, and the *New York Post* carried the story with the headline 'Sex scandal perils the IRA truce'. Martha's career and the talks process were both hanging in the balance. However the *Boston Globe* reported that a number of US officials in Washington DC believed that the *Mail on Sunday* had concocted the story, and carried the reaction of an Irish diplomat, who was quoted as saying, 'This is not about Martha Pope, this is about a smear campaign against George Mitchell.'

I could see how stressful all this was for Martha – she was a person of great integrity and safeguarding her reputation was her highest concern.

Inserting a scandal into the process showed how easy it could be to ruin a good woman's career. She decided to sue the newspapers that carried the allegations, employing Michael Lavery QC as her barrister. Within a matter of days, the libel action was settled and the following week the *Mail on Sunday* and the Dublin-based *Sunday World* published a retraction, agreeing to pay a sizeable sum in compensation.

In the period before the retraction, the British government had taken its time to confirm that the story was false, which left some of us querying whether the rumour had been part of a dirty tricks campaign. Conspiracy theories were to be expected where there was a legacy of malfeasance and cover-ups. Rumours and lies all too easily became the order of the day, displacing any limited sense of trust that might have been built between the parties and the governments. Ian Paisley Snr continued to give the story legs – he wasn't going to let a good crisis go to waste – and he challenged Senator Mitchell about it at the talks.

The senator was in Ian Paisley's sights again after a speech he made in Washington DC. I considered the speech to be one of the most thought-provoking analyses of the peace process that I'd heard. Senator Mitchell identified the twin demons preventing peace as violence and intransigence, though he was careful to point out that there was no moral equivalency between the two. Paisley believed Senator Mitchell was referring to his party when he spoke of intransigence and told the press, 'He's bracketing us with the IRA and I find that highly insulting.' Paisley used what Mitchell had said to question his impartiality and suitability to be chairperson of the negotiations. It felt surreal when Paisley said he was calling on the Fair Employment Commission to carry out an investigation to ascertain the religious and political composition of Senator Mitchell's secretariat staff. I told the Americans in the Belfast office to look on the bright side: Paisley was now finally recognising the need for a Fair Employment Commission.

Crisis after crisis became the order of the day and the next one was the demand for the groups still holding weapons to decommission them. From the start of the talks, the demand for weapons to be handed over had the potential to destabilise the process. I believed that any party holding to principles of non-violence as a way to resolve political differences could not justify holding on to its weaponry. Since no one side could be declared the victor, and all sides had called a halt, I believed that any disarmament process would have to be entered into voluntarily and that all of us around the table would have to create the conditions for that to happen. But dismantling the weaponry was, in part, an issue of timing – not just if but when. Ulster Unionist Reg Empey pointed out that when he called for IRA decommissioning he was referring to guns that were pointing at him and his family. On the other hand, Gerry Adams accused the unionists and the British government of making the handover of weapons their primary consideration. We went through so many iterations of how decommissioning might be achieved that it left me wondering whether we might fare better if the Ulster Unionists and Sinn Féin were to meet face-to-face instead of using the British and Irish governments as proxies.

I knew from my work on domestic abuse that leaving violence behind was a process and not an event. I also knew from that work that attitudes would need to change, so I rowed in behind John Hume when he said that we needed to decommission mindsets. I said that a clenched fist or a punch to the head could be as threatening as a gun – and that if we didn't change the mindsets, all kinds of harm would continue. A church noticeboard that I passed each day on my way into Castle Buildings had what I felt was a message about the weapons for the participants at the talks, and I repeated it many times: 'Let them rust in peace.'

On 23 January 1997 May, Bronagh and I went to London for a meeting with the prime minister, which the *Belfast Telegraph* reported with the headline, 'Major faces tough-talking women'. We spent over an hour in 10 Downing Street giving him the reasons why we believed that the prospect of a lasting peace was being allowed to drift away. The Conservative government's slim majority in the House of Commons meant it was dependent on the votes of Ulster Unionist MPs for survival. Although John Major listened intently and seemed to understand our point of view, he was reluctant to go against them. If we couldn't get past this demand that weapons must be decommissioned before substantive negotiations could progress, it was hard to see how we would ever reach a political agreement.

I had to get back to Belfast that evening to be at Gavin's Confirmation. The meeting ended with a nice touch from the prime minister when he said that he appreciated how difficult all the juggling could be. Following Gavin's Confirmation, I rushed off to yet another meeting – at the Women's Institute in a small rural town. Like me, these women were pinning their hopes on the fact that the peace process was going to work. I felt encouraged by them but it was another one of those long days where I was on the go from dawn to dusk.

In May 1997, Tony Blair became the new prime minister. I was relieved that there was now a party in government with a leader who was on record as saying he would make Northern Ireland a priority, and with enough of a majority in Westminster to move forward on that. I had met Mo Mowlam many times, so I wrote to congratulate her on the historically large number of women elected to parliament. She was the new secretary of state for Northern Ireland as we had predicted, and when she arrived at Castle Buildings, she was a breath of fresh air, greeting each party around the table and giving a few of us a hug.

In the Westminster and local government elections that May, the Women's Coalition ran candidates to reflect what we had set out to do: bring more women from the margins into the political mainstream. We also wanted to widen the choice for voters, but it was hard work for a party as small as ours. Our message was that to make peace we had to listen, talk, communicate and negotiate about everything, whether the subject was marching or reaching a political accommodation. We succeeded in winning a seat in Newcastle, County Down, in the local elections, and Anne Carr became our first councillor.

On 16 June 1997, police officers Roland Graham and David Johnston were murdered by an IRA unit in Lurgan. A few days later, Avila and I attended a meeting with Mitchel McLaughlin, general secretary of Sinn Féin, that had been previously arranged. We confronted him over how these IRA killings contradicted Sinn Féin's policy document 'A Pathway to Peace' and the stated desire to get back into the talks. He told us that the IRA had not sanctioned these killings, and that Sinn Féin had been working since the mid-1980s to find a political solution. Avila kicked me hard under the table after I asked why there had been no rejection of the men who had perpetrated the murders, suggesting that it may have been because Sinn Féin's leaders didn't want to end up like Michael Collins, who had been accused of selling out to the British. I didn't mean to cast aspersions but it was frustrating to see so many issues getting in the way of progress.

After the meeting, Avila and I went on to Castle Buildings, where we ran into Gusty Spence, a leading member of the PUP. When we told him about our meeting, he asked if we would come to their room to repeat to other party members what Mitchel McLaughlin had said. Like most, we felt that there was a very real risk that the loyalist paramilitaries were going to retaliate following the IRA's actions. There had been an unofficial no-first-strike policy between the republicans and the loyalists after the ceasefires, but breaches had already occurred. When we got into the PUP's room the discussion became heated very quickly. The loyalists debated how they should interpret what Avila and I had been told, and what their response should be. Gusty Spence leaned forward and said, 'I think they [Sinn Féin] are telling the truth.' He made the point that if loyalists could not control their renegades, what made them think the IRA could control theirs. As we were leaving, we could tell that the tension in the room was dissipating.

On 26 June 1997, the Irish government had a change of leadership with Fianna Fáil's Bertie Ahern becoming taoiseach. The new entourage included a woman, Liz O'Donnell, minister of state in the coalition government. I was looking forward to meeting her – I'd had a lot of time for her predecessor, Nora Owen. When Nora first came to the table, John Taylor said he couldn't remember her name, referring to her as 'this woman from Dublin – Mary Owen or whatever her name is'.

In addition to Liz O'Donnell, the new Irish government ministerial team led by Taoiseach Bertie Ahern also included Minister for Foreign Affairs David Andrews and Minister for Justice John O'Donoghue. Bertie Ahern had cut his teeth as a successful minister for Labour in the south of Ireland, brokering deals between unions and employers. You could see he was a good listener and was keen to get the business done. His special adviser, Martin Mansergh, deserved credit for spending long months locked up with us in Castle Buildings. Although the Coalition was small, he credited us with punching above our weight.

Because the Coalition hadn't been part of the previous rounds of talks in the early 1990s, we made good use of the services of the Irish and British officials to keep us up to speed. We worked both sides of the street, holding meetings with the ministers in both governments as well as with their officials. Two of them, David Cooney on the Irish side and David Hill on the British, became our 'David times two'. They were public servants of the highest calibre. Department of Foreign Affairs official Seán Ó hUiginn led the Irish team until Irish ambassador to the US Dermot Gallagher swapped roles with him after the first year of the talks. I saw more of the Irish officials – Tim O'Connor, Rory Montgomery, Ray Bassett and Eamonn McKee – than I did of my own family. The British side was headed up by Bill Jeffrey and Jonathan Stephens. I was already on good terms with the directors of the joint Anglo-Irish secretariat: Peter Bell and David Donoghue. I was suspicious at first of Peter Bell, who wrote his notes in Mandarin. I later discovered that he was, in fact, a linguist and this was one of his eccentricities. Chris Maccabe from the Northern Ireland Office – the UK government department responsible for Northern Ireland affairs – became another key person for us. These officials were the 'keepers of the pen' – doing the drafting, working out angles, and protecting the text.

Alan Whysall was a British government official responsible for documenting the proceedings. We knew him first as 'the man next door' – his office was next to mine. We wondered if he had been listening to our conversations; it wasn't just the paper-thin walls, but also the infrared monitors and security gadgets that made it look as if there were bugs everywhere in Castle Buildings. He was another 'keeper of the pen' – or in his case the custodian of the computer disk – banking information at every stage of the process. The politicians ultimately make the calls but the bureaucrats have a crucial role, and I made it my business to get to know them all.

I had taken a few days' break and was on holiday in Donegal when I received a phone call from Sinn Féin's Dodie McGuinness on 18 July 1997. She told me there would be a new IRA ceasefire by midnight and asked if I could meet the party in preparation for its entry to the peace talks. The next day I left Brian and the boys, and navigated my way across the city of Derry, where rubber tyres were burning in stacks across the roads, giving out a sickening pungent smell. The parade season was in full swing, complete with attendant protests. The news on the radio was describing the ceasefire as another moment of history. The British government had announced that it would be another six weeks before Sinn Féin could enter the talks, but the party wanted to get prepared, so when I met Dodie I explained the rules and the set-up in the room.

On 22 July 1997, Ian Paisley and Bob McCartney took their parties out of the talks for the third and last time, in response to what they saw as a lack of clarity from the British government over decommissioning. They had already made their position clear: if Sinn Féin came in, they would go. I told the press that too many people were in their graves and that we owed it to them to move on with the negotiations. The problem was that their departure left the Ulster Unionist Party in a precarious situation, because they had taken a similar stance on decommissioning. Back at the table, David Trimble said that he would use the summer recess to consult with his supporters. He was facing his most critical decision – opinion polls were showing support for the Ulster Unionist Party to remain and civil society groups were saying the same, but it was far from certain that he would return when the talks reconvened after the summer.

The previous year, Sir George Quigley, a retired leading civil servant, had become a cheerleader for the peace negotiations, forming a partnership of business, trade union and voluntary organisations known as the G7 group. In our meetings with him, Quigley advocated that since 'old problems needed new questions asked of them' we should remain at the table. The G7 group increased the pressure on the parties, particularly the Unionist Party, to keep going at this crucial point.

Ian Knox drew a cartoon for the *Irish News* that showed me with a teacher's cane in my hand, guiding the parties through the gate for the start of the new term. But not of all the parties showed up on 9 September – the date the talks were due to reconvene. One new party entered the negotiations (SF), another one (UUP) was considering its position and two parties (DUP and UKUP) had gone and weren't coming back. It felt like progress when Gerry Adams stated what the rest of us had at the start of the talks: his party's commitment to the Mitchell Principles but shortly after we hit another hurdle when Sinn Féin's declaration of support was questioned only two days later. *An Phoblacht* published an interview with an IRA member in which he stated that the IRA had difficulties with the Mitchell Principles. He threw in for good measure, 'But the IRA is not a participant in the talks.' Tony Blair reiterated the British government's position – that the IRA and Sinn Féin were inextricably linked and if the IRA violated the principles, Sinn Féin could not remain in the talks. David Trimble described the republican leaders as 'scoundrels'. Gerry Adams repeated that Sinn Féin spoke for Sinn Féin and intended to honour its commitment to the Mitchell Principles. Taoiseach Bertie Ahern stated that the interview was still a major concern. The talks schedule was once more in disarray.

Just before noon on Tuesday 16 September, a 400lb bomb exploded in Markethill, County Armagh. Most of the parties had returned following the summer recess, but we waited for a few more days to see if the other pro-Union parties who had been at the table – the UUP, the PUP and UDP – would return. The Coalition's change at the start of the talks to the sufficiency of consensus procedure came home to roost on 17 September, when the Ulster Unionists walked back into Castle Buildings with the loyalist parties at their side. The leaders of the PUP and UDP provided the political cover for David Trimble – they were the 'sufficiency' for the pro-Union side, since no one could accuse men like David Ervine and Gary McMichael of selling out. Even though the IRA denied responsibility for the bomb in Markethill – it was claimed by the Continuity IRA, a splinter group that most of us were hearing about for the first time – the Ulster Unionists insisted that the IRA were all the same and issued an indictment that Sinn Féin should be excluded from the talks.

At the table, when it came to the Women's Coalition's turn to address the problem, I said that engaging in the politics of exclusion wouldn't work and that exclusion – be it voluntary or imposed – would only make the task of achieving peace more difficult. I added that it would make more sense for the Ulster Unionists to engage with Gerry Adams, instead of David Trimble saying it was a source of pride that he had never spoken to him. We had worked out the Coalition's position the evening before in my home – that whether Sinn Féin did, or did not, speak for the IRA was something only that party could answer, but that we would be disappointed if Sinn Féin could not reflect the mind or view of the IRA since that was the point of them being at the table. It was also important that we should distinguish between the actions and aspirations of the various armed groups on the republican side: I thought it was too easy to treat dissidents in the Continuity IRA as one and the same with the

Provisional IRA when they were two different factions. I argued that the same fracturing had occurred within loyalism, with renegades in the Loyalist Volunteer Force seeking to sabotage the peace process. I proposed that the indictment be dismissed and that we should move forward with substantive negotiations.

After some wrangling, Trimble and Taylor – the two main Ulster Unionist negotiators – left the room, but were replaced immediately by two party colleagues, Reg Empey and Peter King. The loyalist parties called it a 'sham fight'. It didn't matter to me who was in the Ulster Unionist seats as long as the party was prepared to remain at the table once Sinn Féin entered the room. Pearl admitted to having mixed emotions at the time: 'Sitting down with Gerry Adams is the hardest thing I have ever done in my life. But I am here not for my personal opinions but to represent those who want peace. And if we want peace, we don't have the luxury of who we speak to.' On 24 September, we voted to move the talks to substantive discussions and elected General de Chastelain to oversee the decommissioning issue. It was another historic evening. As the parties stood up to shake hands, I turned to Pearl and said, 'After fifteen months, this is it.'

On 13 October 1997, Tony Blair made his second visit as prime minister to Northern Ireland. Part of his itinerary was to meet the parties, including Sinn Féin, and that's when he shook hands with Gerry Adams. As a result, he was jostled and jeered at during a walkabout in East Belfast. When he came into our office, after the formal introductions were over, I told him that it was better to hold out an open hand than a clenched fist, especially in peace negotiations. I also mentioned that I'd been asked to speak about the handshake on the national news that evening. Alastair Campbell, Blair's official spokesperson, had been trying to rush the prime minister to his next appointment but suddenly made more time for us when he heard my interview was with Jeremy Paxman on *Newsnight*.

One month on from the talks resuming in September, we had not got very far. Davy Adams told me that UDA prisoners were trying to pressurise his party, the UDP, into withdrawing from the negotiations. The lack of progress was causing those inside the prison to lose faith in the process. I assured Davy that we would do what we could – which is how May, Pearl and I found ourselves on our way to the Maze prison in

October 1997. First we ran the gauntlet of Alsatian dogs barking at our ankles; next came the very obvious display of pornography in the prison officers' area. The posters on the office walls were in full view, pinned above the heads of the all-female secretarial staff. I couldn't understand why the women hadn't objected to the pictures of sexualised naked female bodies in their workplace, then I realised it was a reflection of their lack of power. It was my first time visiting a prison. Years later I would return to oversee changes to the prison system.

Already unsettled by the pornographic images and the Alsatians, we spent the next two hours locked up in a mobile hut with Michael Stone, Johnny Adair and Bobby Philpott. For most people, they were the perpetrators of atrocities, but for some in their communities, they were vanguard fighters. Michael Stone mentioned how shocked he was at the television reports showing the treatment being meted out to us at the Forum. I couldn't help remembering his own awful actions at Milltown Cemetery in 1988. The experience in the hut was surreal, with Pearl and the men chain-smoking as May and I sat with streaming eyes. Through the smoke, I told them that the UDP contribution to the talks was making a real difference, and that it would be a loss if Davy Adams and Gary McMichael were to withdraw. As working-class loyalists/unionists, their voices needed to be heard. Mo Mowlam held the same view as us, and went to visit the same men three months later. A secretary of state going into the prison made the headlines – but the gamble paid off when the prisoners announced that they supported the UDP's ongoing attendance at the talks.

As the stance of the Women's Coalition became more widely known, we were sometimes approached by individuals or groups that had a specific reason to want to speak to the parties. They needed passes to come into Castle Buildings, and making these arrangements was how I first met Bill Flynn, Tom Moran and Ed Kenney. Tom Moran was to become a good friend, putting his time and resources into the peace process. He had started his working life as a New York cab driver and ended up CEO and Chairperson of Mutual of America, a position that had previously been held by Bill. Ed was the head of security at the same company. All three used their influence to bring republicans and loyalists to the US to speak to the foreign relations committee in New York. They had succeeded in making the USA more welcoming to unionists, and maintained regular contact with the parties at the table. If anyone deserved credit for making smaller parties like ours feel included when the larger parties were being entertained in high places, it was Tom Moran. I treasured his friendship as well as his insights, and the peace process lost a dear friend when he passed away in 2018.

Rita Restorick was another visitor who made an impact on me. Her son, Stephen, a British soldier, had been shot in a sniper attack in Bessbrook, south Armagh, on 12 February 1997. When she came to our office, she placed Stephen's photograph on the table. She said she missed her son and was campaigning for peace, in the hope that he would be the last soldier to die. She had stood in a solitary peace vigil outside the gates before coming in to face Gerry Adams and Martin McGuinness. She told us that she held no bitterness towards anyone in Northern Ireland and hoped that those who had difficulty supporting the mother of a British soldier would support her as are bereaved mother. She wanted other women like her to have a voice. When I wrote to her later, I was saddened when she said in her reply that she wasn't eligible for compensation for loss of earnings due to ill health caused by the effects of her son's death. She had not met the criteria of being at the scene of the incident or its immediate aftermath, and she wrote in her letter, 'What cold-hearted lawyer or civil servant thinks a mother does not suffer psychological damage unless she actually sees her son being shot?' Gaining reparations for victims would be a hard fight. When I read Rita Restorick's book, *Death of a Soldier: A Mother's Search for Peace in Northern Ireland*, recalling her experiences of the tragedy and its aftermath, I cried. I hoped she had found some consolation in the fact that the peace process was proceeding, however slowly.

Another pass that I had to get but had no prior notice for was Gavin's. He had broken his ankle and was on crutches, so couldn't go into school. He came into Castle Buildings and would either sit quietly behind me at the talks, observing the proceedings, or do his homework in the office beside Ann McCann, who kept her beady eye on him. One day, Gerry Adams and Martin McGuinness walked by. They did a double-take and then came in to speak to 'young McWilliams'. Gavin had heard and read contrasting reports of them – they were either bogeymen or peacemakers – so I was glad he had the chance to meet them to see what he thought for himself. The difference was profound between the informality of this chat and the plenary sessions in the main rooms. At the table, if you wanted to speak, you had to press a button on the microphone directly in front of you. It was often a challenge to reconcile the two worlds.

Substantive negotiations had finally been launched on 7 October 1997, the week before Tony's Blair's visit. The nature of devolved government in Northern Ireland, the north–south relationships with the Republic of Ireland and the east–west relationships between the Irish and British governments were central issues. The 'totality of relationships' had been on the table in previous talks, but this time the outcomes would be different, given the range of political representation involved. In the past, the two governments, the UUP, the DUP, the SDLP and the Alliance Party had tried to reach an agreement, but this time Sinn Féin, the PUP, the UDP, alongside the Women's Coalition and the Northern Ireland Labour Party, were addressing a much more comprehensive agenda. It was clear that since we were the people who were going to be living with any agreement after the British and Irish government representatives went home, we would be the people who had to make the arrangements work.

Seamus Mallon, deputy leader of the SDLP, called the talks 'Sunningdale for slow learners' but I disagreed, not only because of the larger number of parties involved, but also because of the range of issues that were on the table. There had been a notable absence of social and economic issues in previous rounds of talks, but now we had the opportunity to address these, which was especially important since such inequalities had played a role in the conflict. The Coalition's goal was to ensure that commitments to integrated education, shared housing and community development would also be in the agreement. In a process in which 'nothing is agreed until everything is agreed', we recognised the importance of keeping these issues on the agenda in sub-committees day after day. This would ensure that our proposals were 'banked' by government officials, and would have a chance of making it into the final agreement.

Fundamental for the participants at the talks was how to resolve the issue of identity. British and Irish identities were equally legitimate, so any future arrangements would have to give equal recognition to both.

Even the language that both sides used reflected the differences: unionists spoke of the 'Ulster people' when they meant only the unionist section of the population; republicans spoke of 'our people', ignoring those who saw themselves as British. I was conscious that there were those who saw change and movement – any change and movement – as a threat. To counter that fear, I said we now had the opportunity to negotiate a valued place for Northern Ireland not only in the British and Irish contexts, but also in the European one. In emphasising the 'European' dimension, I wanted to get beyond the British/Irish binary, but for some it seemed that having more of a trans-national identity – what the Coalition jokingly described as European Unionism – was a step too far. I had always felt that being part of the European Union had helped us to resolve many of the divisions on the island of Ireland, and I wanted us as parties to recognise that as an advantage. Not everyone saw it the way I did.

We needed a new formula that recognised the allegiances of people who considered themselves to be British or Irish or both. A central pillar would have to be the acceptance that Northern Ireland's constitutional position was different – different to the rest of the island and different to the rest of the UK. If the Irish government was prepared, as it said it was, to remove its territorial claim to Northern Ireland as enshrined in articles 2 and 3 of its constitution, the quid pro quo was that unionists would have to accept the right to self-determination through a referendum about the unification of Ireland. All of this would have to be recognised as part of the deal.

The Women's Coalition proposed that anyone born in Northern Ireland should be able to opt for British, Irish or dual citizenship. If that was the case and if the Irish government removed the territorial claim to the North, we proposed that those holding an Irish passport could act as members in the Seanad – the second chamber of the Irish parliament – and vote in Irish presidential elections. These were creative ideas, and when people around the table asked why, we replied, why not? John Alderdice responded with the well-known saying 'no representation without taxation'. I understood that point of view, but Northern Ireland was different and the ideas we were proposing, we felt, would give greater buy-in to the agreement for those who had an allegiance to their Irish identity. Why should citizenship in a contested territory be a zero-sum game? We asserted that the interdependence and mutuality between the people of these shared islands was more important than any territorial claims.

Another contentious issue was the Irish language. Nationalists and republicans wanted it to be protected, in the same way that Welsh is in Wales. Unionists responded by asking for the same status for Ulster-Scots. I didn't see it as equivalent and joked that when I asked for a translation of Women's Coalition, I was told we were the 'Weemen's Clan'. I could understand the significance of the Ulster-Scots cultural heritage – handed down through music, dancing and language – but the argument for it to be treated in the same way as the Irish language was not a strong one. Most language experts saw Ulster-Scots as a dialect. Symbolic issues, like culture and language, are often the hardest to resolve and that was the case here.

All the parties were in agreement on incorporating the European Convention on Human Rights into UK law. It meant that we would have recourse to the European court at Strasbourg and that the government would have to comply with its decisions. There was also broad agreement on the need for a Bill of Rights for Northern Ireland, but whether it would be guaranteed or not was still in question.

It wasn't a surprise that the parties linked to armed groups were particularly focused on the release of their prisoners. Demobilisation, disarmament and reintegration of prisoners would all have to be dealt with as part of the final agreement. The question we faced was how would these three elements work – in tandem or as separate processes? Should prisoners be released before weapons were decommissioned? We had learned from South Africa that when the circumstances no longer existed in which politically motivated offences were committed, releasing prisoners would be one of the outcomes. The conditions on which the prisoners would be released were crucial if we weren't to be accused of issuing get-out-of-jail-free cards to people who had been given life sentences.

The Women's Coalition proposed that, in order to make the police more representative of the people they were policing, the issues of gender and class would have to be addressed along with religion. Given the time constraints, we agreed that the government should establish an independent review body to take forward policing reform. I proposed that some of the experts appointed should be international to ensure that the review would be as independent as possible. There had been too many instances in the past, such as the Widgery Inquiry, in which credibility was undermined by a lack of independent experts from outside the UK.

In the discussions on policing, the differences between the UUP and the SDLP were stark. Ken Maginnis argued that the police had defended the rule of law while facing an onslaught from those whose only mission was to break the law. It was left to Seamus Mallon to explain why the policing reforms were needed. He drew on his own personal experiences, which were the opposite of those of Ken Maginnis. His argument for a review of policing made sense and he became the driving force in seeing the reforms through. Many police officers now admit that Northern Ireland is the better for it.

The Coalition highlighted the importance of people from working-class areas being recruited into the police. When our representative Barbara McCabe made that argument in the policing sub-committee, the PUP's Billy Mitchell, was in agreement, and stated: 'We need a language that is not about confrontation, relationships that are not based on unionist privilege and supremacy, but on a morality that recognises each other's humanity.' Barbara and Billy were both from Protestant backgrounds and were disillusioned with 'Big House' unionism. The peace process lost these two compassionate and honest people to cancer some years later.

Another idea that the Coalition had adapted from South Africa was that of a Peace and Justice Commission, which we proposed should be established by the two governments. One of the hardest things in any conflict-ridden society is to find an agreed narrative, or narratives, on the causes of the conflict, so having such a commission would be one way to deal with this problem and would also focus on the needs of victims. Our suggestion disappeared into the ether.

From the time we established the party, we recognised the importance of having victims acknowledged and provided for in any agreement. The Coalition had members who were victims themselves. Some called for alleged perpetrators to be prosecuted but others wanted a form of justice that would be more restorative in nature. Ann McCann, our colleague who had lost her brother in the Troubles, wondered whether anyone would ever learn the truth without proper investigations but was just as concerned about the lack of counselling and support for the bereaved. We were determined to do what we could to make sure commitments for victims would be in the final agreement, but we seemed to be a lone voice.

Outside Castle Buildings, fear was stalking the streets, with terrifying loyalist death squads murdering people. On 11 January 1998, Terry Enright, a twenty-eight-year-old community worker and father of two, was shot dead by LVF gunmen outside the nightclub where he worked part-time as a doorman. His funeral was one of the largest I had attended, with hundreds of young men and women in a state of shock. In a coded message to a Belfast newsroom, the LVF said that the killing was in retaliation for the INLA killing of the LVF's Billy Wright inside prison the previous month. Terry Enright's father spoke after the funeral, saying that he wanted people to know that he was as bitter about the political posturing among the unionists as he was about the fundamentalist psychopaths who had carried out the killing. David Ervine described Terry as 'a visionary who had been killed by people with no vision'. The tributes to this young man strengthened my resolve not to give up on the peace talks.

In the months leading up to Easter, loyalist gunmen continued with their campaign of violence. Taxi companies took down their cab signs to stop their Catholic drivers being identified as targets, and Catholic workers employed in Protestant businesses became more fearful of being singled out. In areas near where I lived, six people were murdered. The violence raging outside Castle Buildings was making us nervous inside the room. David Ervine was receiving death threats and because of these he didn't drive his car, so I often gave him a lift. He said that if he were to be killed, it would be by someone on his own side. Brian thought I was taking risks by giving David lifts, and David often said the same, but I wasn't going to let that stop me driving him home.

The talks should have been getting close to the end stage by the time we went to London in January 1998 – it had been agreed that the parties would spend a week at Lancaster House as part of the east–west relationship-building process. This was the place where, famously, in 1979, agreement had been reached on Rhodesia. Reporters were gathered en masse, and a few of them were looking for a sound bite since nothing much was happening – they got what they needed from Jeffrey Donaldson. Before he addressed the press, he cut the Joint Framework Document in two. It had formed the basis for the peace negotiations but the unionists didn't like it. While he spoke to reporters, he made it look as though he was spontaneously tearing the document in half right in front of them.

However, Gary McMichael with his UDP delegates received more attention. The party was about to be expelled because the police had stated that the UDA, the paramilitary group to which the UDP was politically aligned, had violated its ceasefire. I believed Gary McMichael when he said the party had no control over the people who were carrying out the murders. I told the press that if we forced the UDP out of the talks, we would be giving the disaffected loyalists exactly what they wanted and allowing the spoilers to wrong-foot us. The Women's Coalition asked Sinn Féin not to support the indictment against the UDP on the grounds that they could be next – that they could be kicked out too if they were held responsible for the actions of militant dissidents over whom they claimed to have no control. But Sinn Féin did support the indictment, as did the majority of the other parties, and it fell to me to pass that on to Gary McMichael. I suggested that he should leave the talks voluntarily and not let the matter come to a vote, and his delegation agreed to that proposal.

Irish and British representatives David Andrews and Mo Mowlam then stated that the UDP could return as soon as they re-committed to the Mitchell Principles. I told the press that inclusion had to be meaningful in relation to all parties, especially in ensuring that working-class loyalist voices would be heard. Pearl, Avila and I met Gary McMichael and Davy Adams during the four weeks they remained outside the talks. Our promise to reach out to any party during their expulsion had to be put into practice – inclusion for us was not just a paper concept.

I had been looking forward to seeing the 'Propositions on Heads of Agreement' that had been prepared by the two governments, but once again circumstances, this time with the UDP, had overtaken the proceedings. We had arrived in London hoping that we could move on to the serious business of setting out our positions. All we got was more prevarication, with the two governments discussing how to handle the expulsion of the UDP, and the rest of us having very little else to do. That afternoon the British government announced through Mo Mowlam a public inquiry into Bloody Sunday. The other memorable moment was when the UUP's Reg Empey asked Gerry Adams and Martin McGuinness – indirectly through the chairperson – to help him understand how ten men could starve themselves to death in a hunger strike for the sake of a political cause. Questions like this had been missing up until then and it was good to hear a politician on one side express some curiosity about his opponent's ideology.

When the talks moved to Dublin the following month – we'd done east–west, so now it was time to do north–south – we were provided with offices in Dublin Castle. This time it was Sinn Féin that was facing expulsion from the talks. Alliance issued an indictment against the party because of the recent murders that had been claimed by Direct Action Against Drugs, arguing that this group was aligned to the IRA. Once again, I found myself arguing that, instead of serving indictments against parties inside the room, we should adopt a collective stance and not allow external events to undermine the process. The Coalition held a meeting in Dublin Castle with Gerry Adams and Martin McGuinness and came away from it in no doubt that Sinn Féin wanted to remain in the process, despite mutterings that their party was looking for an exit route. Senator Mitchell and the two governments found themselves having to respond to the court application issued by Gerry Adams against Sinn Féin's expulsion. That showed that the party hadn't come this far either to be excluded or to exclude themselves.

When we returned to the table, following the adjournment for the court case, Sinn Féin was absent – the party had been expelled until the following month. In discussions at the table about whether the political centre could deliver a deal without Sinn Féin, I said, 'There will be a deal, but it cannot just be a deal of the centre.' By this I meant the SDLP, the UUP and the Alliance Party. Then, I asked those parties to explain what they meant by 'the centre'. Finally, I asked Fianna Fáil whether it considered itself to be a party of the centre, since it referred to itself as a republican party. I then added that the events of the 1920s should have provided all of us with a much better understanding that 'the centre' was a very dynamic concept in politics.

During our time at Dublin Castle, Enoch Powell's death was announced. John Taylor asked if I would swap my turn to speak so he could attend the funeral with his UUP colleagues. Powell had been elected to Westminster to represent Ulster Unionism in South Down years before but was known mainly in the UK for his pronouncements on race relations and most especially for his famous 'rivers of blood' anti-immigrant speech. I agreed to give up my place and would have done the same for anyone going to a funeral. Before they left the city, the unionist delegation visited the former Dublin home of Edward Carson, which had recently been refurbished by the Irish government. The irony wasn't lost on me that one of the reasons we were having peace negotiations was because of Carson's legacy. The other irony was that both Enoch Powell and Edward Carson had each accused the Conservative party of betraying the Union at different times in Anglo-Irish relations.

The producer of RTÉ's *The Late Late Show* contacted me to see if I would be interested in coming on the programme to discuss the talks. Brian was going to be away for work on the evening of the show, 20 February, so I made arrangements to take Gavin, Rowen and their friend Garrett with me on the train, and to stay over in a Dublin hotel. *The Late Late Show* was to go out in front of a live audience – it had huge popularity ratings in the south of Ireland – and I began to think about what I might be asked. I was also worried about the boys behaving, but they settled down on the floor in front of the cameras. I told the host, Gay Byrne, 'We have this thing in the palm of our hands. We are going to make it.' Even as I said the words, I wasn't certain we would – we still had a month to go – but as the boys looked up at me I felt deep down I just had to be right.

Back at the talks, the pace was heating up with extra days slotted in for a series of questions from the governments. One of those questions was 'Might there be a role for any other institutions such as an all-island consultative forum for bringing together representatives of civil society and the social partners?' If that was the case then the governments must have been giving our proposal for a Civic Forum in Northern Ireland some serious thought in order to have come up with the idea of an all-island one. The secretariat circulated a paper that stated, 'one party is opposed to a Civic Forum in Northern Ireland and others are silent on the issue'. Persuasion was a tactic that we had used before and the time had come to use it again – to build support among our allies to get the Civic Forum agreed.

Just as the parties were starting to exchange position papers, I left the talks for a few days to go to Salzburg in Austria to participate in a discussion on peace negotiations. I was to meet Sinn Féin's Seán MacManus again, ten months after I had met him at the workshop in Harvard, and Jeffrey Donaldson was there to represent the Ulster Unionists. Jeffrey told me that he was attending out of curiosity, which was also the reason why I was there – to see what I could learn that might be put to use back home. The other attendees from Northern Ireland were my university colleague Paul Arthur and former civil servant and friend Maurice Hayes. Dick Spring, the leader of the Irish Labour Party, and Martin Mansergh, the taoiseach's special advisor, came from Dublin. The venue was Schloss Leopoldskron – an eighteenth-century mansion where part of *The Sound of Music* was filmed. Tim Phillips, from the Project for Justice in Times of Transition, had come up with the idea that it would be useful to participate in discussions with others who had lived through years of conflict.

The session I chaired with victims from Latin American countries focused on the terrible atrocities they had experienced over previous decades. Ana Guadalupe Martínez, the female commander of the FMLN, had been kidnapped, tortured and held hostage by El Salvadorian forces and spoke about how she had entered negotiations with the government responsible for that harm. In the discussion that followed, Jeffrey Donaldson spoke about the deaths of his family members who had served with the RUC and the loss of comrades with whom he had served in the Ulster Defence Regiment. Seán MacManus also spoke about his own experiences and how that same day was the anniversary of his son's death – he had been killed in an IRA operation. Jeffrey approached me afterwards to say it had been the first time as a unionist that he had ever heard someone from Sinn Féin speak about their personal loss and he asked if I thought Seán would talk to him. After the introductions, I left them sitting together by the fire. On the way home on the plane, I saw Seán write a note and hand it in an envelope to a colleague at Belfast airport, asking that he pass it on to Gerry Adams. It was many years later that I heard Jeffrey talk openly about what had transpired that evening in Salzburg, describing the conversation as a most enlightening experience. I had learned that sitting around a fire or eating a meal together is when you will often find the humanity in the 'other', and that's what happened that night in Schloss Leopoldskron.

When I got back to the talks, the press were gathering in large numbers outside Castle Buildings and many of those participating in the negotiations were happy to speak to them to get their message across and potentially gain some kind of advantage. Even when it was just one politician talking to a reporter, they were usually flanked by other party members, nodding their agreement. Any time, a comment was made along the lines of 'the country is being sold down the river', David Ervine's characteristically reasonable response was: 'It takes two seconds to say it's a sell-out but two hours to explain why it isn't.' At the same time, republicans were briefing that there wasn't enough in the proposals for them. I could see the same politicians giving snippets to their preferred journalists, leading to media coverage that I felt was not representative of what was going on inside the talks. This contributed to a culture of point scoring that just made things more difficult for both sides. When I listened to what the reporters were being told, it was easy to see that the parties were using the media as proxies to drip-feed information to their own side of the community. And it wasn't the women who couldn't keep a secret.

As spokesperson for the Coalition, I tried to counter the negativity and point-scoring without sounding like a Pollyanna. It was hard to juggle media with everything else that was going on, but it was vital for us to get our message across too. I'd already learnt that I needed to choose my words carefully after an interview in the *Irish News* in which I'd said that compromise was a strength and not a weakness. The reaction to that piece led some of the larger parties to comment that the Coalition failed to understand the risks they were taking and that compromise was the last word they would be using. Compromise was a loaded word, so the next time I wanted to talk about that concept I used the word 'accommodation', a term that sat much more easily with everyone. We all spoke English, but I often felt that the Coalition's role was to interpret what lay beneath the words. It was not always a case of what you said but more how it was heard. As time went on, I emphasised how much the country would gain if an agreement were to be reached and that every party needed to be able to see it as a win-win – that's how negotiations worked. Even as I said it, the question on my mind, and everyone else's, was: Could we make a deal?

10

The Last Week of the Talks

'You do what you can. What you've done may do more
than you can imagine for generations to come.'

Rebecca Solnit

It was getting close to Easter 1998 when Senator Mitchell expressed his
concern at how slow the process had become. Irish government minister
Liz O'Donnell summed it up when she said people had got talked out
– the negotiations were deadening and exhausting, with parties talking
at length over the same issues. George Mitchell set a final deadline for
an agreement to be concluded, telling the press, 'If I don't take action,
the process will rapidly spiral towards failure.' When he set the date for
9 April, the reporters asked whether he knew that was Holy Thursday, the
day before Christ's crucifixion.

The penultimate week of the negotiations was make-or-break time. On
Friday 3 April, we expected to receive the final draft of the Agreement in
its entirety. The finger-pointing started when it didn't arrive, with parties
blaming the secretariat for making a promise they couldn't deliver. In
fact, it turned out that it was the two governments that hadn't completed
the work on the north–south arrangements, but George Mitchell took
the hit, telling us that the secretariat needed the weekend to go over the
final touches. We had been geared up to start work on the draft – it was
the first time we would see all the proposals we'd spent so much time
discussing brought together, so the delay was a major disappointment for
all of us.

I knew we wouldn't have much longer to wait when Martha Pope rang while I was at Avila's house on the Sunday evening to tell us that the three chairpersons had reviewed the papers submitted from each party earlier that week, and that the Women's Coalition would have to choose between its proposal to have a Civic Forum or to have electoral reform as part of the political settlement, as we couldn't have both. Senator Mitchell had said that each party should be able to see its 'imprimatur' on the final agreement – a special stamp, something within the agreement, that you could call your own. While both were important to us, we opted for the Civic Forum – we had set out to widen participative democracy, and we were going to stick to it.

When we arrived at Castle Buildings on Monday morning, we received a memo to say that the meeting that we had all been waiting for – at which Senator Mitchell would present the final draft – was scheduled for that evening. Shortly before it was due to commence, I saw Martha Pope running along the corridor in search of a photocopier. She was holding pages of the draft that were barely legible and urgently needed better copies. Avila went with her to the reprographics room and helped her to reproduce the most wanted document in the land. As soon as that was done, word went out for two senior representatives from each party to come to the room where Senator Mitchell was waiting.

Before he handed out copies of the draft, he impressed upon us that it mustn't be leaked. He added that he had changed a word on a certain page in each party's copy so he would know who was responsible if there was a leak. The PUP's Hughie Smyth told him that if that were to happen, he would have more luck finding Lord Lucan than the source. Hughie was known for breaking nervous tension with humour. Senator Mitchell said he couldn't understand why the parties had asked for so many safeguards – such as the petition of concern and cross-community voting mechanisms – relating to the arrangements for the Northern Ireland Assembly. The SDLP's Mark Durkan – also renowned for his dry wit – told Senator Mitchell a story of a Derry man who had applied for a refurbishment grant for his house, only to wonder afterwards whether the replacement of the outdoor latrine with an indoor toilet was a necessity or a luxury, given that there was now the risk that people would ask to use it. The moral of the tale was that the safeguards were in fact essential and not the least bit extravagant.

The deliberate word changes on the draft turned out to be a ruse but we didn't know that when we headed to the reprographics room to run off more copies. Sinn Féin got to the photocopier just as we arrived there, so we agreed that we would take turns at running off copies. We were going so fast that we got them mixed up. I said not to worry and made a joke that the Coalition wouldn't be doing any leaking. When we read the newspapers the next day and saw that no breaches had occurred, we sensed that all the parties were deadly serious and that we were finally down to the wire.

Despite the relief at getting the draft in our hands, it didn't take long to notice that some of the proposals we had been discussing were missing. We found a British government official, and Bronagh told him: 'Discussions are going on here and we have things to say. We need to have someone we can talk to now that the final drafting has started.' Tony Beeton soon appeared at our office door, declaring he was our liaison person. Bronagh laid it on thick: 'We have been here throughout, to make the dynamic work, to put the partnerships together, but we also have an agenda and we are as deserving of having our issues included as anybody else.' He diligently started to make notes as we went through these one by one – the election system, the needs of victims, integrated education, shared housing, community development, resources for young people, equality and human rights. We had noticed that there were still brackets around the proposal for the Civic Forum so Bronagh left him in no doubt about how much it mattered to us, telling him: 'No Civic Forum and we will have to consider our position.'

Much of the draft focussed on demobilisation and disarmament, but we knew that if we wanted to build a sustainable peace, other issues were important too. The Coalition didn't have as much to bargain with as the main parties, but we were still going to fight for those things that we understood would help in the long run.

The north–south arrangements were a particularly tricky area within the draft. The proposal was that a range of cross-border bodies would work in tandem with the Northern Ireland Assembly. I likened the relationship between the north–south bodies and the Assembly to the black and white stripes on a zebra – they were interdependent and both strands, though separate, were essential to the whole.

In the draft, the annexes that set out the details about the north–south bodies and the North–South Ministerial Council took up seven pages in total, more than any other section in the document. Some of the arrangements still hadn't been agreed, so square brackets indicating which parts might stay or go had to be taken into account. We were also trying to understand which of the cross-border bodies were to be harmonised, which bodies were dependent on cooperation and which of them needed legislation. To try and get to grips with it all, Avila got out a flip chart and Bronagh made lists of the functions of particular bodies and the relationships between them.

It really turned up the heat when John Taylor told reporters that unionists wouldn't touch the agreement with a forty-foot barge pole. John Alderdice went to speak to the world's press, gathering outside the building. His message was straight and direct: 'On Sunday, I spoke to Tony Blair on the telephone and told him he needed to come. Today, it's Tuesday, and if the prime minister wants a deal, he better get here fast.' The unionists were briefing that Sinn Féin had won all the concessions, but Sinn Féin was a long way from agreeing to a Northern Ireland Assembly and was sitting tight, waiting to see who would get the blame if the whole thing collapsed. All the signs were pointing in the direction of the Ulster Unionists. I told the press that we still had time to work on the draft and that 'no one would be going back to war over it'. I was trying to bring things down a notch, sensing that the whole process was about to go belly-up.

Tony Blair had just arrived in Northern Ireland, and told the press from the steps of Hillsborough Castle, 'I feel the hand of history upon our shoulders' – just before that, he had told the media that this wasn't the time for soundbites, but he had just given them one that would be quoted non-stop.

On that same Tuesday, we got news that Bertie Ahern's mother had passed away the previous day. It meant him travelling between Belfast and Dublin for the next few days, coping with his mother's passing and juggling the funeral arrangements at the same time as the tension was rising in the negotiations. He told me later that, after attending the removal of his mother's remains to the church on Tuesday evening, he went for a walk on his own in Drumcondra in north Dublin, to try to get his head around how to proceed. He knew that the hostile reaction from the Ulster Unionist Party to the North/South element of George Mitchell's draft had to be resolved. He took a calculated risk – paring back the Irish government's ambitions on the scale and scope of the North/South arrangements in the hope that that would provide a breakthrough and open the way to an overall agreement. With George Mitchell's deadline still looming over us for the next day, Thursday 9 April, he put the offer on the table. Certain core requirements would remain – the North–South Ministerial Council and a number of cross-border bodies with the authority to operate on an integrated, all-island basis. The Unionist Party had objected to the concept of 'executive' bodies, so in the end a compromise was found by using the word 'implementation' instead. Word changes clearly mattered. 'All-Ireland executive bodies' would not be acceptable to unionists but 'implementation bodies on a cross-border or all-island level' would. This shift from the Irish government was an important moment – at a time when there were still other knotty issues to crack.

Agreement on the identity and scope of these bodies would be delegated to a programme of work to be completed by 31 October 1998. Mark Durkan referred to it as a backstop, clearly worried that the Irish government had left this part of the arrangements so open.

These were very tough days and a mark of Bertie Ahern's and Tony Blair's determination to reach an agreement. Part of a younger generation themselves, they recognised there was now an opportunity for a generational shift in political thinking. During those tense days, there were moments of light relief. At one point Tony Blair thought the Ulster Unionists were asking for the demolition of the rugby stadium in Edinburgh. It wasn't Murrayfield the unionists wanted rid of but Maryfield, the bunker where the Irish secretariat had been installed since the 1985 Anglo-Irish Agreement. The prime minister said he was so tired at that late stage that he would have agreed to knock down the rugby stadium, but when he realised what the real question was, he said that Maryfield could go, much to the horror of the civil servants who wanted to keep the offices to store documents. The Anglo-Irish Agreement, to which unionists had strongly objected when the UK government introduced it without them being directly involved, would now be superseded by a new agreement. This time, the Ulster Unionist Party would be directly involved.

The proposals for the Irish language were also contentious for unionists. It didn't help that the text had double-line spacing and so ran to over three pages, making the provisions look lengthier than other sections. The same formatting had not been applied throughout the document, but I suspected the officials must have been cutting and pasting like crazy to get it ready on time and had not being paying attention to layout. Unionists had already been complaining about too many concessions to nationalists, and they perceived the Irish language proposals as one more. They wanted a similar set of proposals for Ulster-Scots and we ended up in another 'language versus dialect' debate. Tony Blair admitted he'd never heard of Ulster-Scots.

While these negotiations were taking place, the Coalition team was going through the rest of the draft. We pored over the details, suggesting changes such as adding disability to the clause on 'the right to equal opportunity in all social and economic activity, regardless of class, creed, gender or colour.' We noted that the word 'colour' was used rather than 'ethnicity', and would have to be changed. It was good to see that equal opportunities were now being extended beyond the usual confines of religion and political opinion and would include gender, race, disability, age, marital status, dependants and sexual orientation. We had been around long enough to know that an obligation would have to be placed on the state to promote and deliver on these protections and that their enforcement would require the creation of an Equality Commission and a Human Rights Commission. It was good to see this statutory obligation and these two new institutions among the proposals. A Charter of Rights was also there 'to protect the fundamental rights of everyone living in the island of Ireland' as an assurance that the rights of every citizen, whether British or Irish, would be protected irrespective of which jurisdiction they lived in. A proposal for a Bill of Rights was also set out – it would have been better if it had been a constitutional guarantee. Little did I know that the absence of that guarantee would become a problem for me years later.

When we read the Rights, Safeguards and Equality of Opportunity section of the draft agreement, we knew the women who had voted for us would want to see the right to full and equal political participation as one of those safeguards. We explained to our liaison person why it had to go in. He wanted a rationale for its inclusion so Avila quoted Cathy Harkin's words to him: 'We've been living in an armed patriarchy for the past thirty years. That's why we need this right for women's political participation to be in the Agreement.' It was after midnight and he went off to see what he could do. He returned in the early hours of the morning to tell us that the clause had made it into the final document. We knew that the lateness of the hour and sheer exhaustion had worked in our favour – whatever the reason, we were relieved that the role of women in politics was going to be acknowledged, a rare thing in a peace agreement. But it was drafted more like an aspiration and was therefore at risk of not being implemented – we should have gone further and asked for affirmative action to make this happen.

When we looked to see what was in the draft for victims, there were only two sentences. Almost two years before, when the talks started, we had prepared an opening statement in which we made it clear that if any peace agreement was to be meaningful, it needed to commit to supporting and helping victims of the thirty-year-long conflict. Because of the procrastination at the start of the process I'd never been able to deliver the statement at the table, but I found it in my desk, and pitched a few lines from it to address the vague commitment in the draft that 'resources should be set aside for victims'. In the chapter entitled Reconciliation and Victims of Violence, we drafted an additional paragraph and set off to find the relevant people to make sure it went in.

One of those people was Mo Mowlam. She was being jealously guarded by her civil servants, but there was one place they couldn't prevent her from talking to us and that was in the ladies' toilet. Pearl lay in wait and impressed upon Mo the importance of this issue. So, when I handed over the revision on victims, I could say that we had talked to Mo. We managed to get it into the final draft by the skin of our teeth. UUP adviser Stephen King said that when he saw the revision he could see the fingers of the Women's Coalition all over it, but, like most of those in the larger parties, he was more focused on the governance arrangements. He said he was concerned that the proposals for a power-sharing government could lead to a situation in which a Sinn Féin minister could have the education portfolio. I couldn't believe that he was thinking that far ahead, about which party was going to get the top jobs.

These power-sharing arrangements were, however, moving on apace. Downstairs, the SDLP's Sean Farren and Seamus Mallon had been busy negotiating an agreement with the UUP's Reg Empey and Jeffrey Donaldson on the workings of the Assembly. I was very impressed that Mark Durkan had even drafted a pledge of office for government ministers – it was a very ethical thing to do. We had assumed that the SDLP and UUP might have supported our proposal for electoral reform, for the sake of inclusion and pluralism in politics, but they did not. The draft had included a note from the independent chairpersons, in the section entitled 'The Assembly', that stated 'there is disagreement among the participants as to the size of the Assembly and as to whether the election system should provide greater opportunity to small parties to be represented in the Assembly.' It spelled out the options: 'increasing the number of seats from five to six in each constituency and/or providing a top-up of ten or twenty seats.'

The top-up was of greatest interest to us – it was the system that had allowed us into the talks. But we were less concerned about getting ourselves elected and more worried about one of the loyalist parties, the UDP, which was at risk of losing its seats. A similar system was being proposed for the new Scottish parliament, but the larger parties treated it as being off-the-wall and insisted on going back to the system they knew best. This meant that the multi-party set-up that had been key to creating a more inclusive outcome was being frittered away. We wanted the UDP, affiliated to the UDA, to stay within the political system rather than being frozen out. No matter how many times I said that those who had been party to the agreement must be party to the implementation, it seemed to make little difference to the larger parties. As the week progressed, this option fell off the table.

Everything else was being agreed – even the complicated system of consociation for a power-sharing government in the proposed Northern Ireland Assembly, and the arrangements for the selection of a First and Deputy First Minister on a cross-community basis – but in the end our proposal for electoral reform was rejected. Liz O'Donnell came to our office to tell us she had failed to convince the UUP and SDLP and without them, our proposal was dead in the water. Bronagh was dejected:

> Will people look back on us as women and say we faltered because
> we did not hold out at the end? But how could you not sign a
> peace agreement for your country? It's a difficult choice. We have
> to have the peace agreement.

We asked the secretariat to leave the proposal on the record in the hope that others might return to it one day – perhaps after they had seen it working in Scotland, where the system led to many more women getting elected. We put our disappointment to one side after I met Mark Durkan in the corridor and he gave me the news that the Civic Forum would be included in the agreement. That felt like a victory. Another plus was the North-South Consultative Forum on the island of Ireland. Our dedication to participatory democracy was paying off.

The days in the run-up to the deadline were flying by, and when I said goodbye to Gavin and Rowen first thing on Holy Thursday I didn't know that two days would pass before I would see my two boys again. By the time I got to Castle Buildings, everything had started to fall into place like the pieces of a jigsaw. Work continued through Thursday night: we went up and down to the third floor to speak with British and Irish government officials, into the offices of the three chairpersons, back and forth to the parties on the first and ground floors. Communication and lobbying became the skills of the moment. Each of us took turns to sit outside the doors of the draughtsmen (and they were all men), waiting for them to come out for some air. There were still brackets around some vital clauses, which meant they could go either way – in or out. It was a precarious situation, especially since the final changes were not for circulation, and discussions were taking place in corridors and rooms, not in plenary session.

The 'talks tourists' arrived, with parties bringing in people I had never seen before. I didn't know whether the new faces were part of the combatant groups or part of the governments' teams. Someone in our office joked that there were certain bars on the Shankill Road that were empty of regulars that night – and the same on the Falls. When lawyers appeared in other party rooms, I started contacting people we knew who had provided wise counsel over the previous two years.

Shouting problems at the draughtsmen had become par for the course over that week, so I figured it was better to draft suggestions for any changes we wanted to see. I told everyone on our team, 'I need you to bring solutions and not problems' – and we needed to supply these in writing as quickly as possible. To get a sense of what other parties were asking for meant scurrying between the Irish and British government officials and back again. The prisoners' people, the policing people, the human rights and equality people were running past each other on the corridors. Everything was coming at us so fast that my suggestion was 'go to the toilet when you can and not when you need to'. I had to turn over sleeping bodies on the floor – Annie Campbell had taken a catnap – to access the paperwork with our pre-prepared amendments.

Some of the team who had had to go home were phoning to talk to anyone in the room who could keep them up to date – like the rest of us the waiting was killing them. One of our members, Diane Greer, was live on air on Radio Foyle saying she would give up smoking if we reached an agreement. A rumour was doing the rounds that a male delegate from one of the parties had promised to marry his long-standing girlfriend if we could make a deal.

Outside the building, there was a hungry media to feed. I switched mode from time to time to run out and do an interview, and then ran back in again to hear the latest news. The canteen workers had gone home early on Thursday afternoon with instructions from a senior civil servant not to return since the building would shortly be closed for Easter. In the Coalition office we only had a bagful of fruit and some litres of water, so we phoned for pizzas to be delivered. The delivery man was wearing a balaclava as protection against the snow that had started to fall, but he had managed to get past the security man at the entrance who we had persuaded to let the pizzas through. When she saw him in the corridor, the SDLP's Bríd Rodgers said that she was shocked that the paramilitaries didn't have the decency to take off their headgear before they entered the building. The delivery man turned to her and said, 'Ah, missus, no offence, but I'm only here to give the women their pizzas.'

I borrowed a woollen coat from Jane Morrice to face the press. CNN had built a platform on scaffolding for its broadcasters and had installed a rope ladder, but, as I discovered when I arrived to do an interview with them, it wasn't that easy to climb. David Ervine was being interviewed beside me when a message was passed to him to say that Ian Paisley was conducting a middle-of-the-night press conference below in the main press hut. Paisley had returned to the grounds of the building that he had stormed out of a year before and was telling the reporters that the Agreement was a sham. From the top of the scaffolding, David could see his PUP colleagues trying to get in the door to confront Paisley: the last thing he needed was a confrontation between the DUP and the PUP going out live on air. Like Tarzan, he reached for a nearby rope and swung to the ground. The smile was wiped off my face when, from my vantage point on the scaffolding, I saw Pearl entering the melee. I went backwards down the ladder as quickly as I could. As I dashed towards the hut, I could hear Pearl shouting 'What about peace now, Dr Paisley?' All Pearl's life, Paisley had led her to believe that he spoke for the Protestants in her community, but she said that night that he didn't speak for Protestants like her any more. She was furious that he was staging a performance when we were so close to getting an agreement over the line. We walked calmly back into Castle Buildings as Paisley ushered his entourage out the gates.

As the last night wore on, the British government was unsure if Sinn Féin would be in or out. It was an educated guess as to whether it would be able to sign up to an agreement that recognised Northern Ireland's existence as a state. I had built a good working relationship with Pat Doherty, the vice president of Sinn Féin. His wife, Mary, had been a student of mine on the Women's Studies course, and Pat told me how grateful he was that Mary had got such a lot out of it. Pat was able to tell me that Sinn Féin was staying to the bitter end. I met Mo Mowlam shortly afterwards – barefoot, pushing an intravenous drip, with her wig in her hand – she had had chemotherapy some time before – and looking exasperated. She was walking a tightrope, trying to keep all the parties in the loop. Sinn Féin's chairperson, Mitchel McLaughlin, had told the press that morning that there was enough in it for his party but Mo told me they were 'working her over'. I told her that Sinn Féin was staying; she said she would be able to do her job better just knowing that. The larger parties were the big power brokers in the negotiations but, from the outset, members of the Coalition had taken on the roles of facilitator and mediator, and that's the role we played that night.

I knew that if an agreement were to be reached, it wouldn't just involve the demobilisation of armed groups but would also have to include the issue of British army battalions in Northern Ireland – and that's what Sinn Féin had been discussing with Mo. While Tony Blair and Bertie Ahern were stamping their authority on the deal, she was working herself into the ground to bring all the pieces together. She headed off to tell the prime minister what I had just told her.

I went outside to speak to Stephen Grimason, political editor at the BBC, who was sticking it out in the freezing cold night, reporting the ups and downs and, like the rest of us, trying to anticipate what the next hurdle would be. Jon Snow from Channel Four interviewed me about the state of play among the parties. It was an anxious time since we had already passed the original deadline. The question the reporters wanted answered was if and when we would make it over the line. Optimism was a rare commodity at that late stage, so I told the press that we couldn't afford to fail. If we did, we would only have ourselves to blame.

On Friday morning, no one told us that the canteen was open as a special favour to the parties and that Ulster frys were being served up. Instead, we sent out for supplies. Coalition delegates brought sandwiches and Martin McGuinness, who was abstaining from meat on Good Friday, had got wind of the fact that they were meat-free. He came into our office offering to recite one of his poems in return for a couple of sandwiches. The deal was duly made – it was definitely one of the easiest negotiations that Good Friday. We joked that the governments were starving the parties into submission, hoping that between hunger and exhaustion we would give up and agree to anything.

The small drinks and coffee bar was packed with people squeezing in to watch the television and see what was being reported. It was wall-to-wall coverage. As soon as the local BBC news programme went off air, someone changed the channel to Ulster Television. When anyone made a strong statement, everyone clapped. If they scored a direct hit on the spoilers – those denouncing the agreement before it had even been reached – a cheer would go up. When the hero or heroine re-entered the coffee bar, they got a round of applause.

When I went to speak to Paul Murphy, British minister of state, I noticed airline tickets sitting on his desk. Like Mo, Paul didn't stand on ceremony and was able to tell me that Tony Blair was hoping to get away for an Easter break in Spain with his family. George Mitchell had told his wife Heather that he would be home to celebrate the holiday with baby Andrew. Each time I saw Senator Mitchell that week, I joked he would be facing a divorce if he wasn't back in New York for Easter. The information about the trips made it clear that the Good Friday deadline was now a real one – if we didn't reach agreement, the process was over.

We were finally beginning to see what a deal would look like. A United Ireland had been taken off the table but the constitutional right to self-determination remained. For unionists, the status of Northern Ireland would remain the same as long as the majority of people in Northern Ireland were prepared to give their consent to remain part of the United Kingdom. The quid pro quo was that each citizen had the right to be British or Irish or both. Reforms to the police and justice system meant a totally reformed Northern Ireland. The new north and south of Ireland arrangements for the island of Ireland meant being connected in a way that we hadn't been before. We could disagree about the past and even have suspicions about the present, but at last we had drafted a framework for the foreseeable future.

When the journalists asked how I was feeling, I said that out of the dark clouds of the week had come the sun. Somehow it sounded right. The weather had changed from snow to rain and hail and was as surreal as what was happening inside Castle Buildings. But no one could be certain of what was to come. There was euphoria at 11 a.m., when a final copy of the Agreement arrived from the secretariat with a cover note that read, 'This is, in all likelihood, our last memorandum to you. We take this occasion to thank each of you for your courtesy. It has been a pleasure to work with you.' In the middle of the night I had drafted a speech for my final statement but was beginning to wonder at what hour of the day that might happen.

It was early morning on Friday and the secretariat staff hadn't slept for seventy-two hours. Having done all they could, they were now waiting it out. Senator Mitchell was having a sleep, raincoat over his head, so I didn't want to wake him to give him the Aran jumper that we had bought for baby Andrew. I also left the Red Sox stress ball that I had brought home from Boston and wrote a note to say that I was giving it to him as compensation for acting as the chairperson of the peace talks when he could have been the chairperson of the American Baseball Association. The Irish government officials and advisers were also starting to celebrate – we spied a forty-ounce bottle of whiskey being brought into their offices.

Back in our office, we made a presentation to the US staff – Martha Pope, Kelly Currie and David Pozorski – knowing we were about to say goodbye to three good friends. Brian had cooked a few dinners for them over the previous two years as a way of saying thanks. After two years of talking, we said it was now over to us to deliver on what had been agreed.

Secretary of State Mo Mowlam arrived in our offices, as shattered as the ten shattered women she wanted to speak to. We could hardly say a word, given the tension. Mo played a blinder that night, as did Liz O'Donnell, and we told them so. I said that I hoped they, along with Martha Pope, would get the recognition they deserved.

And then we hit a hurdle. Senator George Mitchell's schedule began to slip. I was talking to David Ervine when he mentioned that the Ulster Unionist Party was having a meeting from hell. We were expecting the final plenary to take place at any moment, and then we got word it was off. It started to feel like torture. A woman bringing tea to the UUP office had been told to clear off after she had knocked politely to tell them it was ready. She was still in a temper when she told us how she had gone out of her way to make them tea at that late stage in the day and had shouted through the door, 'I bloody well made it so you can bloody well drink it.' She had abandoned the tea trolley in the corridor.

Shortly after that, Jeffrey Donaldson was seen leaving the building. Reports circulated that he wanted a guarantee that decommissioning of weapons would be tied to prisoner releases, but that hadn't been on the cards. The process of transferring prisoners from England and the south of Ireland had already begun and an accelerated programme for the release of prisoners had been agreed the previous evening. Gerry Kelly and David Ervine had been arguing over the prisoner release period. David told me afterwards that he knew that people would object to a one-year prisoner release scheme, but both Sinn Féin and the PUP were committed to ensuring that prisoners would be released, so they settled on two years. The governments agreed to reduce the time scale from five years to two on the condition that the ceasefires would remain unequivocal and the prisoners would stay on board with the peace agreement. The agreement was that those still in custody two years after the scheme commenced would then be released. Proposals for individuals who were in 'voluntary' exile or 'on the run' from court proceedings had been relegated to the category of 'too hot to handle'. When this came up at our meeting, the civil servant in charge of security had flown off the handle when Avila and I suggested that the 'on the runs' should be discussed since the issue could come back to haunt us one day. Avila asked for a sunset clause to be inserted, committing the parties to resolve the issue of those 'on the run' from the state as well as the return of young people forced into exile because of disputes with paramilitaries. Such issues were part of the 'normalisation' process in other post-conflict societies. Prisoner releases weren't Women's Coalition issues per se; we had a list of our own but we were prepared to facilitate the resolution of some of those from other parties as well. But we didn't want the process to be viewed as serving only the interests of the warring groups.

I met Gusty Spence and David Ervine in the corridor. They told me that 'horse-trading' was going on between the Ulster Unionists and the prime minister. Tony Blair was trying to satisfy the Ulster Unionists' demands on decommissioning, but he wasn't going to change what had already been agreed. The rest of us weren't party to those discussions. Rumour had it that the prime minister had given a promissory note to David Trimble, outlining a date for decommissioning. David Ervine predicted that the chickens would come home to roost if that was so. He held that any date for decommissioning should have been agreed with parties like his that would be expected to direct the decommissioning of weapons. His question to me was a good one – was the promissory note worth the paper it was written on?

I was worried that the agreement that we had thought was possible was beginning to slip away. As we waited it out, I gave Avila's daughter, Aoife, the job of going around the parties and the two governments with a copy of the final draft agreement, to get their signatures as proof of who was present on Good Friday – even then, I had a feeling that this might become a historic document. She came back with them all, and the other parties began to follow suit.

Martha Pope came to tell us that the situation could go either way.

President Clinton had phoned earlier to try and instil confidence in those who were still unsure. David Kerr, the Ulster Unionists' press officer, later said that he became convinced by what the senior member of his party, Ken Maginnis, had said as they were coming close to making a final decision. He had recounted the number of times that the Ulster Unionists had said no to an agreement – each time they rejected the deal, there was less on the table when they returned to start another round of negotiations. David Trimble had to make the final decision. I later heard that at around 4.30 p.m., he read out the 'comfort letter' he had been given by Tony Blair. Trimble told those in the room that the letter was enough for him. He said that those who wanted to come with him, could follow him now. Most of them did. To bring your people with you when there are so many doubting the direction you are taking is a very tough thing to do. Trimble made that call on Good Friday.

At around 5 p.m., word came through that everyone needed to get to the room for the final plenary. There was no time to lose in case the Ulster Unionists changed their mind. The plenary would not be open to debate. The room was packed. We had drawn lots for who would occupy the three seats behind Pearl and me, but when I saw the size of the gathering I sent word to Ann McCann to tell the others to come up from our office, as the numbers were not restricted. People who had tried to kill one another were now standing next to each other. The former IRA general Joe Cahill was standing alongside well-known loyalists. I watched as he gripped the back of Hughie Smyth's chair because he needed it for support. I wondered if that would be the way of things in the future.

Senator Mitchell completed his last tour de table, asking each party in turn to say if they were in favour of the Agreement. I was the third person to say, 'For the Agreement.' Gerry Adams was fifth. He stated that while he thought more was needed, he would put a positive recommendation to the party. The Ulster Unionists were the eighth and last party seated at the table and when it came to David Trimble, he nodded his head and said 'Yes.' And that was it. The British and Irish governments and the parties had made their declarations. All were in favour. The governments were the guarantors of the international treaty. I was an oral signatory. Only 3 per cent of women around the world were signatories to a peace accord, and it felt good that I had helped to increase that number.

Finally, all the parties could make a closing statement. In mine, I acknowledged Bertie Ahern's leadership, saying his mother would be looking down on her son who had helped to make the peace agreement. I was proud to be able to say that the Agreement was built on mutual acceptance, equality and parity of esteem. The well-crafted sentences of the Agreement exuded hope of a new beginning, while leaving space for a menu of national aspiration and identity that circumvented narrow notions of citizenship. It was principled and pragmatic as well as a win-win for a country that had so long been mired in political stalemate. I concluded:

> We owe it to those who have died to build a society that will stand as a living testimony to the victims and if we are to achieve this task we have to do it together. Not by monopolising power, but by sharing it. Not by seeking to shatter the aspirations of any sector of our society, but by creating a space for them. Not by being restricted by a politics of anger, resentment and rigidity, but by daring to envisage a politics that can be open and imaginative, and even courageous. That the principles of equality, inclusion and human rights were not a victory for one group over another: they were the bedrock of our future. It is my belief that there are many around this table who through their actions today have shown that such a politics is possible.

I told the women around me that when the Agreement was announced, they should hold back on their tears. I didn't want the cameras showing women sobbing at such a crucial moment – we had to hold our nerve. But as soon as Senator Mitchell said, 'It is now over to the people of Northern Ireland to make this peace agreement work,' men started to cry and I could hear sobs at the back of the room. I turned to Coalition member Elizabeth Meehan, who was standing behind me, and said, 'It's okay to cry now,' and she did.

I was fourteen years old when the Troubles began, so for the best part of my life – three decades – I had lived through conflict and most of the Coalition team had done the same. It was a day without precedent, and we had travelled a long way since Avila and I had met up at that cafe on the Lisburn Road.

After the sign-off, I did the round of press interviews, going from camera to camera with print and broadcast journalists from around the world. They already loved John Hume's 'We have a new dawn', but they were still looking for more. I had come to know Hervé, a French journalist, and had joked with him that because there were no chimneys at Castle Buildings to send out a smoke signal, I would throw away my papers like my students do at the end of their exams to indicate to him that the parties had reached agreement. So when it came our turn to speak to the press – we were the very last party – we threw our now redundant papers high in the air. I'd kept my promise to Hervé and photographer Derek Speirs captured the moment – the picture was syndicated and made the front pages of a vast array of local and international newspapers.

As calm descended, we gathered up our detritus, hoping that this would be our last time in the concrete block. My car was parked down the hill at the Stormont Hotel, where I ran into George Mitchell with his suitcase, heading home to finally see his family. I went home to my own family, after thanking the women who had stood with me through thick and thin. We were all too tired to do anything more than say, 'Hope to see you on Monday.' Easter holidays or not, the agreement was now to be put to the people of Northern Ireland, and we needed to get ready for the referendum.

When I got home on Good Friday evening, Rowen was on his skateboard. I shouted to tell him that we had just made peace. He said that was what I was supposed to be doing and skated on down the street. Gavin was watching the proceedings on TV and jumped up to hug me. He asked if it was true what they were saying – that we had succeeded in making peace – and I told him we had finally reached an agreement. It was the question that followed that brought me back down to earth: 'Does that mean all the protests will stop, and will the killings come to an end?' I had to tell him the truth – that making peace was an unfinished business. He stopped me in my tracks once more when he asked, 'Then what did you sign today?' I thought about that and about how difficult it would be to deliver on what we had achieved.

My neighbours poured in, bringing their own euphoria, and it became another long night. When I finally got to bed, I thought long and hard about what Gavin had said and the work that lay ahead. We needed to have many more days like this one.

11

Referendum and Election to the Assembly

'As if "Get a grip"
might elicit a new broom.'

Jean Bleakney, from '*Jean*'

The day that the Good Friday Agreement was signed, I told reporters outside the building:

People in Northern Ireland have always said, 'If only the politicians would sit down together and talk, and reach an agreement.' Today we have done it. We have interrupted the culture of failure in Northern Ireland. There is no going back.

The violent conflict was starting to unwind after thirty long years, but getting politicians to a resolution on the community divisions was a different matter. We didn't even have an agreed name for the deal we had achieved – the dual nomenclature of the Belfast/Good Friday Agreement reflected that. The front cover of the printed copy that was posted through my door that Easter weekend showed a family walking into the sunset. I was hoping it was the North Coast but was told it was the Cape of South Africa – the rush to get a copy of the Agreement out to every household in the land meant the government had to use whatever image was to hand.

A referendum on the Good Friday Agreement had been set for 22 May 1998. Ian Knox's cartoon summed up the choice facing the people of

Northern Ireland – the Yes side was represented by the Agreement's cover page that said, 'This Agreement is about your future: Please read it carefully. It's Your Decision'; the No side by an image of the three main politicians on the anti-Agreement side, with Ian Paisley holding hands with a dissident renegade loyalist wearing a balaclava, and the words underneath that said: 'Disagreement is about the past. Please Repeat Endlessly. It's Your Lot.'

The referendum was the first all-Ireland poll since the general election in 1918, before partition, and although we only needed 51 per cent north and south in favour of the Agreement, we figured that at least 60 per cent of the people in Northern Ireland would have to vote Yes since anything less would cause a problem for the unionist community.

On Easter Sunday, we started preparing the ground for a Yes vote. The referendum campaign was going to be another white-knuckle ride – the nationalists were overwhelmingly in support (though somewhat muted from Sinn Féin), but the situation within the unionist community was much more uncertain. As before, we had to run the Coalition's campaign on a shoestring, falling back on the inventiveness that had taken us to the peace talks. We hired an open-top double-decker bus, from which we waved and shouted 'Yes, we must' as we travelled from town to town. Our children were strapped in on the top deck as we moved along the coast of County Down and then back to Belfast by a different route. Our slogans were written on wallpaper in purple lettering and our makeshift banners were stuck to the windows with masking tape. As always, we chose green, white and violet (which was actually purple) to match the suffragette colours, but we ended up with too much green. In a place where green and orange represent the different sides of the political divide, our ratio of colours caused us some bother, but it was soon sorted by adding more purple on the banners. As we approached unionist strongholds in North Down and Ards, we could see lots of red, white and blue on the posters flying from the lampposts on the dual carriageway, but they all belonged to the anti-Agreement side.

The No side had a habit of issuing a statement that the press would report as fact the following day, with the No supporters then citing the article as a reason to vote against the Agreement. We had to stop this, so we invited reporters to join us on the bus. The anti-Agreement side had mounted a high-profile campaign, declaring, 'No terrorists in government.' People were getting overloaded with negative messages – we had to reach those who were wavering or had misunderstood the facts of what was included in the Agreement. May Blood shouted on a loud hailer from the top deck: 'Come out and vote for peace'. The children on the bus thought she was amazing. Rowen was telling everyone how the class above him had been doing their Eleven Plus tests and had written that anti-agreement was the opposite of agreement. The referendum campaign was so bitter that 'anti' seemed more accurate than disagreement. The No people on the street pulling down Yes posters were scornful of those who disagreed with them. Civil society crusader Quintin Oliver was leading the multi-party Yes campaign, and we became part of that as well. We used its mocked-up road signs that read 'Straight ahead and no dead ends'. That image of a dead-end junction was a powerful one, capturing the idea that if we didn't move ahead, we would end up going nowhere. Coalition members Helen Crickhard and Martin Carter even put Yes stickers on green traffic lights but they had to be removed following a warning from the roads authority.

Newcastle had arcades with dodgems and amusements, which kept the children – and us – entertained for a while before we got on with the more serious job of persuading the locals to support the Agreement. Anne Carr was our party's representative on the local council and knew that middle-aged and elderly voters were concerned about prisoner releases and what would happen to the guns. We asked anyone who had concerns if they thought that by voting No they would achieve decommissioning of weapons. Without a political process in place, there would definitely be no progress on the issue. A young man on the street, all in black, announced that he was in the dissident Loyalist Volunteer Force. He tore up the Yes leaflet I gave him and threw the pieces back at me, then gave me a Hitler salute. He had a stick that he pretended was a gun, and pushed it into my face. Then, he pointed it at my head and shouted bang. I didn't flinch but I did ask him why he was so agitated and angry.

Newry, a largely nationalist town was, as expected, very positive about the Agreement but there were also some republicans there who declared that Sinn Féin signatories were traitors because they had sold out on a United Ireland. The nearby town of Banbridge was predominantly unionist and had had more than its fair share of IRA bombings, along with loyalist assassinations of local Catholics. This bitter history was evident in the way people responded to us – some quietly endorsed our position and thanked us for bringing our referendum bus to their town while others gave us a two-fingered salute. As we travelled back to Belfast on the bus, the children were the only ones with any energy left.

The media focused on No campaigners, mostly dissident Ulster Unionists who had joined the DUP and UKUP. Their No manifesto asked voters to 'Have a heart for Ulster', and played on people's worst fears, such as encouraging them to believe that terrorists would come pouring out of the prisons as a consequence of the Agreement. They used a hard-hitting anti-Agreement advertisement in the *Belfast Telegraph* that showed an elderly woman contorted with grief to make their point. David Trimble was having problems with this portrayal of the deal and had his own concerns, with six out of his ten MPs at Westminster declaring their opposition to the Agreement. These anti-Agreement UUP members combined forces with the DUP to form the United Unionist Campaign under the slogan 'It's right to say No.'

Things looked up on 18 April, when David Trimble received a boost, with seven out of ten of the ruling council delegates at the UUP meeting giving the deal their backing. And then the rollercoaster plunged again – the Grand Orange Lodge, the ruling body of the Orange Order, and a constituent part of the Unionist Party, called on its members to vote No. It was easier for those opposed to the Agreement simply to tell voters to say No, in contrast to those of us on the pro-Agreement side having to explain the nuances involved in the 'fair deal'.

On 21 April Adrian Lamph, a Catholic civilian, was shot dead by the LVF at the council yard where he worked in Portadown. He was the first victim to be killed since the signing of the Agreement – and a signal that the renegade loyalist group were not going to allow us to live in peace. Just a few days later they struck again, killing twenty-two-year-old Ciaran Heffron as he walked through the village of Crumlin. It was claimed in the newspapers that those responsible had attended an earlier anti-Agreement rally in the nearby town of Antrim. The murders reminded me of what can happen to a woman after she leaves a violent relationship – it can be a very dangerous time for her because the perpetrator doesn't want to lose control. We were facing that same problem from dissident paramilitaries. Those on the republican side, in the 32 County Sovereignty Movement, had issued a statement rejecting the Agreement, saying it was 'fundamentally undemocratic, anti-republican and unacceptable'. When those opposing the Agreement on political grounds, which they were perfectly entitled to do, used violent forms of militancy to advance their position that, to my mind, made *them* undemocratic and unacceptable.

Nationalists were outraged by an anti-Agreement rally at which some of the audience were singing 'The Billy Boys', a vicious, sectarian anti-Catholic song. Unionists were just as appalled at the display put on by Sinn Féin in Dublin on 10 May. The British and Irish authorities had agreed the temporary release of four men who had been involved in the Balcombe Street Siege to attend a special Ard Fheis that had been organised by Sinn Féin to rally support for the Agreement. When the television pictures showed the audience celebrating as though these men were making a triumphant return, the publicity was far from helpful to the pro-Agreement side. Unionists voters were wavering over prisoner releases already, as I had seen on the stump in Belfast, with No voters screaming at me, 'You let those scum bags out of jail'. What some people didn't understand was that the prisoner-release scheme wasn't an amnesty – conditions would be imposed, and the seriousness of the offence would be taken into account. But those who shouted, 'You gave them a get-out-of-jail-free card' did not seem to be aware of that fact. Not for the first time, I had to explain that ex-prisoners would be returned to prison if they didn't abide by the conditions of their release. The anti-Agreement side deliberately ignored the details and made it sound as though the releases gave prisoners carte blanche.

At their Ard Fheis, Sinn Féin members voted to change the party's constitution to allow candidates to take their places in the proposed new Assembly – a historic moment, as the party had refused to participate in institutions of government in Northern Ireland for seventy-seven years. But for unionists what was positive in this decision was overshadowed by seeing prisoners on temporary release sharing a platform with Sinn Féin; it only increased their concerns at a time when many of them were still deciding which side to come down on.

On 11 May, the Yes campaign took another downward turn when the prominent loyalist prisoner Michael Stone was released on parole to attend the UDP's Yes rally in the Ulster Hall. He was one of the three men whom I had met during the Women's Coalition visit to the Maze Prison the year before; the man who had thrown grenades and fired bullets in Milltown Cemetery. I could only imagine what his victims felt – probably the same way the victims of the IRA had when prisoners were paraded as heroes. If the combatants on both sides had come to say that the war was over, that would have fitted in with the rationale for prisoner releases. Instead the scenes on stage made me think of a paramilitary mural I had seen in the Village area of South Belfast. It depicted the Norwegian artist's painting *The Scream*, with words underneath: 'Show no mercy and expect none in return.' That mural made my blood curdle – we needed to reassure people in the referendum that there would be no going back to that way of thinking.

The copy of the Agreement that I always held in my hand was useful when I was confronted on village corners by people declaring it was a terrorist's charter and that there was nothing in it for victims. I was able to point to the proposals in the part that said, 'The achievement of a peaceful and just society would be the true memorial to the victims of violence.' But it was difficult to convince objectors that that was our aim. If we had agreed to stick together and sell the Agreement in its entirety, our campaign would have been much stronger but there was no single, united effort. The Ulster Unionist Party had refused to join Quintin Oliver's shared Yes campaign. They were worried that joining up with the rest of us on the pro-Agreement side would further upset the hardliners in their party. Each of us had parts of the Agreement that we found hard to swallow but we had said on Good Friday that there was enough in it for everyone. It was my belief that if you continually tell people they are losing, they will eventually come to believe it.

With all the noise that the spoilers were making, the possibility that the referendum could end up in chaos was staring us in the face. After the two years of hard work at the negotiating table, it was torment to watch the agreement being torn apart. A group of us – Ken Maginnis (UUP), Barry McElduff (SF), Joe Byrne (SDLP), David Ervine (PUP) and me – tried to turn that around on the platform we shared in Omagh Leisure Centre.

Some of the audience approached us afterwards to say that our responses to their questions had helped them to vote Yes in good conscience. David Ervine and I had known all along that visuals of parties publicly selling the benefits of the Agreement together in local communities would make all the difference. At a time when David Trimble had the political wind in his face instead of at his back, with an increasing number on the unionist side going against the Agreement, he needed all the support he could get. Even Jeffrey Donaldson confirmed he would be voting No, saying that parts of the Agreement were too difficult for him. The meeting in Omagh was the only multi-party event on the pro-Agreement side that ever took place; for me, that was a let-down.

On 19 May, less than a week before the referendum, the polls were reporting that the 'Undecideds', especially among women voters, were the key. New and first-time voters were saying that they would be voting Yes. And then came an upward trend after 'Doctors For Yes' made their moving appeal. These medics had been on the front line dealing with trauma for more than three decades and it was heart-wrenching watching them, some in tears, as they described how they had dealt with the aftermath of the bombs and the bullets. To hear directly from those doctors and nurses, and first responders, greatly helped the Yes camp. The next lift came when Chancellor of the Exchequer Gordon Brown announced a £315 million investment package. He said that the money was 'not conditional' on a Yes vote, but it made sense that the peace settlement would need to hold for the investment to be successful.

One of the meetings that May Blood held was in the predominantly Protestant housing estate of Rathcoole. She had brought Mo Mowlam to speak to a group of two hundred women. May said afterwards that 'people think women get up and just run off at the mouth, but there were women in that audience that had sat down and really thought about the Agreement.' She knew that when anyone said, 'Well, I haven't really read it yet' that meant they had but were still making up their mind. Engaging with the public, giving talks and answering questions was how we would get people over the line on the unionist side, but I couldn't see any of the bigger parties doing what we were doing – translating the details of the Agreement into a language people could understand. While the women in the Coalition were firing every ounce of energy we had into the campaign, the men in the main parties were more focused on getting ready for the elections that would come afterwards, assuming that there would be an affirmation of the Agreement. We were leaving nothing to chance and the loyalist parties were doing the same. Given the rancour within unionism over the Agreement, the leaders of the PUP and the UDP should have been given more credit for the work they were putting in on the ground.

Margaret Logue was holding public meetings in Derry where women reported a new interest in politics. The peace agreement had given them a curiosity about how things might work in the future. Women were living through a time when opportunities they had never experienced before were starting to become available. The political experience of the referendum campaign had bumped up women's confidence: as one woman said, 'It lets you see that you can do it. It doesn't require magical skills – you don't need to be anything but yourself.'

Mo Mowlam was certainly being herself the day she threw pebbles at the windows of our Belfast office on Elmwood Avenue to attract my attention. The windows had already been broken by a bunch of anti-Agreement hooligans trying to intimidate us. The same louts had also broken the windows of the architects' office on the floor below. The last thing I wanted was for Mo to end up doing the same. We were glad to see her since she had come to lift our spirits. She had heard of the postcards that we had sent out for the Yes campaign, bearing the office address; they had been returned with epithets scrawled across them, like 'Get back into the kitchen where you belong' and 'Whores'.

On 18 May, there was a free gig to support the Yes campaign for 2,500 young people at the Waterfront Hall, with U2 headlining and local band Ash also on the bill. Bono invited David Trimble and John Hume on stage. The two men had their jackets off and looked relaxed as they shook hands in front of the crowd. It was a symbolic moment and the first time they had appeared together during the referendum. The one-minute silence in remembrance of all those who had died was a reminder of all that was at stake in the referendum and the responsibility to make the peace agreement work.

Polling day was 22 May, and there was a turnout of 81.1 per cent in the north and 56.3 per cent in the south. That meant that more than

The election poster that caused such a stir.

A get-together in the White House with President Clinton and many of the key players involved in the Agreement on St Patrick's Day, 1999.

© John Harrison

Former Secretary of State for Northern Ireland Mo Mowlam in the Coalition's office in October 2002. Just one of the many meetings she had with us over the years.

Getting to YES. Making it fun.

Taking the Agreement to the people, May 1998 referendum.

With May Blood outside Belfast City Hall.

Canvassing in the Assembly elections, 1998.

More meetings in Parliament Buildings with Jane Morrice who
was elected Deputy Speaker.

Presenting the advice on a Bill of Rights to the UK government with my fellow commissioners, 10 December 2008.

Enjoying chatting to Jimmy Carter – who has achieved so much out of office – at the Nobel Peace Prize Forum in 2015.

With friends Melanne Verveer (on my left) and Miriam Coronel-Ferrer (holding microphone) at Georgetown, September 2015.

One Million Women for Peace during the
Colombian referendum, 2016.

Brave women in Barranquilla the day before the
Colombian peace agreement was signed in 2016.

Employment and counselling working in tandem
in the healing process in Rwanda, 2019.

eight out of every ten people were showing up to vote in Northern Ireland – the highest turnout in years. With Coalition supporters out in force, going from polling station to polling station, food, hot coffee and flasks of tea were the order of the day. I met people who were very emotional, saying it was the first time they'd had an opportunity to vote on their future. Others who turned up with the wrong identification went back home and returned with the paperwork they needed. The whole country seemed determined to exercise their franchise. The No campaigners got a shock when police officers at the polling station near Taughmonagh – who they'd assumed would be on the No side because of the reforms to policing – started telling anti-Agreement supporters how much they wanted a different future. Just before the polls closed at ten o'clock a young woman ran past me at Rosetta polling station. When she came out and declared that she had flown home from London to vote Yes, I wanted to give her a hug.

But the close of the poll didn't mark the end of my work that night. I had to phone around friends to ask them if they'd help take down the posters – we needed the backing board for the Assembly election. I got a gang together and we set off in our cars, armed with ladders and shears, to prune hundreds of posters from the lampposts. We weren't the only ones out after midnight in Belvoir housing estate. At around 3 a.m. six other cars arrived – the story had gone out from the Yes campaign headquarters that whoever got to the posters first could keep what they needed. The No campaigners were taking down as many Yes posters as we were, but it wasn't the place to be having a row over hardboard. Their presence indicated that the No side were anticipating an election, which meant they were expecting the Yes vote to prevail. It was enough to put us on a high. We raced around all night to recover as many posters as we could under cover of darkness. We finished at 4 a.m. and headed to the home of John McGettrick – another of the Coalition's stalwarts – to store the liberated materials in his garage.

During the night, the ballot boxes were opened in the King's Hall for verification of votes. Kate Fearon was the Coalition's nominee to observe that process. She reported back that she couldn't see much as the papers spilling from the boxes were all face down. But when the count started the next day, we got a good initial indication from the bundles of Yes votes stacking up on the long red Formica tables. Brenda Callaghan and Pearl were able to see from the stacks that even in DUP strongholds, one third of votes were returning a Yes. The real surprise came from the middle-class unionist areas, where the number of Yes votes was higher than predicted. But we had to wait for the tallies to start to get the full picture.

Yes votes were being counted into layers of forty thousand. The tally people counted the layers, checking the percentages with each other every thirty minutes. We knew that the unionists needed a decent majority to tick the Yes box, and it was a given that would be the case for nationalists. We waited to see if the Yes layers would grow higher. By midday, people in the hall became more confident that we would get a good result. There was hustle and bustle at the front when Pat Bradley, the chief electoral officer, stepped on to the platform. I told everyone from the Coalition to make their way to the podium where the announcement was about to be made. To the right, Ian Paisley was asking his son for a calculator, getting more and more anxious as he waited for the outcome. When it came, it showed over seven out of every ten people had voted Yes. My friend Jane Wilde was standing beside me, as she had done throughout the campaign, and smiled as she said it was the first time she had ever been on the winning side. A scuffle broke out between members of the PUP and Paisley's people. There were shouts of 'You're finished' as Paisley attempted to push past jubilant PUP supporters – with this fork in the road the two parties were now heading in opposite directions. As Paisley Jnr shouted, 'You better watch out. Rest assured we will be back,' we stayed focused on the fact that the people of Northern Ireland had said Yes in numbers that couldn't be contested.

I loved that the hard-working women in the Coalition were jumping for joy. The picture of Jane Morrice and Ann McCann hugging each other made the front page of the *Observer*. By the time the Irish minister for foreign affairs, David Andrews, whom I had come to know during the peace negotiations, called to congratulate us, I was holding a pint of Guinness in the King's Head pub across the road. He was able to tell me that in the south of Ireland over nine out of ten people had voted for the Agreement. I rang my mother to tell her the good news. After she'd said how relieved she was, she asked me to kindly put down my pint before doing any more interviews.

The thought of another election in four weeks' time brought all of us back to reality. We hadn't planned on the Women's Coalition remaining as a women's party, having thought we might dissolve it after the peace talks. But our dilemma was that if you weren't elected to the Assembly, you couldn't participate in the implementation of the Good Friday Agreement. Since a space had momentarily opened up to transform a society that had been largely blind to issues of gender and class, I wanted to ensure that things didn't revert to the status quo. The main political parties had rejected a constituency-based system with twenty top-up seats that would have helped to guarantee more women entering politics. The only option for us to increase the number of women in politics and with it the proportion of women in the Assembly was to run in the election ourselves.

I had once heard that it takes the same number of years for people to come out of conflict as the number they have been in it, so even if I wasn't best known for my patience, I wanted to help with the transition – I hoped it wouldn't take thirty years. As part of the bottom-up movement that had helped lay the foundations for a new society, I was conscious that a peace accord was not just a matter of discussion: it had to involve the rebuilding of damaged relationships and the creation of a new way of living that helped to sustain livelihoods, make people feel safe, and deliver the basic rights that we had promised. I was up for all of that.

In the election for the Forum and talks, we had been able to hoover up votes across the country, but now I was going to have to stand for the party as a candidate in a single constituency. It was a solo run in my own area when I would have preferred to be in a cross-country team. The idea of forming a People's Coalition was mooted because it would be difficult to attract men in a single constituency to vote for a Women's Coalition candidate. But we decided against becoming a People's Coalition and instead stuck to our record as the Women's Coalition. We felt that the skills and confidence that we had forged in the furnace of the peace talks had to be turned to some advantage.

Our first task was to raise money for the election, which had been set for 25 June. Shannon O'Connell had volunteered with us during the referendum and came back from Boston to help in the election. She told me that in the USA you aimed high and just asked for donations, and that's what I did in the States. Donors there liked to feel involved. Back home in Northern Ireland, I was almost ashamed to ask for money. With Shannon coaching me from the sidelines, I finally got into the swing of cold-calling and in time began to confidently ask for donations from people I didn't know, which was a major achievement for me.

Carmen Suro-Bredie opened her home to host fundraisers in the USA and it never ceased to amaze me that a woman from an Ecuadorian background was prepared to do that for a group of women that she hadn't heard of until the day Jane Morrice met her at a conference. Carmen helped in every way she could, including putting me in touch with a lawyer to register the party in Washington DC, so as to be allowed to raise funds as a foreign entity. Each time I had gone to stay with her during the St Patrick's Day events, I had the cosy basement in her house in Chevy Chase all to myself. Carmen often reminded me that I needed to 'have an ask' – that I shouldn't ever leave a meeting without making a request. The 'asks' did not come naturally to me and I had to force myself to make them, knowing that the benefit was for others and not for me personally. I was also fortunate to have the support of Melanne Verveer, whom I had met when she was Hillary Clinton's chief of staff. She came to Belfast many times, and became my rock; Catherine Shannon and Olga Reissman took on the same role in Boston.

Two weeks after the referendum, I invited Colette Rhoney, who had helped with our fundraising in the States, to come back with me to see the work we were doing on the ground. When I brought her to the Elton John concert that Mo Mowlam organised in front of Parliament Buildings to celebrate the Yes vote, Colette remarked that she would always remember the night when thousands of people sang out in unison, hoping for a very different life. Mo also enjoyed the occasion – as she waved from the stage that night, fifteen thousand waved back.

The forthcoming election would be the Women's Coalition's fourth. We had raised enough money to run candidates in eight constituencies. Seven days after the referendum, we were ready to take part in another historic poll. On 30 May we had held our largest monthly meeting since the start of the Women's Coalition. Carmel Roulston gave a presentation on proportional representation and the single transferable vote. As a cross-community party, transfers from other parties would benefit

with the cuts to social security
the government subsidies ran
back to the USA with his millio
at the factory in West Belfast
Back to the Future. A creative re
– that led to nearly one in fiv
1980s – was the development o
This act of defiance reminded n
Co-op in Swatragh that my fa
and that was still going from s
default, like the multi-millionair
had borrowed money they coul
Donegall Street started a not-fo
our meetings, to spend our mon
The pub was named after the po
right of his Protestant ancestors t
my grandfather came here / and
waste.' That was more than coul
At the same time, the Poverty
Payments for Debt Act. Some pe
'Payments for Death Act' – it was n
The legislation, first introduced in
deductions from social security be
by those who had participated in
The legislation was then amended
recoup money from any claimant i
Rosie Nolan, a young, single moth
this act. As well as her benefits bei
the waiting list for rehousing becau
the block of flats in Turf Lodge wher
there had been diagnosed with dysen
Depression among mothers was hi
day after day. Rosie Nolan ended h
words, which I recalled from my
happens when a dignified life is no lo
money and little hope, it can be impo

erence votes cast. Getting the surplus votes
eats as well as the transfer from candidates
would be key. This required an understanding
y to do well – we couldn't just rely on people
also needed to convince voters to give us their
that the people of Northern Ireland had
o political leaders: they wanted a future that
way from conflict, one in which people and
esponsibly. To get the manifesto out on time
ilde and Shannon O'Connell worked in the
l leaflets ready for circulating to candidates.
ast East; Jane Morrice in North Down; Anne
n Cosgrove in South Antrim; Marie Crawley
Tyrone; Annie Campbell in Lagan Valley; and
d Armagh. I was the candidate for South Belfast
part of it, along with the towns and villages
ndidates were running. And running was what
n and out of the office like a yo-yo. It was quite
ld Ann McCann that I'd lost a few pounds, she
to the donations. John McGettrick acted as my
ed a line to use as we went from door to door
u think I would be out here canvassing instead
Cup if I didn't believe this woman has a serious
ings were looking up when I heard a child say to
hat lady is everywhere.'
darker side, like the anonymous phone calls that
we had the right as a 'bunch of feminists' to stand
as the sexist insults that got to me the most: the
ice, instructing me to 'get back to the kitchen',
nistic drawings of penises on posters. My sons
behalf. Gavin later told me that he got bullied by
s supported another candidate in the constituency.
ne, and to my children, that they saw the Women's
ion for their votes. I made it just as clear that we
where elections were meant to be free and fair. But

it still saddened me to hear that my sons were having to deal with this kind of thing.

I invested in a very large billboard for the election. Rowen first saw it on his way home from school on the bus when one of his friends shouted, 'There's your mum.' He assumed that I was standing at the bus stop, but instead found himself looking out at a six-foot-high poster of his mother. I had requisitioned a site beside traffic lights, and when the lights turned red, no matter what direction motorists were coming from, that image was in front of them. My prospects of getting elected weren't that high but I was hoping the billboard would put a name to the face. Posters that said 'Vote Smyth' or 'Vote Wilson', as if candidates didn't have a first name, struck me as strange so I used both my surname and first name to add a more personal touch and put it at the top, above my photograph. I didn't like having my picture displayed in public like this, and never got used to it.

On doorsteps across the constituency, people would tell me that they were voting for the big men, meaning John Hume or David Trimble. Even when I said, 'You know they're not standing in this constituency', they still viewed voting for them as a proxy vote for the person they saw as their leader. To many people, I was 'that blonde woman' from the Women's Coalition but that wouldn't be on the ballot paper.

I roped in my cousin Ann-Marie to help us put together the party political broadcasts for the television stations. Rather than going for the usual newscaster-to-camera straight shot, with a photogenic party stalwart delivering the message, we scripted a plot that included the World Cup. Even the hardened hacks enjoyed the way we portrayed the notion that politics was worth watching just as much as the soccer matches. It took five or six takes before we got it right, but it became a game changer. It gave people something to talk about, especially in comparison with the standard party political election broadcasts that bored their socks off.

Visiting areas where we were least likely to do well – predominantly republican and loyalist areas – was hard work but as a cross-community party we went everywhere, asking at doors for second-preference votes if I wasn't going to be people's first choice. Bit by bit, we covered the constituency of forty thousand voters that bordered on areas of east and west Belfast. Occasionally we got mixed up about exactly where the constituency began and ended. The houses with the largest gardens necessitated a long trek up to the door and another long trek back down again. In working-class housing estates, homes were quicker to canvass, as they were in 'Nappy Valley' areas, where young families lived. I was thankful that the gardens were not as big or as well fenced as those in more affluent areas where it took us hours to move from door to door.

I moved from residential homes for senior citizens to schools, supermarkets and parish halls, and as I went along I checked the register to see who was eligible to vote. That was another complication – working out which nationality was eligible, especially if they were citizens of the European Union. My lead-in line was 'Do you know there's an election on? Are you registered?' If it turned out that they weren't, I would encourage them to do so before the next election, and then keep moving. Every night more of the map would be shaded in as we marked off the territory we had covered.

The university area was a nightmare – students were saying they'd vote but it turned out that either they hadn't bothered to register or they were going home to vote. Sundays were also hard work, as we canvassed people before and after church services. We started early and finished after midday, distributing leaflets into five thousand pairs of hands. I offered one to a man coming out of church, only to hear him say, 'I've got five of your leaflets. I got one at the church, I got one at the supermarket, I got one at the school, I got one through my door, and I got one walking along the street. If you don't get elected after this I don't know who will.' People were beginning to say openly that they would be voting for me as number one. Some had shifted their position, moving me up from number two to pole position. I began to believe that politics was the art of the possible.

The last week of campaigning was non-stop. I spent a half day in Newcastle, another at Bangor market and then went down to Fermanagh on the Thursday to canvass with Marie Crawley, our candidate there.

Jane Morrice went up and down the commuter trains delivering our message to a captive audience. By talking loudly to one person in the carriage, she was selling it to everyone. Everyone got a copy of the Coalition's manifesto and all were impressed, just as I was, that she could make canvassing such fun. I loved her infectious laughter and enthusiasm as well as her passion for politics. By the time Jane left the train, everyone knew her name.

The weather changed, from wet nights to hot, sunny days. As ever, canvassing wasn't without incident. One of the men supporting me found himself in a tricky spot. In the last week of the campaign, he drove into a loyalist area to replace some posters that had fallen down. He got out of the car and recognised some local men cruising along the street. They pulled up alongside him as he produced one of my posters. They asked him 'Are you with her?' When he said he was, he got the reply 'Oh, she's all right.' I was glad that they felt the Women's Coalition candidate could pass. It also made me realise what great supporters were on board – this man was not in the least worried about canvassing for the Women's Coalition.

On the day of the election, my eighty-four-year-old mother took over duties at a polling station while Mary went off to get the boys from school. It was cold and wet outside, so my mother stood inside the polling station to shelter from the rain. She was handing out leaflets when one of the polling station staff told her she wasn't allowed to do that on the premises. In the end, the staff took pity on her and let her stay, sitting on a stool in the porch. Instead of handing out leaflets, she simply asked people to vote for me by telling them my name. When someone told her, 'Well I'm voting for her, she's doing a fine job,' it made her day. My two brothers had also come up from the country and I watched them chatting with the loyalist party workers. On the left was the PUP, on the right the UDP, and in the middle were John and Terence. I could see that the investment in building friendships with other parties had been worth it. Sharing our fish suppers with other canvassers also drew comment as sharing anything on election day wasn't that common.

As I went from station to station, I could see the extent of the battle that David Trimble was having inside his own party. His future rested on the outcome of this election. Rev. Martin Smyth, the MP for my constituency, was on the anti-Agreement side of the Ulster Unionist Party, and his supporters were annoying Michael McGimpsey, who was also in the UUP but on the pro-Agreement side. They were scoring out Michael's name from his posters, an indication of how bitter things had become in the UUP. Each time Michael McGimpsey's supporters left a polling station, his posters would be torn down within minutes. The men who were doing this told me that nothing in the Agreement would ever make them happy. I wondered what world they were living in.

Even at closing time, our party workers were still handing out leaflets at polling stations. My US friends Catherine Shannon and Mary Myers were soaked to the skin – Catherine looked like she had shrunk by six inches, and Mary resembled the Michelin Man in her thick layers of coats. I couldn't believe they were loving every minute of it. I was hoping for their sake that their investment in us would pay off and that one or two of us would get elected.

We still had work to do to prepare for the count the next day. I had invited a couple from Dublin, Mary and Tony, as experts in tallying votes to join the training with Avila's team in my house that night. Mary and Tony were trying to work out what way the transfer of votes would go from parties on the pro- and anti-Agreement sides. They stayed up all night to design a computer programme that listed the party candidates and the various stages of the process. I needed to find an office for their computer in Belfast City Hall, where the count would take place. I called David Ervine to ask if our tellers could use his council office and back came his reply: 'You're going to be in our space all day, you're going to be in our face all day, but it doesn't matter – you can have the office.'

I gave Mary and Tony the good news. They were nervous about their Dublin accents and joked that they'd have to sign to each other in the PUP office, but by the time I arrived they were chatting away, surrounded by loyalist paraphernalia on the walls. Things went so well that after Mary and Tony had finished calculating my votes, the PUP tally men asked them if they'd do theirs as well. So they extended the programme, and the more data they entered the more accurate the predictions became.

When the first boxes were opened, I was getting 10 per cent of first-preference votes but it was the second preferences that would make the difference. I was disappointed to hear about the elimination of the UDP's Davy Adams as we had become close friends. 'Elimination' is a harsh word and my heart went out to him. I genuinely believed that candidates like Davy would have made a great addition to the Assembly: he had shown such political acumen during the peace talks. All I could think of was the loss to the process of a very insightful thinker who would have continued to work hard to break the sectarian logjam. As the day wore on, a young man wearing his school uniform showed his dislike of the Women's Coalition by kicking me on the ankles and telling me to go home. My feet were already sore enough from all the standing about. I told the young brat that he needed a good kick up the arse.

As more of the votes were counted, I could see that we had succeeded in attracting a working-class, cross-community vote; the canvassing in these areas, with second preferences from republican and loyalists voters, was paying off. The percentage of transfers was rising but Avila was muttering that someone should have sponsored training in proportional representation for Sinn Féin voters. They had voted only for their candidate and not expressed preferences for any of the others on the ballot sheet.

In the media interviews I stayed focused on the cross-community support that I had worked so hard to get and that was making the crucial difference. In the middle of the afternoon, I took a break and went to talk to the team across the road. My family were with May Blood in Jurys hotel in the city centre, glued to the TV on which commentators were trying to work out if I would still be in at the final count. The punters drinking their pints gave me the thumbs up but in reality I was only hanging on by the skin of my teeth.

Walking back to the City Hall, I could feel the pressure building up. The tellers' predictions were looking good but I was running neck-and-neck with two other candidates and there were only two seats for three people. The nine hours of waiting had taken such a toll that I told Ann McCann, 'Never, never, never again.' But just as I said that, people started to come forward, offering their congratulations. There hadn't been a declaration but they knew enough to confirm that I couldn't be beaten – there weren't enough votes left for either of the other two to overtake me. But I still waited for the returning officer to step up to the podium to declare that I had been elected. Only then would I accept that I was to become a member of the new Northern Ireland Assembly.

My acceptance speech was short: 'Women have watched and waited for too long. Our time has now come.' I told reporters that I hoped my voice would make a difference even if I were to be on my own in the Assembly – I still wasn't sure if Jane would get elected. I was the only cross-community candidate in the constituency and mentioned how proud that made me feel. I was happy that another woman would also follow me into the Assembly, with the SDLP's Carmel Hanna winning the last seat. The cameras were still running and showing me live as I called Brian to say: 'Tell the children I've just been elected!' It was after midnight but the boys were still up. They loved that they could see me on the TV and simultaneously hear my voice down the phone.

Shannon O'Connell was still by my side, even at this late hour, and I appreciated how she, as an American, phrased her congratulations by saying: 'I cannot describe how potent this sense of justice is to see you becoming a law maker'. After all her hard work, it was good to hear her add that it had been one of the most thrilling days of her life. Once the result was announced, we went down to the PUP office to pour champagne into plastic cups to celebrate – both David Ervine and I were toasting each other. I promised Billy Hutchinson that I would bring a bottle back for him if he managed to get elected the following day. I knew he was a teetotaller but I wanted to keep his hopes up. On the way out I passed the Sinn Féin offices, where party workers were hard at work analysing the figures for West Belfast. They poured out into the corridor to give me their congratulations. Win or lose that night, everyone was showing appreciation for those who had entered the rough and tumble of the electoral process.

On the way home, Brian phoned to say that the party he had promised, no matter the result, was in full flow. I hadn't expected the neighbours to be out on the street, cheering and dancing. One of them said that after years of voting he had finally got someone who had hit the jackpot. There is still the mark in the room where the cork from the champagne hit the ceiling. In the speeches, I singled out Avila who had been there from the very start, walking with me every step of the way. I had to postpone downing too much of the bubbly stuff since I was still waiting to hear whether Jane was going to get elected in North Down.

It was to be another long day waiting for her results. She was still in the contest, and I knew what a difference it would make if she were to get elected as well. Rather than me being the lone voice in the Assembly, we knew that the Women's Coalition would have full party rights if two or more members of any party were to be elected. Jane felt she was in with a chance – she was also relying on transfers from across the political spectrum. She had taken a bet with a BBC commentator who had predicted that she would be beaten – but when the electoral officer got up on the platform to announce the result, the journalist changed his tune and agreed to take Jane to dinner to celebrate her win.

We had broken new ground by showing that a small autonomous women's party could get elected in its own right. We didn't have a big political machine behind us, but we had worked tirelessly across our different cultural traditions and once again had achieved our goal. We had endured humiliation and sexual harassment but, with a small group of like-minded men and women, we had faced down the macho politics of Northern Ireland. It felt like we had scaled mountains. Annie Campbell put it best: 'We are part of a tapestry of activism making positive change. We were not in any hero mode – we are part of a group – so you do what you can and everyone else does what they can, and together you can make that change.' Time would tell if that was enough.

12

The First Assembly

'A wise enemy is better than an ignorant friend.'

Persian proverb

The first sitting of the Northern Ireland Legislative Assembly was on 1 July 1998, and I was still coming to terms with the fact that I had been elected to represent South Belfast. It was another historic day as Sinn Féin was present for the first time in a legislative body in Northern Ireland. Republicans who were opposed to the Good Friday Agreement had accused the party of accepting the partition of Ireland by taking their seats. But that day Sinn Féin members were also encountering their opponents on the other side of the community divide, the DUP seated opposite, for the first time.

However, it wasn't either of those parties that challenged the new system first – it was us. All members had to sign the register, and indicate whether they were nationalist, unionist or other. Since the Women's Coalition had members who were all three, I took the pen and signed the book, stating my designation as nationalist, unionist and other. My fellow Coalition member Jane Morrice did the same. We were expected to sign in as 'other', but this wasn't accurate for us and did not reflect the diversity of our party. The Good Friday Agreement had made provision for us to be British or Irish or both, and that's the point we were making.

One hundred and six other Assembly members were watching to see what would happen next. The initial presiding officer, John Alderdice – who was later elected speaker – was having none of it, saying his role was to make the proceedings go smoothly. He called an adjournment, during which we explained our reasons to him. We hadn't intended to engage in subversion. We had no wish to hold things up on the very first day. It wasn't our fault that the rules were too narrow to accommodate a party like ours. We went outside to explain our position to the press.

The adjournment didn't last long – the advice that John Alderdice had been given left us with no other option but to designate the Coalition as 'Inclusive Others'. As I stepped forward to write that in the roll book, Peter Robinson raised a point of order, stating, 'The two members of the Women's Coalition seem to be in some sort of political drag as other/ unionist/nationalist'. He wanted to know how the matter had been cleared up, and John Alderdice explained. The issue of designation for cross-community parties has never been satisfactorily resolved; nor has it lost its urgency.

When it was his turn to speak on behalf of Sinn Féin, Martin McGuinness said how delighted he was to meet the DUP in person for the first time, but that he hadn't recognised Sammy Wilson with his clothes on. It was a jibe about a holiday picture that had been published in the *Sunday World* and for which Sammy had successfully sued the newspaper. Not everyone heard Sammy's immediate retort: that he hadn't recognised Martin McGuinness without his balaclava. The proceedings were being transmitted live and showed David Ervine and me laughing. We were sitting next to each other because the parties were allocated seats in alphabetical order.

Brian was in his office, watching the proceedings live on TV, when one of his co-workers – who didn't know that Brian was my husband – remarked that the rumour about David Ervine and me having an affair had to be true since the filming showed the closeness between us. Brian feigned surprise and then told them that he'd be cooking dinner for David and his wife Jeanette that evening. When Brian told us the story later, we agreed that the best way to deal with the gossip was to ignore it. The rumour, which I'd known about for some time, was intended to damage me, as invariably it is the woman's reputation that's on the line when these kinds of stories circulate. This is another peril for women entering public life. My friendship with David and Jeanette reminded me of the words in John Hewitt's poem, in which a Protestant speaker walks with his Catholic friend: 'You must give freedom if you would be free,/ for only friendship matters in the end.'

David Ervine and I came from two very different backgrounds; he was a Protestant from east Belfast and I was a Catholic from a market town in County Derry. In the two years leading up to the agreement, we often talked about what David called 'the rotten stinking war'. When anyone asked about his role in the UVF, he would reply, 'That was then and this is now,' meaning that someone's past shouldn't define their future. Nor did it mean that he couldn't have a positive and progressive influence on politics. What I liked most about David was his ability to rattle my thinking – to make me see things from a different perspective. He was the only man I knew who could get away with saying that he was 'lusting for peace'.

He had joined the UVF in 1972 on the day that he said changed his life – it became known as Bloody Friday because of the death and destruction caused by the IRA's twenty-two bombs in Belfast city centre. Vengeance came in the door and reason went out the window. He said he had been shaped in that crucible of hatred but came to realise its futility during his time in the Maze prison, where Gusty Spence asked each new inmate, 'Why are you here?' It was a soul-searching question – he was not looking to find out about their sentence, but rather to discover what the new arrival felt was being achieved through bombing and bullets.

David's East Belfast constituency bordered mine, and we worked together to tackle sectarianism. He was right when he said, 'I can smell sectarianism a mile off. It doesn't grow wild in a field; it is tended in a window box'. Father Stephen McBrearty, a mutual friend, had been worried about the problems in his parish of St Anthony's in the predominantly Protestant area of Willowfield, which bordered on David's constituency. The church had been attacked regularly from the time it was built in the 1940s when its altar had been desecrated during the building's construction and a worker had been murdered. A relative of mine, Father Robert Fullerton, faced serious sectarian abuse when he became the parish priest: a pig's head was hung on a tree outside the church door with a sign 'Cured at Lourdes'. More recently, mourners at a funeral had been on the receiving end of yet more insults, such as, 'Pigs get out of our area.' Parishioners still use a side entrance to the church, to avoid drawing attention to themselves as they attend Mass. When David heard about the church windows being stoned, he undertook to find out who was responsible and to get them to stop. His intervention worked.

He took risks, big and small, to help build peace on either side of the community. Because of the threats to his life, his home was fitted with steel doors, bulletproof glass and security cameras. He often joked about Ulster Unionist Party members who expressed concern about the risks they were taking for the Agreement; he knew he was at much greater risk from disaffected loyalists, and he often told me that if he got hit, it would be with something of a higher velocity than an umbrella or a handbag. When our mutual friend from New York, Tom Moran, met both of us in the Europa hotel, Tom often agreed to David's request to switch seats. What we didn't know, and only discovered later, was that David himself never wanted to sit with his back to the window.

On the first day, the Assembly met in the same room in which the Agreement had been signed. The chamber in Parliament Buildings was still being refurbished following a recent fire and we had to decide whether the new legislative body's home would be located there. I was the Coalition's chief whip – the strangest title I ever held – which made me a member of the business committee with responsibility for that decision. The chief whips from each party agreed to walk up the hill to Parliament Buildings to see what debating chamber now looked like.

Parliament Buildings had a long legacy: for nationalists, it was the place from which so much of the discriminatory legislation had emanated. So, it wouldn't have been the first choice for them. I reminded those standing beside me of how the Bolsheviks had handled their historic buildings following the Russian Revolution – instead of pulling them down, they recalled the craftsmanship that had gone into them, and for that reason alone deserved to be retained. I also thought it was a waste of public money to start construction on a new venue, especially when we didn't know for sure how long the Assembly would be in place. A number of statues from the previous era were still in full view – Carson was on his plinth at the front of the building and James Craig, the first prime minister of Northern Ireland, was prominent in the entrance hall. These were men who were acceptable to the unionists but not to nationalists because of the decisions they had made at the time of partition.

As we stepped through the front door, I thought it augured well for the future that Peter Robinson was holding the door for the next person, and that next person turned out to be Sinn Féin's Alex Maskey. But things went downhill after that. It became clear to me, when the parties started fighting about where they would sit in this proposed new chamber, that the alphabetical seating arrangements that we had used in the negotiations were going to be abandoned. The main parties planned to revert to the status quo of days gone by, when unionists sat on one side and nationalists directly opposite. This would mean that the First and Deputy First Minister, despite holding joint positions in the new government, would be facing each other, creating a needlessly adversarial atmosphere and giving the impression they were in opposition rather than working side by side.

When the colour of the carpets and the curtains came up for discussion, members who had previously been elected to parliament decades before said they preferred the chamber's old red velvet colour and not the current blue. Things were still tense on the streets in the run-up to the July marching season, and here we were discussing interior design. Another issue that had to be resolved was the logo for the new Assembly. The argument over that continued for months: given its legacy, the old logo wasn't acceptable to nationalists. Women's Coalition member Eliz Byrne McCullough suggested the flax flower that had once made Northern Ireland famous for its linen. Coincidentally, John Alderdice made the same proposal, and that's how the new logo was decided. I was anticipating a quip such as 'trust the women to want a flower' but there was no such comment. I hoped the way was now clear for us to get on with more substantive business but the issue of the Drumcree parade flared up once again.

The Parades Commission was in place by then and it had banned the parade at Drumcree – a decision that went against the wishes of the Loyal Orders and another stand-off between them and the Garvaghy Road residents began. I was asked by a women's group in the area if some of the Women's Coalition members would visit them – they said they had been hemmed into their area and couldn't come to see us, so we agreed to meet them in the local community centre. On our way there, Ann, Kate and I were stopped at a police checkpoint below the Drumcree church where thousands of men were gathered in the fields above us. The officers checked the car and signalled for us to pass. When we reached the community centre, the women there were fearful that the police couldn't hold the line up the road.

Philomena Gallagher, a former student from my women's studies class and a member of the women's group, asked if I would do an interview on their pirate radio station. She escorted me into a hen house that was doubling up as a studio. I said a few words of reassurance about how the rule of law would have to be upheld and that everyone's safety was a priority. As I came out, I looked up to see a Chinook helicopter hovering over my head, reminding me of the opening scene of *Apocalypse Now*. On the way out of the estate, soldiers were swarming everywhere and I got the sense that trouble was brewing on the hill. Over time, the protesters melted away but before they did, something happened that broke my heart: I got the news that three young boys, Richard, Mark and Jason Quinn, had been burned to death in their beds in their Ballymoney home. As part of the protest against the march being banned, a number of loyalists had thrown a petrol bomb into their house, setting the place alight. The night before the funeral, Gavin and Rowen wanted to know how someone could do such a thing to children the same age as them. I explained that since the Agreement, the more agreeable we became, the more some very violent men would try to block our way to democracy by burning and bombing people out of their homes. As I looked at my two boys, I wondered how I would cope if I lost them in such circumstances.

The next day that terrible thought stayed in my mind – it was overwhelming watching the Quinn family having to bear the unbearable. I cried as the little white coffins were carried down the aisle. The children's aunt read a poem that described what had been so special about Richard, Mark and Jason. She spoke of their little touches, their kisses, their unconditional love, and once again I was reminded of the costs of sectarianism. Colin Parry was standing beside me outside the church and I knew that the funeral must have brought back memories of that awful day in Warrington, when his son Tim had been killed by an IRA bomb.

When the *Irish News* asked me to write a piece about the tragedy in Ballymoney, I said that it was a time for sorrow. Referring to what had been happening at Drumcree, I also made it clear that the days of making angry speeches full of hatred from hillsides were over. I said that there was no quick fix, that we had a very high mountain to climb, but for the Quinn family we would go on climbing it.

The year before, in April 1997, on my way to my parents' home in Kilrea, I'd stopped in Randalstown to show Gavin and Rowen the remnants of the Catholic church that had been burned to the ground that week. As we looked at the still-smouldering embers, I explained that the arson attack was the result of sectarianism. Mutually exclusive narratives, honed by inherited tales and stories, seemed to justify acts of destruction as a distorted way of protecting each side's heritage – GAA halls and Orange halls getting burned to the ground were the outcome of this. Some were too slow to condemn the arson attacks, arguably becoming guilty of collusion through their silence.

In my own constituency, in South Belfast, the July period had passed off peacefully even though the Ormeau Road had been a flashpoint in the past. We had succeeded in keeping lines of communication open between the residents, the RUC, the Ballynafeigh Orange Order and the local political representatives. Communication worked. We had a majority of people in favour of the Agreement and a majority of parties ready to implement it, but the peace process was facing so many challenges that it was difficult to believe that we could sustain it.

In the days before the Twelfth, the Assembly had been told to close up early because of outbreaks of civil disorder and subsequent cancellation of public transport. In spite of the unofficial curfew, I stayed on in Parliament Buildings to finish up some work. By the time I left, there wasn't another person in the building. My usual exit was locked so I climbed through a window on the lower floor and headed for the gate lodge. No one was there either and the barrier was down but luckily the security man was sleeping peacefully in his hut. When I woke him, he told me that the dual carriageway had been blocked by loyalist protesters, that I wouldn't be able to get through in my car, adding a snippet about some protesters wielding baseball bats. He advised that I should tell them I was a nurse but I was doubtful that ruse would work – my posters had been on every lamppost. I phoned David Ervine to find out how things were where he lived as I knew that one option for getting home was to go through the Braniel estate. He mapped out a route that avoided the hotspots, and then said, 'If you run into any bother, let me know.' I weaved my way back home where Brian was waiting for me, and we went for a walk on the Ormeau Road. Two American students were throwing a frisbee to each other in the middle of the road, clearly enjoying the emptiness of the streets. I picked up the evening edition of the *Belfast Telegraph*, and saw the quip, 'Will the last person leaving Belfast please switch out the lights'.

What had happened in Ballymoney was shocking, and more was to come on 15 August. I heard the news on holiday that a bomb had exploded in Omagh, killing 29 people and injuring some 220. I would go on to work with families caught up in the atrocity at a later stage, but all I could do that week was watch silently on television as families buried their dead. I knew the town really well, having spent many of my holidays as a child nearby on my Uncle John's farm, and once again my heart went out to the people there.

Gerry Adams stated, 'I am totally horrified by this action. I condemn it without any equivocation whatsoever.' It was the first time that anyone had heard Sinn Féin use the word 'condemn'. On 4 September, he went further: 'Sinn Féin believe the violence we have seen must be, for all of us now, a thing of the past – over, done with and gone.'

As that terrible summer passed, the Shadow Assembly took its first tentative steps. The designated First Minister (David Trimble) and the Deputy First Minister (Seamus Mallon) were acting alone because an Executive had yet to be put in place. This also meant that direct rule from Westminster was still operating. The decommissioning of weapons had become a sticking point: the Ulster Unionists argued that Sinn Féin could not assume their ministerial posts until the IRA handed over its guns and explosives. The IRA, for its part, was insistent that until an inclusive government was set up, there would be no decommissioning. It was stalemate.

In December 1998 Tony Blair and Bertie Ahern were back in Northern Ireland, trying to work out a compromise, but it proved elusive. Their efforts were hampered by recriminations and accusations of bad faith. The exchanges in the Assembly on 18 December showed how far apart the parties were. The Reverend William McCrea, who was against the Agreement, was accusing the pro-Agreement Ulster Unionists of treachery. Peter Weir, who had defected from the pro-Agreement side and joined a group called Union First, was demanding that one third of the IRA's arms be destroyed. In my response to him in the Assembly, I said, 'No doubt, next time we return to the chamber, it will become two thirds,' and argued that the political vacuum, which I referred to as 'subsidised inaction', echoing Mark Durkan's phrase, to reflect how tax payers money was being wasted, had gone on for too long: that we had been elected to do business and it was time to get on with it.

The debate became slightly comical when Ulster Unionist Dermot Nesbitt described Sinn Féin and the IRA as being in a marriage that didn't work, in which the husband and wife should divorce. I said that anyone who knew how a marriage worked understood that agreeing to live with difference and allowing for independent decisions in which one party does not force the other into discordant agreement was the only way forward. I pointed out that 'the uncertainties of today' were better than 'the mayhem of the past', and that the only certainty was that the people had voted overwhelmingly in the referendum to make the Agreement work. This required compromise, rather than any one side holding out for 100 per cent of its demands to be met. I argued, 'We have concentrated on decommissioning and the politics of ultimatums. Perhaps one day we will have a healthy debate about other issues which were also in the Agreement ... the inclusion of more women in decision-making in Northern Ireland's politics or on community development'.

I told the Assembly members, 'We do not often hear about people who are beaten in their homes. When we talk about what constitutes terror, let us include all the unacceptable forms of violence.' I also emphasised again the importance of a functioning Executive, saying, 'We must try to create the cornerstone that will make this a place in which everyone's traditions are respected. Both sides fear that one day they will be an alienated minority. Only the Agreement can end that fear, and it is time that we set up a government.'

I had referred to how party members were working in a collegiate manner in committees and were an example of how we should behave in the plenary sessions, and made a suggestion to the DUP members: 'They should head not simply for the door, as they would like to do, but up the stairs, where the work is being done.' There followed an exchange between me and Sammy Wilson:

Mr S Wilson: I would not go upstairs with you at any time.
Ms McWilliams: Mr Wilson knows little about sexual relationships,

and he ought not to lecture people about where in this building they should go ...

The Initial Presiding Officer: Order. Two Members should not be on their feet at the same time. I heard an intervention which was neither a point of order nor a point of information. It may not be on the record.

Ms McWilliams: For the record, Mr Initial Presiding Officer, I shall repeat the cheap, scurrilous jibe made by Mr Wilson. He said that he would not go upstairs with me at any time. Ha, ha, ha.

The Initial Presiding Officer: It will certainly now be on the record.

Ms McWilliams: Apart from Mr Wilson, no one is laughing.

Just before that Christmas of 1998, the party leaders as joint signatories to the Good Friday Agreement were invited to the Kennedy Library in Boston, where JFK's daughter Caroline presented us jointly with the Profile in Courage award that was named after her father. The tour of the library was memorable because I got to watch John Kennedy Jnr and his cousin Bobby crawling under the desk that President Kennedy had used in the Oval office. They wanted to see the scrawls they had made on the wood when they were children. When I sat beside Caroline that evening, I told her I had already met her Uncle Ted Kennedy and her aunt, US Ambassador to Ireland Jean Kennedy Smith. The circle was complete for me when I later met Ethel Kennedy. These were the Kennedys who had fought for civil rights, who had impressed me in my formative years, and I felt fortunate to have met so many of them in person.

The next stop was Washington, where John Hume and David Trimble were both in good form as they were going to Oslo a few days later to receive the Nobel Peace Prize. We were being presented with the Averell Harriman Democracy award, and, during the ceremony, we were asked to reflect on the achievements of the Good Friday Agreement. It was the first and last time we ever had an opportunity to do that together. When I looked at the list of the previous award recipients, it was heartening to see that we had been raised to that level. We'd all got on well during that trip and I hoped we would bring some of the goodwill back to Northern Ireland.

The next time we got to meet President Clinton was when he arrived in Parliament Buildings in 1999. Each party lined up in the Long Gallery in their assigned spot. The DUP was first in line. I surmised that Gerry Adams's visa to the US shortly after the ceasefire in 1994 was the source of the heated exchange between Ian Paisley Snr and the president. I had heard that Trimble and Mallon had taken bets on whether or not the president would look awkward when the newly arrived US Consul General introduced me as 'Monica' – the scandal about him and Monica Lewinsky had hit the news. The Consul General was struggling to remember my surname, and kept repeating my first name: 'This is Monica, Monica, Monica ... McBride.' The president smiled, saying he already knew who I was. The next day the *Belfast Telegraph*'s story read, 'Big Bill meets Harmonica'.

Hillary Clinton had travelled to Belfast separately to host a conference with Vital Voices, the organisation she had set up to bring together women from different conflict regions and had promised to bring it to Belfast when Pearl and I met her at the White House. The news of the tension between the Clintons was dominating the media. I felt sorry for Hillary Clinton and Monica Lewinsky, as the media was hanging both of them out to dry. But I wasn't there to talk about that in my interview with CNN outside the Waterfront Hall, the venue for the conference. I was fixated on the secret service frogmen scouring the river for explosive devices as the CNN introduced me: 'And today we have here the leader of the Northern Ireland Women's Coalition, Monica Lewinsky ...' Once again, I carried on and somehow CNN managed to erase those words before it went out on air. The reporter said he would put the piece in the can for the Christmas party that year.

I was due to meet Hillary Clinton again, but fate intervened. I had received an invitation from Ken Wollack, the CEO of the National Democratic Institute (NDI), to make a presentation to her at the Averell Harriman Democracy award ceremony on 24 September 1999 in Washington DC. During the first leg of my plane journey, from Belfast to Amsterdam, I started to feel pain on my right side but I didn't think too much of it. John Hume also happened to be in the terminal en route to Austria. When John told me he wasn't feeling well, I thought his illness sounded much worse than mine, and I said he should see a doctor. He said the same to me, but instead of taking each other's advice, we both found ourselves in hospital shortly after arriving at our destinations – John ended up having lifesaving surgery in an Austrian hospital while I faced an emergency appendectomy in George Washington Hospital. John wrote to me afterwards, joking that I had stolen the limelight from him. When I called home to explain that I had just had my appendix out, Brian agreed that he would wait for the boys to wake up before he told them the news. But that was pre-empted by an early morning radio report, which made my non-appearance at the NDI event for Hillary Clinton sound so much worse than it was. Rowen was set to do his school transfer exam later that same morning and was shocked to see the newspaper headline: 'McWilliams Recovering After Washington Drama.' I called him to tell him not to worry; that I was the cat with nine lives.

By then the hospital had discovered the reason why I was in Washington DC and had started to treat me like a VIP. That contrasted with the way I had been treated on arrival at the reception desk the day before, when it had seemed like I would be turned out if I couldn't produce proof of medical insurance on the spot. The VIP treatment didn't last long – I was told twenty-four hours after surgery that I would have to find somewhere to recuperate since it was time for me to go. I crawled into a wheelchair and went to stay with Martha Pope in her house on Capitol Hill. When I arrived, she told me that she had refurbished her kitchen with the settlement she had received as a result of the Gerry Kelly scandal. I almost burst my stitches when she said her new kitchen was due to a man she'd never met.

Unfortunately, my hospital visits weren't over – I had to return when I had an allergic reaction to mosquito bites that I'd got when I fell asleep in my wheelchair in Martha's garden. I was in Washington much longer than I'd planned because I wasn't allowed to travel until the stitches were removed. When I finally got home to Belfast, the boys hugged me and said they never wanted to let me out of their sight again. There was also a kind letter from Hillary Clinton, in which she commiserated with my misfortune.

Mo Mowlam set a target date of 10 March 1999 to trigger the procedure to nominate ministers to serve on the Executive, and that deadline prompted Sinn Féin and the Ulster Unionist Party to agree to talk face to face for the first time. It was hard to believe that they had signed up to a peace agreement without having said a word to each other. The absence of any engagement meant that Tony Blair, who had taken on the role of Mr Fix-It, had now replaced round-table meetings that involved all the parties with meetings between the leaders of only these two parties in Downing Street. As a result, in spite of her best efforts, Mo Mowlam was unable to make the other parties feel involved in the implementation process. Inclusion had gone out the window.

We rolled our eyes each time David Trimble walked into our office asking, 'Well, ladies, where are the buns?' On a couple of occasions, he argued with Jane Morrice about the benefits of the UK's membership of the European Union. Jane gave as good as she got and Trimble would likely have known that she was the former head of the EU Commission office in Belfast. I was a big supporter of the European Union and Trimble's negativity amazed me. It was the same with the Agreement. He saw it as a stick with which to beat the republicans – with whom he had to work – and a triumph for unionism as a result. But the Agreement, as I saw it, was neither of those things, and needed to be more skilfully nursed by people in leadership positions. We had been on a mutual adjustment journey, helped by the constructive ambiguity embedded in the Agreement. Now, some collective certainty was needed in order to move forward.

Several times during those first few months of 1999, Women Together – a cross-community group that Women's Coalition member Anne Carr headed up – stood in the cold outside the Waterfront Hall trying to persuade the Ulster Unionist Council to support the decision for Trimble to remain in the Assembly. Already, some members had left the party and others were threatening to follow. Although the opinion polls continued to show that a large majority of people wanted the Agreement to work, David Trimble wasn't having much success inside his own party. The polls showed that the people were ahead of the politicians.

In 1999, Good Friday fell on 2 April and Tony Blair set that as the date by which the Northern Ireland Executive should be established. The British and Irish governments asked the parties to gather in Hillsborough Castle for yet another round of negotiations in the days before the deadline. The two governments thought a pressure-cooker approach might work so we were kept inside the castle for several days. In all-night negotiating sessions, the two premiers had come up with what they thought was a resolution: weapons would be put 'beyond use' and verified as such by the international decommissioning body. However, the Ulster Unionists were disinclined to accept this because of their concerns that the weapons could be recovered and used again. They insisted that weapons should be destroyed and confirmed as such. Sinn Féin reacted negatively to the UUP's demand since neither that nor a timeline had been made explicit in the Agreement. Because there was no chance of a political representative of the PUP joining the government, and the UDP hadn't won a seat in the elections, there was no discussion about loyalist weapons. The entire emphasis was on the IRA's guns since Sinn Féin would be in government. Each time Tony Blair told us Coalition members that we weren't a problem I surmised that it was because we didn't have any guns. They had become the price of the entry ticket to all of the negotiations that were now taking place – the rest of us were left to sit it out.

I had been talking to Sinn Féin during the night as key players milled around, waiting to be consulted on decisions. Gerry Adams and Martin McGuinness were in and out of the building, and the Ulster Unionists speculated that they were leaving to talk to the IRA Army Council. The build-up of tension was apparent. Pressure was mounting on Sinn Féin to sign up to a deal on weapons, for them to jump first, but they weren't for budging. I was aware that republicans were facing the threat of disaffection, given the growing number of factions forming both inside and outside the party. They also had the problem that there was an ever-growing alphabet soup of re-named and nuanced republican groups that were accusing the Sinn Féin leadership of treachery. It wasn't just the Ulster Unionists who were struggling with party unity – there was serious strain on the pro-Agreement republican side as well. David Ervine had predicted this would happen as he had faced the same thing within the PUP. He said that such tensions were inevitable when you take risks for the sake of peace, but he was prepared to do that.

Hillsborough Castle was packed with people as Trimble wanted his entire Assembly group to be present, and other parties had followed suit. Anti-Agreement protesters were demonstrating outside the gates. It reminded me of the protests that had taken place outside Hillsborough Castle during the signing of the 1985 Anglo-Irish Agreement. The difference now was that Ulster Unionists were on the inside and David Trimble was being called a traitor, just as Margaret Thatcher had been back then. Every time I went out into the Castle grounds, I could hear them shouting, 'Monica, Monica, Monica – traitor, traitor, traitor.' I thought better of shouting anything back across the fence.

It proved to be a long night as party members spread out on the hard wooden floor in the Throne Room. I took a picture of Sinn Féin's Mitchel McLaughlin and Bairbre de Brún seated comfortably in the actual thrones. Ken Maginnis was asleep upstairs, having been allocated a proper bed in the Queen's room by Tony Blair. I was chatting to Sinn Féin's Martin Ferris, who I'd met before at an American Ireland Fund function in Boston, but I was getting dagger looks from some of the UUP members, who thought I was being over-friendly with the likes of him. As the clock struck midnight, Mo Mowlam came to tell us that the protesters had laid siege to the castle, and the police expected their numbers to increase. She gave instructions on how to get to the back door, where a bus was waiting to move us to a hotel. I waited to see who was going to make the first move. But, having captured the attention of everyone in the room, Mo Mowlam laughed, clapped her hands and announced, 'April Fool'. It was past midnight on 1 April. 'Now', she said, 'for the real craic, I'm off to tell Sinn Féin that the Brits are getting out of Northern Ireland.' She took our minds off the hard floor that we were about to sleep on. The next morning, it looked like we had trashed the place, with cushions and cups of strong coffee strewn everywhere.

The two days in Hillsborough Castle had involved most of the pro-Agreement party representatives twiddling their thumbs while waiting to see what was being cooked up between the two governments. It was depressing to see how the 'sufficiency of consensus' – for which the Women's Coalition had worked so hard – had been allowed to dissipate like this. When what became known as the Hillsborough Declaration was announced on 1 April 1999, it proposed that putting weapons 'beyond use' would be best achieved by a 'collective act of reconciliation'. The problem was working out what this actually meant. Was it some form of reciprocation – and if so, whose guns were to be included? Had the British army and the armed groups agreed to what I considered to be a token gesture? There had been no round-table discussion on the feasibility of this 'collective act of reconciliation', and as I sat on the steps listening to the two governments' talking to the world's media, I wondered if this was just another deal to save face.

Expectations were raised on 15 May 1999, when Downing Street declared a new deal had been agreed between the three main parties. But they were dashed the same day, when David Trimble's Ulster Unionist colleagues rejected it on the grounds that they had not been party to it. That soured relationships even further. Since devolution to the Scottish Parliament and the Welsh Assembly was due to take place on 1 July 1999, Northern Ireland was in danger of being left behind if it didn't form part of the UK's new constitutional framework. To speed things up, both governments agreed that an inclusive Executive exercising devolved powers and the decommissioning of weapons should be achieved by the next deadline of May 2000, under the auspices of the Independent International Commission on Decommissioning (IICD). I issued a press release to say this was the first time since the Good Friday Agreement that all the parties had agreed that they should work to make decommissioning happen without the threat of sanctions hanging over anyone's head.

I took no comfort from waking up on 12 July 1999 to a large group of men banging drums and playing flutes in front of my house. I assumed they were protesting about the Parades Commission decision to re-route the Orange Order parade through the local Ormeau Park. I had been mediating between the local Ballynafeigh Orange Order and the Lower Ormeau Residents in an attempt to find a resolution. Neither side was content with the decision, even when the day turned out to be peaceful. It was another step towards normalisation, but the men outside my door were showing their displeasure at the decision. I had known that it would be hard to settle these disputes but the difficulty was driven home the day that I found my newsletters on a bonfire in Taughmonagh, in south Belfast. They were to have been distributed to people's houses, but the newsletters had found their way into the hands of local paramilitaries. Ann McCann and others from the Coalition, scoured the housing estate, picking up the debris left on the ground from the burnt paper.

That autumn, Mo Mowlam was replaced by Peter Mandelson as secretary of state, after senior members of the UUP made public their complaints about her. I could see the toll the peace process had taken on Mo. No secretary of state could have pleased all sides, though – the nationalists disliked Peter Mandelson. I said his insistence that the British government negotiate solely with 'the main players' would be a major problem as it flew in the face of the principle of inclusion. It made it difficult to see where the accountability for implementing the Agreement lay. I insisted that he include all the parties, especially David Ervine's, since it made sense to include the loyalists if a resolution to the decommissioning issue were to be found. He told his civil servants not to talk to me after that. Peter Mandelson's approach was short-term crisis management. None of the other parties outside of the UUP and Sinn Féin were briefed, but we were expected to go along with whatever was decided. Sheer peace process weariness drained the energy from me and I suspected it was the same for most of the people watching the proceedings from outside.

To get around the problem, the Coalition proposed an implementation committee to include all the parties that had been involved in making the Agreement. But Sinn Féin's Bairbre de Brún came to the Coalition office to tell me that her party and the Ulster Unionists had developed a better working relationship. She argued that the implementation committee that we had proposed would only get in the way. I decided to withdraw the proposal. It was a mistake not to insist on the committee, since it would have helped to build consensus in the same way we had done during the negotiations. Without it we were going nowhere.

Like the rumblings of a volcano, the negotiations about the decommissioning of weapons were like *Alice's Adventures In Wonderland*: 'Down, down, down. Would the fall never come to an end ... There was nothing else to do, so Alice began talking again.' The story provided the solution – more dialogue was needed. When Senator Mitchell was called back to conduct a review in September 1999, I told reporters, 'By now we should have been weaned off having to rely on Senator Mitchell, but he is here and let's hope we can get on to solids soon.' Parties should have been talking directly to each other and finally did at Winfield House, the US ambassador's residence in London, where Ulster Unionist Reg Empey referred to the UUP's first meeting with Sinn Féin as the most difficult dinner he had ever sat through. Senator Mitchell optimistically said, 'It may not be trust yet, but it's an important start.' He completed his review within two and a half months, outlining a series of steps that would be undertaken, and remarked that he believed there was a basis for the parties to move forward.

Based on the outcome of the review, the logjam on 'no guns, no government' was broken. On 29 November 1999, ministers were finally appointed to a mandatory coalition. It was mandatory in the sense that the parties with the most significant Assembly representation had to be offered an Executive position. It took the form of a consociational government, in which the four main party leaders chose the ministerial positions in proportion to the numbers of seats they held in the Assembly. When it came to Gerry Adams's turn, he nominated Martin McGuinness as Minister of Education. There were gasps from the unionist side of the chamber; I also overheard hissing and booing from the public gallery. Cedric Wilson got up and left the chamber, saying it was an obscenity for anti-Agreement parties like the DUP to be joining a government with a terrorist party. The tension cranked up a notch when Alliance's Seamus Close mocked the DUP's anti-Agreement stance. According to him it was hypocrisy, since its 'pseudo-reluctant Ministers' were grabbing office with tears in their eyes and claiming to do it all for Ulster.

The two women in the cabinet – the SDLP's Bríd Rodgers and Sinn Féin's Bairbre de Brún – were left with the last two positions, Agriculture and Health. It was a shock to me that no other party had prioritised these positions but seeing two women alongside the eight men was at least a plus. The other plus was that instead of sending deputations to Westminster for decisions, these ten men and women would have to take responsibility for governing Northern Ireland. Gerry Adams tried to strike a mellow tone when he asked, 'Couldn't Mr Paisley in the twilight of his career work with Sinn Féin for the sake of the children of the nation?' What he didn't seem to get was that the nation to which he was alluding was every republican's dream but for the unionists on the opposite benches, it was a nightmare they couldn't begin to contemplate.

On 2 December, the Assembly powers were finally devolved from London. Apart from that being yet another historic occasion, it also meant that I was in a more secure position, having taken a hit on my salary as a university lecturer. If the Assembly were to collapse, it would put anyone with a family, like myself, in a very precarious situation. Little wonder that so few women, and young men for that matter, contemplate a career in politics.

On 14 December 1999, the *Irish News* ran with a headline 'Another step on the journey of hope.' It was a new era for north–south and east–west relationships, with the inaugural meeting of the North–South Council in Armagh and the British-Irish Council meeting in London. The image of the Irish government ministers snaking toward the Armagh council offices in twenty-two black Mercedes had a whiff of the Celtic Tiger about it. But it was the first time in history that members of the Republic's cabinet were going to sit down with the Northern Ireland Executive. Bertie Ahern set the tone when he told reporters, 'For too long, conflict and political division led us to turn our backs on one another, rather than to deal face to face. That era is over now.' Mutual cooperation between Ireland, north and south, had begun. Martin McGuinness said, 'There is logic to all of this – if we work together to end the division on the island, then all of us can look forward at some stage in the future to a united Ireland'. The Ulster Unionist reply was that the British-Irish Council 'will actually be the revolutionary one', to emphasise that, for them, it took precedence over everything else. I wondered how we would square that circle.

I didn't have long to wait for the answer. On 11 February 2000, David Trimble offered his resignation to Peter Mandelson. Trimble's letter led to a countdown that had me staying in my Assembly office waiting to find out if I would still be there the next day. One minute the letter was making its way from the Ulster Unionist HQ and the next Sinn Féin was making an announcement that it was engaged in last-minute discussions on decommissioning. At six o'clock, I finally heard that Peter Mandelson had triggered a suspension of the Assembly which, among other things, meant I was out of a job.

The following week, Jane, Kate and I met with Brian Cowen, the Irish minister for foreign affairs, in the Wellington Park Hotel in Belfast. He was in a foul mood, telling us that the Assembly had to be up and running again the following week. I was certain he knew that the Assembly wouldn't be back that soon. The manner in which the suspension had happened had left most of the parties in a state of shock and the same was clearly true of the Irish government. The constituency work continued while the Assembly was in abeyance, but it was an uncertain time. Each time the Assembly went down so did my morale.

Clinton came back for his third and last visit as president to meet Assembly members at Stormont in December 2000. It was a busy day as I rushed between the various venues. Hillary Clinton gave a speech at the 'Women Raising Their Voices for the New Northern Ireland' event in the Grand Opera House. I met her that afternoon in the Odyssey arena before President Clinton's keynote address to 8,500 people. When Prime Minister Tony Blair said 'peace is a process and not an event', I knew he had first heard that from me.

A terrible feud started on 19 August when loyalists from the Shankill Road viciously turned on each other. The LVF had been causing trouble in the Mid Ulster area since the time of the peace talks but I was shocked to see the extent to which paramilitaries from this group had infiltrated areas of West Belfast. They had joined up with ex-UDA members, who were described as drug barons and racketeers. In the Assembly, I listened as David Ervine called for the attacks to end. Billy Hutchinson summed it up in the *Irish Examiner* saying, 'Paramilitaries live in a macho world and their code is if you live by the sword, you die by the sword.'

May Blood asked for Coalition members to support a march that she was helping to organise on the Shankill Road. That evening, as we passed the Rex Bar, which was the site of a recent skirmish between the two opposing loyalist groups, we didn't know if our presence would cause offence – but we were determined to stop the outrage as it was, as usual, mothers and children who had been forced to flee their homes. Johnny Adair (aka Mad Dog) was finally arrested, and I wasn't the only one asking why he had been allowed to rampage around for so long, causing so much damage to so many people's lives.

An act of decommissioning was finally carried out on 23 October 2001 and was enough to convince David Trimble to try again to get his party over the line and get the Assembly back up and running. On 2 November 2001 the designation issue – Unionist/Nationalist/Other – raised its head again as a majority of votes from both sides of the political divide in the Assembly was needed for the appointments of the First and Deputy First Ministers and the UUP's votes weren't stacking up to secure Trimble's position – he needed three more. That's when the Coalition came back into the picture.

The only way to save the situation was to apply some creativity to the Assembly rules. These allowed for members to redesignate and to revert to their original designation within six weeks. And that's exactly what Jane and I did. The Coalition members had agreed that to maintain our cross-community ethos, Jane would re-designate as unionist and I would redesignate as nationalist, and go back to being 'Inclusive Other' once the vote for Trimble had gone through. We pushed the Alliance Party to do the same, even though they were understandably furious at the idea that some of their members would have to redesignate from centre/other to unionist. A few of their votes added to Jane's would be enough to put Trimble in as First Minister.

The debate preceding the vote was hot-tempered, with Jane on the receiving end of anti-Agreement invective. She used her usual sunny disposition to explain the reasons why the Women's Coalition had taken such a step, and joked that she would have to learn to tie up her children's swings on a Sunday so as to observe the rules of a proper unionist, alluding to the insistence of local unionist councils that parks be shut on the Sabbath. I thought it was a nice touch when she described herself as a 'European Unionist'. Ian Paisley Jnr looked at us as he asked the Speaker, 'Are they unionists, nationalists, others, or just rescuers of whatever party is in trouble?' Strange as it might have seemed, lending support to a party on the pro-Agreement side that was in trouble wasn't a problem for us.

When the Alliance Party's David Ford agreed to allow his party to lend three votes to make Trimble First Minister, the UKUP's Bob McCartney declared him to be 'a self-confessed horse's ass'. A DUP member entered the chamber dressed up as a pantomime donkey. The anti-Agreement side found a blocking mechanism that delayed the vote by another twenty-four hours but, eventually, the vote went through and David Trimble and Mark Durkan – who had taken over from Seamus Mallon – took up their positions as First and Deputy First Minister on 6 November 2001.

After the final votes were taken, members poured out into the hall, where the First and Deputy First Minister were making their first press announcement. A massive scuffle broke out. I had a perfect view of it from the steps in the Great Hall. Pro- and anti-Agreement members were shoving each other, with some kicking other people's ankles, to prevent being caught on the overhead cameras. Staffers were trying to stop their elected representatives from taking a swing at the opposition. The security man shouting 'Gentlemen, please', was ignored. MLA John Kelly described it perfectly to me as a case of 'hold me back … let me at him.'

When Presiding Officer John Alderdice called the chief whips, of which I was one, to a meeting to discuss what the media called 'the brawl in the hall', I was waiting to see if allegations would fly about who had thrown the first punch, but no one was forthcoming. The cameras hadn't recorded anything of worth, and it was left at that. I returned to my office to find Ulster Unionist James Leslie waiting there with a bottle of champagne. He said, 'My party should be thanking you for what you have done today. You took abuse for another party when you didn't have to.' He was one of life's gentlemen and I thanked him for his generosity – there wasn't much of it about. Because of the stand taken by the Coalition and the Alliance Party, David Trimble was now First Minister.

I met RTE's Tommie Gorman for the first time that day. I came to trust him as a journalist, a rare enough thing in politics. While other journalists focused on 'who' the Women's Coalition were, Tommie was prepared to focus on what we wanted to achieve. Since we were neither orange nor green, it meant we had to present our analysis in a way that people could digest – that was far from easy in a divided society. The media offered a precious platform and I had to learn to make the most of it, but we often found that too many of the political commentators and reporters were as hidebound as the established politicians they covered.

In an Assembly debate that followed, I focussed on issues that got less coverage in the press. 'In the acrimony of parliamentary debates the suffering of the victims is sometimes forgotten … We should be ashamed of ourselves if we do not bring Northern Ireland out of the limbo that it has been in.' The endless friction had led to dysfunctional behaviour. It was left to Mark Durkan as the new deputy First Minster to build bridges, but even with his congenial personality, it was asking a lot of him. He certainly tried his best.

Now that the Assembly was back in session, the Women's Coalition put down a motion opposing double-jobbing, arguing that elected representatives should dedicate themselves to one elected position rather than holding multiple seats. The Assembly had twelve members who were also in the UK parliament, as well as more than half who were local councillors. I believed it to be physically impossible to be even half effective holding all these roles. New voices were being held back by the seat-hogging that had gone on for years. Hansard records what Sammy Wilson said of our motion: 'They ask for crèches, nurseries and facilities to free them from the sink and get them out to work … If there is a way to interfere in people's lives, the Women's Coalition will find it.' It turned out that our 'interfering' proposal for 'one person, one elected position' was ahead of its time. It was defeated that day, but double-jobbing was eventually abolished.

Hardly a day passed without some contentious issue surfacing in the Assembly. In June 2001, one of the issues was abortion. The law that applied in Northern Ireland was based on an 1861 Victorian statute and was shrouded in confusion. I pointed out that because of the way the law had been framed, doctors had concerns that they could be accused of performing illegal terminations in cases of rape, incest and fatal foetal abnormalities. I asked that Jim Wells' motion on behalf of the DUP – that 'this Assembly is opposed to the extension of the Abortion Act 1967 to Northern Ireland' – be referred to the health committee so that we could hear evidence from the gynaecologists, obstetricians, midwives and medical experts and make a report within six months as an alternative to the hard-hitting exchanges on the chamber floor. I said that as Assembly members we would have to have the courage to admit that we didn't have all the answers and needed to hear the scientific facts. Instead, we had a four-hour Assembly debate that became a carnival of absolutism on a matter that was far from black and white. That day in June, there was no referral to the heath committee and Jim Wells' motion passed. Many people assumed that the Women's Coalition would be pro-choice, but in reality the issue was divisive within our own party. Some of our members felt I should have pressed for the extension of the 1967 Act; others thought it was a conscience issue, something that shouldn't be a party policy; still others thought that the legislation should stay as it was. It was something that came up on the doors when we were canvassing, and I wondered what impact trying to make it a public health issue would have at the next election. It was to take another two decades before a resolution could be found.

As a member of the Assembly during that year, a serious case of child abuse was brought to my attention following the disclosure that a dormitory prefect at Campbell College had abused a young boarder in the prep school some years before. The abuse had been made known to the school principal at the time. Following my own enquiries about safeguarding procedures, the Department of Education undertook an investigation. Its report catalogued a history of mismanagement in relation to the allegations and, as a result of a court case, the school was forced to pay out a large sum in compensation. I found working on these cases that involved so much suffering emotionally exhausting.

Other events, of a kind that should have been left behind us, continued to flare, such as the turmoil that erupted over access to Holy Cross Girls' Primary School. The school was situated near the Protestant Glenbryn estate in Upper Ardoyne and was literally a stone's throw away from the Catholic area of Ardoyne. The dispute started in June 2001 when a loyalist flag was put on to a lamppost outside the Catholic school. When a man got out of his car and tumbled the ladder of the flag erector, it started a fight that went on for months and went far beyond the two men initially involved. A loyalist blockade of the school ensued, with disastrous consequences for the 250 children there. Police blocked off the main access street in order to escort parents and children to and from school and to maintain their safety from the loyalist protesters who subjected them to an onslaught of stones and bricks. It made me think of my recent visit to Bosnia, where neighbour had turned on neighbour, despite having lived cheek by jowl for decades.

Two women activists from the area, one from either side of the community, could not work together because the dispute created so much friction between them. Neither the Executive, nor direct rule minister Jane Kennedy, who was in charge of security, could find a resolution. Some of the ideas they came up with – proposals to change the bend in the road or put a security gate across the route that would be unlocked when the children were going to or coming from school – were non-starters.

Although the dispute died down over the summer holidays, it reignited when the new term began. I watched the TV footage on 5 September in horror. A blast bomb had been thrown at a group of parents and children – the terror on their faces was unforgettable. David Ervine had been watching the same pictures and told Billy Hutchinson to go back in and help defuse the situation. Billy rang me and asked if I would come to a meeting in a local community centre with those involved on the Glenbryn side. It was Halloween and fireworks were exploding outside, making me think of gunfire. I said that their proposal that the girls should walk to school through the grounds of a nearby school for older boys wouldn't work. I told them that I didn't think that any parent would be happy with what they were proposing. And, in any case, the children had a right to walk the shortest route to school. They said they'd go away and think about it.

During the dispute, Father Aidan Troy played a heroic role. He had arrived a few months before as the parish priest and chaired the school's board of governors. He remained calm in the face of insults and catcalls as he walked to the school each day. The abuse went on for months and I was shocked at what I heard the day I walked alongside Aidan Troy. I had a little girl's hand in mine and I joked with her to try and shut out the toxic atmosphere. Anne Tanney, the school principal, was standing at the gate waiting to greet us. She too was heroic, standing firm and resolute in support of her children who were, as she said, the core of the school community. My two-hundred-yard walk up and back down the road again was memorable, and not in a good way. Police officers in riot gear lined the route to prevent missiles that included bottles of urine hitting us. Well-armed soldiers were lined up on the other side of the road. Mothers told me that their children were being prescribed anti-anxiety medication – the toll of this lengthy dispute could be seen on all their faces.

When a senior civil servant rang to ask why I was getting involved in a dispute in North Belfast, I asked her, 'What part of "women" in Women's Coalition do you not understand?' I was there to support the mothers who had asked me to come. The local women's group had organised the visit, and when I showed up, one of them said, 'Your solidarity is much appreciated.' We'd had the same response when local women said how glad they were to see us marching down the Shankill Road during the loyalist feud.

At the Assembly, decommissioning continued to dominate the agenda. Little attention was being paid to poor housing conditions in places like the Glenbryn housing estate. The persistent social disadvantage that working-class communities on both sides of the divide were experiencing was being ignored at a time when those kinds of issues should have been the priorities. The Coalition had succeeded in having a clause inserted into the Agreement, stating that young people from areas affected by the Troubles were to be supported by special community-based initiatives, but nothing concrete had come of it. Too many young men had come to regard paramilitary fighters as role models; too many young women were being cast as trophies on the arms of the macho men in gangs masquerading as paramilitaries. If we were meant to be building a post-conflict society, this had to change. I was in politics to work for transformation through education and training that would make a difference to young lives. The Coalition drafted a Private Member's Bill for a Commissioner for Children and Young People, and agreed to pass it over to the Executive – it became one of its first pieces of legislation.

On 11 September 2001, planes hit the World Trade Centre – it was morning in New York and afternoon with us, and I watched in horror the pictures of the twin towers collapsing. US Consul General Barbara Stephenson came to the Assembly to hear expressions of condolences from party leaders. After I had expressed my sorrow to the victims' families, I made the point that the US had not been called upon to deploy military force in Northern Ireland, as it had in some other conflicts in the world, but instead had sent teachers, trainers and sports players whose work with our young people had paid dividends through the years of the Troubles and it was our turn now to reciprocate.

The following month, when a group of us from the Assembly and the new policing board were in the US to meet the New York Police Department, we were taken to Ground Zero, where we held a short memorial and laid a wreath. As I stood there in silence, I thought of the devastation caused by the massive loss of innocent people's lives. Coming from Northern Ireland, I had experienced the depth of loss. I sensed that things would never be the same again.

In May 2002, the Queen and Prince Philip visited Parliament Buildings. Sinn Féin didn't attend, though this refusal to recognise royal visits was to change later. Protocol required unionists to line up on the right and nationalists (minus Sinn Féin) on the left, with the rest of us in between. Jane and I were among the first to meet Prince Philip. The clerk introduced the two of us by saying, 'This is the Women's Coalition.' He had to repeat it after Prince Philip asked, 'The Women's What?' When I explained who we were, he said, 'That sounds like a very sexist party.' I was so taken aback that I mumbled something about how that was ironic, given the rules on royal inheritance that were then in place. But I am not certain he heard me as he was swiftly ushered up the line by the clerk.

One of the last debates in which I spoke was just before the Assembly's dissolution. It was on maternity services, which had been one of my priorities from the time I had given birth to my sons at the Royal Victoria hospital. I had seen the inadequacy of the facilities in its maternity unit – the shortage of showers and the queues for the toilets – and I became determined to get the antiquated conditions upgraded. Consultants working in obstetrics and gynaecology had written to me to ask the Health Committee, of which I was a member, to initiate an inquiry to tackle the services in Belfast and beyond. The location for the new regional maternity unit was the cause of much controversy between the parties. Bairbre de Brún, as the minister of health, was accused of prioritising the Royal Victoria Hospital in her West Belfast constituency, and for making the decision without first going to the Executive for approval. The issue became a political football, and less focused on the needs of mothers and babies. In my last speech on the floor of the Assembly I said I sincerely hoped that I would be able to tell my constituents one day that there would be a purpose-built unit to meet the needs of women in Belfast.

I had two other priorities. One was improvements in cancer services, working with specialists in the field – Paddy Johnson and Seamus McAleer – who provided me with policy briefings. It gave me great satisfaction to see the cancer centre being built at the Belfast City Hospital. It was not only the best in Northern Ireland but also rated as one of the best in the world. I wasn't to know that one day I would have need of it myself.

My other priority was better mental health facilities. I set up and chaired an ad hoc committee of Assembly members and invited practitioners and groups working in the field to make suggestions about how best to support them in their work. One of those pieces of evidence was that more people were dying by suicide in Northern Ireland than anywhere else in the UK. It was an issue I cared deeply about, as my younger sister was suffering from depression and it was proving difficult to find the mental health services that she needed. I could also see the shortage of trauma services for victims of the conflict – we had fallen far behind in delivering what had been promised in the Good Friday Agreement.

On Friday 4 October 2002 I opened my office door at the Assembly to see thirty police officers in black boiler suits and baseball caps running past on their way to Sinn Féin's office at the bottom of the corridor. I could hear Bairbre de Brún remonstrating with them, demanding to see their warrant before they could enter their office. Gerry Kelly was telling them they were up to their dirty tricks for removing computer disks from his office. I overheard the police saying the warrant had been signed by P. O'Neill, justice of the peace, which made the whole thing sound even more farcical since this was the pseudonym the IRA used for its public statements.

It was yet another episode that rocked the already fragile peace process. An earlier event, when Castlereagh police station had been broken into and sensitive documents stolen on St Patrick's Day 2002, had also sent shock waves through the Assembly. Martin McGuinness denied that the IRA had anything to do with the burglary and put the blame on 'the securocrats'. With 'intelligence' from inside the police blaming the IRA, and the IRA making counter-claims, it sounded like something rotten was going on. No one knew for certain if 'Stormontgate' – which is what the

Coalition staff were now calling it – was related to the Castlereagh break-in, but because they came close together, and both involved intelligence gathering, both events generated more disaffection, making it seem as if the peace process was faltering.

Given all of this, and adding in the violence that year – there had been 96 shootings, 69 bombings and 86 explosive devices, with the finger of blame pointing mainly towards loyalist paramilitaries in the UDA – it was getting near impossible to believe that we had actually made a peace agreement. The continuing lack of engagement between the Ulster Unionist Party and Sinn Féin remained. David Trimble, at his party conference, remarked that Sinn Féin needed to be house-trained. Both sides believed the other was acting in bad faith. Once again, I thought that if we'd been working to the agreed principles of the Good Friday Agreement and committing to political means to resolve disputes, we'd be much further down the road.

In April 2002, General de Chastelain reported that he had overseen IRA weapons being 'put beyond use'. It was not enough for Trimble, who downplayed the report by stating that the IRA had not made known 'the precise nature of what they had decommissioned'. The public took to the streets for a Belfast rally against sectarianism, but Sinn Féin turned it into an argument about loyalist paramilitaries causing the most grief. The trade union Unison banner made more sense: 'Stop All The Killings'.

There were also some bad days in the office. I held an open day each Friday so that constituents could talk to me face to face. I sensed there was something not quite right with a very thin, ill-looking man who walked through the door. His eyes were starry and he couldn't sit still – so I asked my constituency worker, Maureen Murray, to come in from the corridor. As I stepped outside my door to call her, the man tried to rush past with my bag in his hand. I hadn't spied the screwdriver in his back pocket but the ever-vigilant Maureen had her wits about her, and as I tried to block his path, she shouted, 'Let him go.' He shoved me out of his way and made a run for it. He was caught later, stealing money from the nurses' locker room in the Mater Hospital. I took comfort from the fact that he had only got away with money and my cheque book, and not my address book – there were important contacts in it. I got the bag back later, minus the money.

And trouble came to my door again – this time at night and in my home. Joy riders, most probably in a teenage gang, burgled the downstairs rooms while we were sleeping. Having found the keys in the hall, they stole my car, which was later found abandoned on vacant ground in West Belfast. The area had been designated as off-limits to police officers, which meant that Brian and I had to go there to see for ourselves how much damage had been done. The irony was that I had been responding to complaints from residents' associations about the increase in car theft in south Belfast. I had reminded them that this was to be expected now that roadblocks and soldiers at checkpoints had been stood down. We were returning to post-conflict 'normalisation' but it still felt odd to say that this was 'everyday' crime and something we'd have to get used to.

I hadn't anticipated the spike in the figures for domestic violence as a result of victims being able to make reports to the police in a way they couldn't before. Most of the public thought it was because paramilitaries were at home more often following the ceasefires, or because of prisoner releases. I could show from my research that the spike was due to the more rigorous data as well as the police being able to focus more on domestic violence in the aftermath of the Agreement. While there was no comfort in seeing the figures go up, at least now we had a better sense of the true extent of the problem.

In September 2002, David Trimble was instructed by the Ulster Unionist Council that unless the IRA disarmed and disbanded he must pull out of the power-sharing Assembly by January 2003. Once again, republicans accused unionists of being rejectionists who feared change, but unionists responded by saying that Sinn Féin was crying crocodile tears and that the IRA's activities posed the more serious threat to peace. It was history in the unmaking.

In the plenary session on 4 October, I tried once again to highlight this point by saying:

Let us be honest: the Assembly and the Agreement have not failed. It is the political parties in the Assembly who have failed ... to trust each other and be worthy of trust. They have been secretive and aloof and have only looked after their own interests. If a peace agreement is about anything, it is about looking after the interests of others as well as your own. If the Assembly is plunged into limbo, either by resignations or suspension, we must be clear about what that means. The institutions will be disrupted, leaving a very dangerous political void. The only people who will clap their hands at that prospect are those who never wanted it to work and used very violent means to ensure that it did not.

Rescuing the Assembly was out of the question, and an election was called for May 2003.

The Women's Coalition geared up for this date and then, at great expense for a small party like ours, we had to stand the campaign down following the postponement. We started the election preparations again for November 2003, but the glow from the Good Friday Agreement had dissipated and I sensed that the run-up to the election would be a dispiriting experience. A group of stalwarts, led by Ann Hope and John McGettrick, came out to canvass once again, leafleting areas on freezing cold, dark nights. We were doubling up in the canvassing that November as Eileen Cairnduff was the Coalition's candidate for Castlereagh Council. We were glad of Paddy Hillyard's camper van for breaks during the long counting session in the King's Hall. The Coalition's candidates for the Assembly and the local councils stood together under the slogan 'Change the Face of Politics'. But the new-found faith in politics that I had experienced after the Agreement was now gone, and the writing was on the wall for the Women's Coalition. It was to be my fifth and last election – now I knew what it felt like to be eliminated. Of the smaller parties, only David Ervine in the PUP survived.

It was hard to listen to the ridicule that we received when we lost our seats. A cynic described Jane Morrice as 'toast'; Jane was her usual upbeat self and replied, 'I am like yeast and still rising.' I preferred the African proverb, 'Fall down seven times; stand up eight' and convinced myself that even if the Women's Coalition departed the political stage, we could still play an active role in civil society. After Patricia Wallace – our last serving elected representative – lost her council seat in 2006, we stood down the Coalition and held a party to celebrate our ten years of existence. We joked that we knew the time had come to decommission.

That November 2003, the fulcrum shifted and with it the balance of power. The DUP and Sinn Féin had overtaken the parties considered to be the moderates. The British government suspended the Assembly and direct rule returned for the next four years. Ian Paisley Snr did an about-turn when he formed a Coalition government in 2007 with his former nemesis, Martin McGuinness. By then Rev. Harold Good and Father Alec Reid had reported to the Independent International Commission on Decommissioning that weapons had not only been decommissioned but also put beyond use. The debacle was over, but the years in between had leached much of the confidence out of the peace process.

I discovered that there was indeed a life after politics and returned to my job as a university lecturer. I was looking forward to a quieter life, and relieved to be out of the eye of the media. I could get a night's sleep without someone ringing me at a late hour looking for something that could have waited until morning. And I didn't have to worry about what I was going to wear. I was back at the University of Ulster, in the Transitional Justice Institute, undertaking more research on domestic violence.

A window had opened in 1996 and for seven years I had found myself in an extraordinary situation – an accidental activist and politician. Looking back, I realised that the job was like no other. I was reminded of that after hearing Pete Buttigieg's comment, following his withdrawal from the 2020 US presidential race: 'Politics at its worst is ugly. But at its best, it can lift us up. It is not just policy-making. It is moral. It is soul craft.'

When I left the Assembly I remembered something I had said in 2002 on the floor of the chamber: 'This is not the end: this is the beginning of a new and difficult phase of the peace process. There is no question that, if we are political representatives and if politics is about the art of the possible, we must find a way out of this serious crisis.

I held on to my belief that one day we could make it work.

13

Human Rights For All

'If one member is afflicted with pain,
Other members uneasy will remain.'

Bani Adam, 'Sa'adi' (translation of thirteenth-century Persian poem)

The Women's Coalition had worked hard to get commitments on human rights and equality into the Good Friday Agreement. I believe that the lack of civil rights in Northern Ireland, and the response of the Unionist government to the peaceful demonstrations in the late sixties, laid the basis for the eruption of violent conflict that became known as 'the Troubles'. Since then, my engagement with the victims and survivors of the Troubles and my advocacy for them had reinforced my commitment to human rights and my desire to be involved in that work. Since 1993, I had been supporting the work of WAVE, the largest cross-community victims' organisation in Northern Ireland. That started when I met Myrtle Hamilton in the university canteen, and she asked me to get involved. Myrtle's husband, Tommy, had been murdered by the IRA on 26 November 1974 in his shop, close to their home. She had two young children at the time and was pregnant with her third, and I was inspired to join when she told me: 'I could have chosen to get bitter but this work has helped me to survive.' Adversity had come in different ways to each of the women I met at WAVE but they had become agents of change through the work they were doing together.

Over the years, I've been involved in a range of fundraising activities for WAVE. My favourite is the most recent, when I volunteered for a Strictly Come Dancing competition, and dressed up in bobby socks and a polka-dot skirt for 'Greased Lightning'. I looked like mutton dressed as lamb but the five other couples helped to take the ageing teenager look off me and my partner Alan McBride, better known as WAVE's spokesperson. Avila's daughter, Aoife, and her partner, a volunteer from Germany, won the prize for the best solo dancers but Alan and I got the prize for being the most popular. I was over the moon until I realised that we had to do a lap of honour – dancing our cha-cha-cha once again to 'Uptown Funk' by Bruno Mars. I stuck to walking the Belfast marathon after that, even if it was only the nine-mile part – it was a much easier way to raise funds.

Sandra Peake, the director of WAVE, introduced me to Families of the Disappeared in 1998. Their loved ones had been abducted, murdered and secretly buried – and they had been searching for them for as long as two or three decades. My involvement began when I launched an appeal for WAVE, asking members of the public to come forward with information using a confidential telephone helpline. But the campaign had an unfortunate outcome when a caller gave misleading information that led to gardens in West Belfast being dug up needlessly. For years, the Families of the Disappeared had been told not to ask questions or to seek information, but we hadn't realised the extent to which that intimidation had extended to the local communities or to relatives who were too afraid to speak out.

Kathleen, wife of Charlie Armstrong, and Mary, mother of Gerry Evans, felt that the only safe place to talk about the disappearances of these two men was at morning Mass in Crossmaglen. At one of the annual Palm Sunday Masses in Armagh Cathedral, the priest pointed to the cross hanging on the wall and made a prayerful plea for those responsible to allow the families to put down the cross they had been carrying for so long. I was moved to tears by the moral injury that had been caused.

A turning point came in 1998, when Mags McKinney, whose son Brian had been disappeared in 1978, went on a visit to the US. Mags became determined to find her son, having experienced cruelty at its worst. Not only had her son been disappeared but she had been sent Christmas cards supposedly from Brian, which she presumed were to make her believe that he was alive. She took the opportunity to ask President Clinton for assistance, and when he appointed Jim Lyons as

Economic Envoy to Northern Ireland, the president asked him to take an interest in her case. She referred to Clinton as 'my president' after that.

The Independent Commission for the Location of Victims' Remains followed in 1999, set up jointly by the British and Irish governments. That same year statements from the IRA and the Irish Republican Socialist Party (IRSP), a republican group aligned to the INLA, admitted responsibility for disappearing ten individuals. While that still left some of the Disappeared unaccounted for, the statements opened up a line of communication that allowed for a flow of information. Individuals were asked to come forward on the understanding that anything they passed on would be treated as privileged and used solely for the purposes of locating the remains. Assurances that anyone with information would not be incriminated were guaranteed in law. As an academic, I was familiar with the concept of transitional justice and this approach was seen to be in keeping with that approach. But the commission realised that opening up lines of information was not enough. Digs were being undertaken in the wrong places because people's memories weren't always accurate about the exact location of the bodies. When a search across the border for Charlie Armstrong's body was unsuccessful, I watched as his wife Kathleen lit candles at the site and prayed more accurate information would be found. It was a painful scene. Sandra Peake went to some very lonely places to lend support to the families during the digs, and occasionally I went with her.

When Mitchell Reiss became US Special Envoy to Northern Ireland in 2003, he advised the group about a specialist forensic team that had successfully recovered the bodies of Irish railroad workers buried in Pennsylvania. As a result, forensic specialists were recruited for this work in Ireland and, over time, more families were given the news by the Commission that the remains of their loved ones had been found. After Charlie Armstrong's body was found in County Monaghan on 29 July 2010, I was moved to hear his daughter Anna say, 'This is one of the happiest days of my life.' I watched as his grandson carried the coffin into the church – back when his grandfather disappeared in 1981, he was only a baby. Michael McConville was also a child in 1972, as were his nine siblings, when his mother Jean was murdered by the IRA and secretly buried on a beach in County Louth. I felt a sense of peace myself when each of the families talked about the peace they got from having a proper memorial and burial place for their loved ones.

What I liked about the families at WAVE was that they didn't sit and curse the darkness but focused their energies on keeping their issues in the public eye. Mark Kelly did exactly that – he had lost his legs in a loyalist bomb in 1976, when he was just eighteen – and continued to campaign for WAVE, quipping at times, 'I'll always stand up for victims and survivors, even on tin legs.' Each year, the Families of the Disappeared climbed the hill at Stormont for the All Souls' Day Silent Walk as a reminder to politicians that there were more bodies to be recovered. Anne Morgan, whose brother's body was eventually found in France, designed a 'forget me not' lapel button and we each wore one. In 2005, Lisa Dorrian disappeared and is believed to have been murdered. Those involved included people who may have been associated with a loyalist paramilitary group. The Dorrian family got support from WAVE's Disappeared group, while the Commission for the Location of Victims Remains provided the PSNI with expert guidance with its intensive searches.

Shortly after Good Friday 1998, I was asked to join with others involved in the peace negotiations to unveil a Reconciliation Sculpture at Parliament Buildings. We hadn't spent any time discussing the issue of reconciliation and I was glad of the opportunity to do so on that day. The sculpture was of a man and woman, arms wrapped around each other in grief. The stones we laid at its base came from war-torn countries and mine came from Beirut. It has often been remarked that the Northern Ireland conflict was relatively small in comparison to those of war-torn societies in the global south and other parts of the world. But if the numbers of dead and injured were to be applied to Great Britain, in proportion to its population, then the figures of 108,000 deaths and 1,118,000 injured gives us some idea of the scale. As I stood looking at the grief depicted in the sculpture, I was reminded of a story, believed to be of Cherokee origin, of a girl who is troubled by a recurring dream in which two wolves are having a vicious fight. Seeking an explanation, the girl goes to her grandfather, who is highly regarded for his wisdom. He explains what the dream represents: there are two forces within each of us struggling for supremacy, one embodying peace and the other war. The girl is distressed by his answer and asks her grandfather who wins. He replies, 'The one you feed.'

The sculpture made me realise how far we were from being reconciled – and at peace – with those who were different to us. The 'feeding' of war comes with fighting for supremacy over your neighbours; the food of peace is equality and the dignity of human rights for all.

In Northern Ireland, as in other conflicts, arguments and counter-arguments persisted over how to deal with the past. Getting to the truth about atrocities and human rights violations during the conflict had become a victim of political expediency. I found this hard to stomach, since the search for truth took a huge emotional toll on those involved. My friend Ann Hope described the impact of this when she had to talk about what happened to her on Bloody Sunday:

> You think that you are not affected by what happened during the Troubles but when I had to give evidence about Bloody Sunday to the Inquiry, it all came back to me and I wasn't able to speak. I sat in front of them, obviously traumatised, and they just sat there and looked at me. It was my solicitor who went and got me water and sat with me until I was able to carry on. It made me realise what people who had lost loved ones or were caught up in bombings were going through every day of their lives.

The day I met the Families of the Forgotten in Parliament Buildings in 2002, I thought about what Ann had said. These families had lost loved ones in the Dublin and Monaghan bombings of May 1974. They wanted the UK Government to expedite the supply of all relevant documentation to the Barron Inquiry, set up in 2000 to investigate the attacks in which thirty-three people had been killed and more than three hundred injured. Two babies, aged fifteen months and seven months, had lain unidentified because no one knew until the following day that their parents had also been killed. It was one of the worst things I ever heard. What made this even worse was the fact that the inquiry couldn't reach any conclusions in any of its reports – due to missing police files in the south and the north and to lack of disclosure from the British authorities.

In the Good Friday Agreement, all the parties had agreed 'to acknowledge and address the suffering of the victims of violence as a necessary element of reconciliation'. But in both the north and the south, victims and relatives had lost faith in the institutions, which, through government actions, omissions and denials, were preventing the full disclosure of events. I meet victims and survivors who still feel a huge sense of betrayal because of the delays and backlog of cases. Two decades later they are still waiting on a process to deal with the legacy of the past. All of the parties and victims' groups in Northern Ireland are critical of the UK government for proposing what they see as a de facto amnesty for those who committed crimes during the conflict. Building peace is messy. As I know, it involves uncomfortable compromises and requires a lot from those from whom so much has already been taken. I tried to drive home this point during the peace negotiations when I said at the table, 'We owe it to victims and survivors to care for them, but more than that, we need to show them that we care.'

In spite of my commitment to human rights and my passion for the work, I still had mixed feelings when I saw the advertisement in 2004 inviting applications for the post of chief commissioner to the Northern Ireland Human Rights Commission. I was enjoying being back at the University of Ulster and very happy to be out of the public eye. I wasn't living at such a frantic pace and had more time with my family. But I was drawn to the post. The Good Friday Agreement was in my mind – its promise of a 'new beginning' and the commitment we had all made 'to dedicate ourselves ... to the protection and vindication of the human rights of all.' I knew the job would be far from plain sailing but I could see that it was a way of delivering on what had been promised, and that was hugely important to me. Eventually, I argued myself into a position where I felt I couldn't not apply.

I had been following the progress of the Human Rights Commission, which had been established in March 1999 as a result of the Good Friday Agreement. The Agreement committed the UK government to incorporating the European Convention on Human Rights into domestic law, and that resulted in the Human Rights Act 1998. The legislation was designed to protect the most vulnerable and was especially important for a society like ours that was still recovering from conflict. If I got the Chief

Commissioner's job, I would be the second post-holder, following Brice Dickson. I would be heading up a team of nine other commissioners who, like me, would be appointed through an independent process. That was a core requirement of a UN-recognised human rights institution, which the one in Northern Ireland was. Uniquely in the world of national human rights institutions, and because of the mandate of the Good Friday Agreement, the human rights commissions in Northern Ireland and the Republic of Ireland, were required to work together on a range of cross-jurisdictional matters.

The application process started in 2004 and went on for four months – there was the paperwork on how I might meet the competencies and skills required for the post, followed by an interview and a presentation in front of a panel in London. More than ten months passed between the interview and the phone call from Secretary of State Peter Hain to confirm the appointment. I had given up on it, especially when I had had to ask the *News Letter* to print a retraction about a story it had published, informing its readers that I had got the job – they had agreed they were in the wrong. I finally took up the post in September 2005.

Lord Laird, an Ulster Unionist peer, was particularly opposed to my appointment. He had already stated that Northern Ireland did not need a Human Rights Commission and that it would be a waste of money to appoint another Chief Commissioner. He tabled parliamentary questions in the House of Lords about when and where my interview had taken place, who was on the interviewing panel and whether I had been contacted beforehand about the position before it was advertised. Laird followed up with snippets of information that had clearly been leaked to him by an anonymous source. I felt I was being scrutinised for no apparent reason, and it reminded me of how I had been made to feel in the Forum. The irony was that, following my appointment, the Northern Ireland Office passed his PQs to the Commission for me to answer. When I visited the House of Commons to give evidence to the Joint Committee of Human Rights, or to explain proposals for amendments to legislation, Laird treated my fellow commissioners and me with such disdain. It was as if our advice counted for nothing. As it turned out, he had to answer to parliament for a scandal in which he had been paid to place PQs. The House of Lords Standards Committee suspended him for four months.

I wasn't long in the post when, on 13 December 2005, Ian Paisley Snr used his parliamentary privilege in the House of Commons to say in reference to my appointment as Chief Commissioner: 'She is not fit ... she should not be there ... the sooner the government remove her from her position and replace her with a neutral person, the better it will be for everybody.' I was fortunate that David Ervine took to the airwaves to defend my reputation following several references to my religious background. I made the point on the UTV news that the use of sectarianism or sexism to undermine a person's integrity is the reason why so many people are reluctant to take up a public position. I had thought long and hard about my own decision and I was beginning to doubt if I had done the right thing in taking up this role.

In that same parliamentary debate, Paisley said he was against the Commission being given investigatory powers through Westminster legislation, while the SDLP's Eddie McGrady advocated that the powers should be granted to make the Commission more effective. The battle lines had been drawn. I continued to advocate for these powers to make the commission fit for purpose and to bring it more in line with the requirements of a UN-approved human rights institution. They were particularly important in a place like Northern Ireland that was making a transition out of conflict.

The negative attitude to human rights to which I became accustomed would usually surface, during investigations or a training session, along the lines of, 'It's all very well, this human rights guff, but if you ask me, the only human rights you need in the modern world are the right to private property and the secret ballot.' If I raised the issue about the right to life, back would come the response, 'Of course you need the right to life because without it, you couldn't vote, or own property.' Some would often claim that an institution to deal with human rights was only needed in the developing world. But I would unravel this argument by pointing out that the rights that the commission was charged with defending were intrinsic to the notion of humanity: the right to life, liberty and security of person; the right to a fair trial; protection from torture and inhuman and degrading treatment; freedom of thought, conscience, religion, speech and assembly; the right to marry; the right to free elections; the right to fair access to the country's education system; and, to top things off, the right not to be discriminated against. I asked the doubters which of these rights they wouldn't want, and that normally stopped the questions.

When I first took up my post, the US was detaining terror suspects in Afghanistan and Iraq, subjecting them to torture and renditioning them to Guantanamo Bay. Occasionally US aircraft used airports for transit through the UK and I wanted to ensure that the British government wasn't using the one in Northern Ireland. The Irish Human Rights Commission in Dublin requested the same assurances about Shannon airport, and we raised the issue in our Joint Committee meetings. Maurice Manning, chief commissioner in the south of Ireland, and I succeeded in getting both governments to provide assurances that any involvement of airports on this island in rendition would stop.

From time to time, the Commission took cases to court, either in its own name or intervening where there was a public interest. The cases we took, such as those raising the question of enforcing the right to life by effective investigative processes when life is taken, were instrumental in the court setting down the procedural requirements of an effective investigation under article 2 (right to life) of the European Convention on Human Rights. This applied to everyone killed, whether by the state or by armed groups.

I recalled what my sister Mary had said in 1996, following the inquest into the death of the young man who had driven into her car. The forensic investigation stated that his car had been 'substantially on the wrong side of the road'. Mary said she felt vindicated as the cause of the accident was now public knowledge, as was the fact she was not to blame. She knew that was the case but the burden had been lifted as there was no longer any doubt about what happened that night. During those long weeks in intensive care, she kept asking questions and I had told her that one day we would get to the truth. When that day finally came, part of her healing came from getting some of the truth, even if she didn't get all of it. Her experience helped me to empathise with victims and survivors in their search for the truth.

The need for investigations for victims and survivors was brought home to me when I met with the victims of the Omagh bombings. Following our meeting, I issued a joint press statement – with Maurice Manning from the Irish Commission in Dublin – calling for an inquiry and a recognition that the investigation would have to involve both jurisdictions. More than two decades later, the families are still waiting.

Also in my mind when I thought about this issue were the men murdered in the 1980s and early 1990s near Kilrea – in circumstances that prompted allegations of collusion – and how important it was for the state to be held accountable. But in a contested society such as ours, some politicians were quick to accuse the Commission of being anti-state when we raised matters like this. Cases that applied to British soldiers deployed in Northern Ireland were among the most contentious, and still are.

I had been at the negotiations at Weston Park in 2001 when the British and Irish governments agreed that a judge would be appointed to examine cases that involved allegations of collusion between the state and the paramilitaries, and to decide whether those claims merited a full inquiry. Even when it was decided that there was enough evidence to warrant an inquiry, such cases were contested by the government on the grounds of national security.

One such case was the murder of the lawyer, Pat Finucane. In 2008, Judge Cory – the Canadian judge who had been appointed following the decision at Weston Park – ruled that there should be a public inquiry in this case. Pat Finucane was murdered at home in February 1989. It took thirty years for the case to make its way through the courts in Northern Ireland and Europe. Prime Minister David Cameron's apology for 'shocking collusion' and the fact that the government had refused an inquiry added to the family's frustration. When the case finally reached the Supreme Court, the family submitted that no one in authority had been held accountable to any degree for 'facilitating and furthering the murder', or for perverting the course of justice, and that the authorities had never had to explain themselves in public. The Supreme Court ruled in their favour and after years of disappointment, the decision gave Geraldine Finucane some hope of getting justice for her husband. Since the judgement still hasn't been implemented the Committee of Ministers of the Council of Europe has decided to reopen its consideration of the steps taken by the UK government in response to the European Court of Human Rights decision in this case, to ensure the measures taken are adequate, sufficient and proceed in a timely manner. After thirty years, Geraldine is still waiting for that to happen.

Another case that I was involved in at the Commission and that is still not fully resolved is that of Denis Donaldson. I knew him as Sinn Féin's administrator at the Assembly – his office was down the corridor from mine – and he was one of three members arrested during the 'Stormontgate' episode back in 2002, though he had subsequently been released. Soon afterwards, Sinn Féin revealed that it believed he was involved with the state intelligence service. He went to stay in a remote cottage in Donegal, and it was there that he was murdered on 4 April 2006. I was in the Human Rights Commission when I heard the news on the radio. I was horrified.

I got to know Denis Donaldson's daughter and her husband when they came to the Commission to discuss the proposed inquest. I raised the issue with the Irish Commission, since it was a matter of cross-jurisdictional interest, and on 5 May 2011, both commissions issued a joint statement in which Maurice Manning – on behalf of the Irish Commission – stated: 'We are concerned that five years after Mr Donaldson's murder this inquest has still not taken place. Additionally, we have heard from the family their concerns about the lack of disclosure and information from the coroner and the Gardaí. Human rights law requires that the family in these types of cases must be involved in the investigative proceedings to safeguard their legitimate interests.' I added to that: 'Article 2 of the European Convention on Human Rights places a duty on the state to protect life and also to investigate death. One of the questions that should be addressed at inquest is what, if anything, did the PSNI and/or the Gardaí know of a risk to Mr Donaldson's life and, if they knew there was a risk, what measures did they take to protect him.'

Denis's case showed the limitations of state authorities' compliance with the European Convention on Human Rights in both jurisdictions. As part of the Good Friday Agreement, the Irish government had incorporated the convention into domestic law. The Agreement had also envisaged a charter of rights for the island of Ireland. During my time at the commission, the Joint Committee of the two Commissions drafted the charter and presented it to the Speakers in both legislative bodies in 2009. It has been gathering dust on their shelves ever since. The charter was meant to reflect and endorse 'agreed measures for the protection of the fundamental rights of everyone living in the island of

Ireland'. But the levelling up had not happened in Denis's case, so I asked both governments how they intended to address this issue. The inquest into the circumstances surrounding Denis's death has been postponed more than twenty times. The family's complaint about the role of the police and intelligence agencies has now passed through the hands of four consecutive police ombudsmen. With no remedy in place, the family has been left in limbo.

Since our conflict had originated from exclusion in one form or another – political, social, cultural or economic – I felt it was important to adopt a human rights lens to help rebuild civic trust. It needed to be built along horizontal lines, between groups on each side of the divide, as well as vertically between the state and its institutions. For me, the understanding that one group was more likely to live in safety if the rights of the other group were protected was the only way forward. But that was easier said than done.

The Irish language was another issue from the Agreement that required a rights-based resolution. The proposals in the Agreement stated that the Irish language should receive formal recognition and support. I wrote to the secretary of state in October 2007 to enquire how he intended to bring these proposals forward, since nothing much had been done since 1998. At that time, any official document from the DUP carried the strapline 'Getting it Right'. Ian Paisley Jnr's response to my public stance certainly didn't match that motto when he publicly remarked that 'the Human Rights Commissioner should quit meddling in devolved matters'. The row over the Irish language has been like a see-saw, with the UK government making a commitment to legislate at St Andrews in October 2006 and then pushing it back to the Assembly, only for the DUP to reject an Irish Language Act and the UK government having to take that on. The toing and froing doesn't augur well for the future.

I found myself having to defend the Commission after we had intervened in the Holy Cross School case at the House of Lords. The loyalist protest that prevented the children from getting to school and in which I had tried to mediate, had run for months from 2001 to 2002, and the parents argued that the police should have done more to protect the children's right to education. The case had gone through the courts of Northern Ireland and was eventually decided at the House of Lords in 2008, where the Commission's challenge on a point of law was successful but the parents' case was dismissed. Such was the toxicity at the time that even when the Commission was successful in court, some unionist politicians accused us of wasting public money. Taking a position on something might not be popular, and might even be disagreeable to one side or the other, but upholding human rights standards was what I was there to do.

The Commission also had the powers to undertake investigations into places of detention such as prisons or institutions – all public authorities had a duty to comply with the Human Rights Act. A significant part of my job was dedicated to carrying out investigations into the conditions for men and women in prison at Maghaberry, Magilligan and Hydebank. When a person goes through a prison gate, the social contract between a government and its citizens doesn't dissolve but becomes even more important because a prisoner is within the physical control of the state. However, that contract tends to be portrayed by conservative-minded politicians as a villains' charter, as if human rights were a gift rather than a duty of the state. So work on prisons raised much controversy.

Many of the women I met in prison should not have been in custody – they were there either because they were too poor to pay fines or because they were suffering from mental ill health and were a danger to themselves and others. There were women who had defaulted on fines imposed for not paying their television licences. I brought pressure for a change in the law, providing evidence of the toll imprisonment took on families, and of how much imprisonment cost the state. Later, when I became involved in overseeing prison reforms, I advocated for alternatives – such as community orders – to be put in place, but the wheels of the criminal justice system turn slowly and it took several more years before there was any real progress.

During the Commission visits to prisons, I met women with severe personality disorders who said they felt safer inside the prison than outside, which was an indictment of our mental health system. Research in which I was involved pointed to the fact that many women in prison have experienced violent and sexual abuse from partners. Probation officers have also raised this issue in their reports to the court. Non-UK-national women who had overstayed their visas were also being detained in prison because there was nowhere more appropriate for them to go. That was another indictment of the immigration system; it has since been changed. Since Northern Ireland had no other facility to house women who had been trafficked, they were also being held in prison or sent to Dungavel Immigration Removal Centre in Scotland. Northern Ireland didn't have such a facility so I went there to assess the conditions and met women who spoke of their fear that their families would be targeted if they named who had trafficked them into the UK. The advocacy work that proposed trafficked women should be accommodated in places of safety took more time, though Women's Aid is now able to provide the help they needed.

One of my very first cases turned out to be a contentious one. A man from Sierra Leone had been convicted of rape, had served his sentence in Northern Ireland and was waiting to be deported. The man should have had a psychiatric assessment before his removal to Sierra Leone but the prison ombudsman's office got in touch to say that it wasn't going to be done as officers had been instructed to get him out of the prison as quickly as possible, put him on a plane and hand him over to Sierra Leone to deal with him.

I wanted to ensure that safeguarding measures would be in place in Sierra Leone – as it was, the rights of women and girls there would be jeopardised given the risk of repeat offending from this man. The Commission took the case to court, asking that an emergency assessment be undertaken before the man left the country and that this assessment accompany his deportation from Northern Ireland. When the prison service informed the Commission's lawyer that the man would not speak to a woman, it made me even more concerned. But before the case got to court, a newspaper ran with a story about how I, in my role a the new chief commissioner, wanted to keep a foreign rapist in a Northern Ireland prison instead of sending him back to where he came from.

A BBC producer then asked if I would participate in *The Nolan Show* in response to concerns raised by the Rape Crisis Centre. Its director, Eileen Calder, and I knew each other, and on the show we discussed what needed to happen in a calm and rational manner, which wasn't what Stephen Nolan was expecting. I explained that human rights were universal, and, when applied to this man, they meant that the British government had a responsibility to ensure that mechanisms were in place for an assessment that could be sent ahead to Sierra Leone before his return. The prison service as well as the politicians who had objected to the assessment needed to appreciate that human rights are also in place to prevent a reoccurrence of abuse, whether at home or abroad. The parties who had been opposed to my appointment remained opposed to much of my work as Commissioner, so every time there was a controversy, they weighed in. None of it was helped by continual leaks about the work of the Commission or by the source of the leaks being well protected.

The most contentious visit I undertook was on 23 March 2009 to the serious crime suite at Antrim, where twelve suspects were being held under the Counter-Terrorism Act. Two members of the Commission staff accompanied me in order to make an assessment of the facilities where the detainees were being held. By agreement with the PSNI chief constable, Hugh Orde, we were able to undertake the visit. His willingness to be subject to the Commission's scrutiny – he could have demanded a period of notice but allowed us immediate access – indicated how far human-rights-based policing had come in a relatively short period of time following the Patten reforms.

It was my job to scrutinise the operation of the counter-terrorism legislation recently introduced at Westminster. The new regulations permitted twenty-eight-day detention without charge – which made it one of the longest periods of internment in Europe – and was a retrogressive step. I had made a previous visit to the Antrim custody suite and was aware that there was no outdoor space, which meant that it didn't meet the standards expected for twenty-eight-day detention. The station only ever held individuals for short detention periods and, unlike the detention centres in England, it was not a purpose-built facility. That was the conclusion I was going to put in my report to the Policing Board, but before I had even exited the building, I was told that press reporters were waiting outside to speak to me.

Information had been leaked by an officer inside the station. I hadn't expected this, but I also knew that in times of crisis, a national human rights institution such as ours would be tested and that's what I said that night to the reporters and again the following morning when Ian Paisley Jnr called *The Nolan Show* to complain that I had been 'looking after terrorists'. I was able to state that although changes to the facility would be needed, the public could be reassured that the police investigation was in keeping with human rights standards. The call from Paisley Jnr that the Commission should keep its nose out of the police's business and let them get on with their work didn't hold up since oversight of the police had become fairly routine from 2001 onwards due to the Patten reforms.

The press reported at the time that Daphne Trimble – a recently appointed commissioner – had issued a press statement opposing the visit to Antrim police station. It was clear to me that human rights would be meaningless if those charged with their oversight were to be thwarted in that task. At that time, the Commission met to discuss how we were all responsible for protecting the Commission's independence from undue interference – otherwise we wouldn't be able to do our work.

I had succeeded in getting the Northern Ireland Commission recognised as an A status human rights institution by the UN International Coordination Committee. We were the first in the UK to be awarded this accreditation – before Scotland and GB – and I was proud of this achievement. This status could be challenged if the Commission was perceived to be allowing political parties to dictate what it should be doing. The Commission was in place to uphold everyone's rights, whether in or out of prison.

One of the most difficult cases that I encountered as a human rights commissioner was the dissident republican prisoners' dirty protest in the separated unit for paramilitaries at Maghaberry prison in 2011. The dispute centred on the right to 'free association' and the prisoners' opposition to 'strip-searching' – more generally known as full-body searches – and an issue with which I was familiar from decades before. The prison service used the searches to check that drugs or weapons were not being smuggled into the prison, but the prisoners argued that they were being overused and that they were unnecessary and they refused to comply with the searches. As a result, the republican prisoners were forcibly stripped and searched. The protective clothing that I wore to assess the conditions made me look like a Ninja Turtle. The stink was overwhelming, but the cleaning up was rigorous – costing £10,000 per week. The separated unit – Roe House for republicans and Bush House for loyalists – was a difficult place to work, with officers instructed not to get 'too close' to the prisoners because of death threats. The dissident republican prisoners were opposed to the prison regime and refused to cooperate with the system, and the situation remains the same today.

In 2013, two years after I had left the Commission, Minister of Justice David Ford asked me to join Patricia Gordon and Duncan McCausland to monitor the implementation of the recommendations of a review into the prison system. I was particularly keen to see if an alternative could be found to full-body searching. I remembered what it had felt like to be asked to remove my clothing in the departure terminal at Leeds Bradford Airport in the early 1990s. I was involved in a series of workshops with other academics on 'gender-specific abuse' over a number of weekends and the irony was not lost on me that I was the subject of a body search – involving a female security officer searching beneath my clothing in a separate cubicle at the airport. If I felt humiliated by that, I could only think how much worse it must be for women in prison who would feel more disempowered and less able to object.

One of the alternatives I was asked to check as a replacement for body searching was the BOSS chair – aka Bodily Orifices Security Scanner. I volunteered to sit in it – to see how it worked – and I was able to say that, despite its name, it didn't contravene a person's dignity. But it wasn't considered to be an option since it could only detect weapons and not drugs. At last, a solution was found for the women's prison – the half-door cubicle. Women could hand over their garments from behind the half-door in a sequence of steps. Any body searches after that would be based on risk assessments. All this proved that the guidelines for the protection of individuals inside an institution benefited from a human rights framework.

Reforms to the prison system came later than the reforms to the RUC and benefited from the lessons of that process. Policing reforms had been part of the architecture of the Good Friday Agreement, so I was glad to see the final draft of the Agreement state: 'The Commission [on policing] will be broadly representative with expert and international representation among its membership'. Getting to a situation of shared values and shared ideals was never going to be easy, but getting proposals on police reform agreed was going to be a very tall order. Chris Patten, a former Conservative MP, headed up the commission on policing and decided to undertake a series of public consultations before the commission published its report in 1999. As I crossed the university quad with Avila on my way home after the public consultation at Queen's, two young men spat directly into our faces. Neither of us had made a contribution at the meeting but I wondered if they recognised us as being from the Women's Coalition and opposed our public stance in support of policing reforms. We were amazed at how young they were.

Barbara McCabe and I had submitted evidence to the Commission the previous year, in 1998, in which we had supported affirmative action when it came to police recruitment in order to redress the imbalance of religion and gender. We were well aware that the idea wasn't a popular one. Maurice Hayes, one of the independent commissioners, told me afterwards that because the commission was expecting to be criticised for recommending a 50/50 quota for Catholic/Protestant recruits, they wouldn't be going beyond that to recommend a quota for women. He understood, but many others didn't, that affirmative action was in keeping with the international human rights standards – and could be permitted in order to address imbalances resulting from exclusion or discrimination against members of a minority group. I thought it was a missed opportunity not to include a gender quota – it reminded me of the time in the mid-1970s when we had to fight to have the Sex Discrimination Act extended to Northern Ireland because the government's singular focus of attention was on religion.

When the policing report was published in September 1999, it followed the terms of reference as set out in the Agreement: that the service had to be effective and efficient, fair and impartial, free from partisan political control, accountable and representative and conform to human rights norms. But Ian Paisley Snr objected to its findings, telling the press, 'It is an unconstitutional attack upon the democratic rights of the Ulster people,' while others in his party claimed it would be 'the death-knell of the police'. As I was preparing to speak to the press about the policing recommendations in the Great Hall in Parliament Buildings, I overheard David Trimble tell reporters that he had been let down by the British government who had guaranteed that the RUC would remain intact. But the Patten Report wasn't the British government's report; it was the outcome of the deliberations of eight independent international experts. Following the reforms in 2001, the newly established Policing Board commissioned Keir Starmer QC and barrister Jane Gordon to produce its annual human rights reports. When we linked that work to what the Human Rights Commission had been doing, I could see how a human rights framework on policing in Northern Ireland would stand the peace process in good stead.

To mark the tenth anniversary of the PSNI, in 2011, I was invited to speak at a public event. I said that I was glad to see that the term police force had been changed. I noted that the term 'police service' – which the Patten police reforms had made part of their new title – said much more about what was expected in terms of policing with the community, and quoted the clause in the Agreement that stated that 'the arrangements ... should be unambiguously accepted and actively supported by the entire community'. I knew we had some way to go in building confidence in policing but I also knew that there was nowhere in the world where the police are unambiguously accepted and supported by the entire community.

The work I am most proud of during my time at the Commission is drafting the advice on a Bill of Rights for Northern Ireland. The mandate for that work came from the Good Friday Agreement, with its proposal that the Commission examine the particular circumstances in Northern Ireland and take account of international instruments and experience in scoping out the advice. In the Commission's consultations, we discovered disagreement between the Unionist parties over rights. Unionist parties claimed that the inclusion of any social and economic rights would undermine the government's policy decisions and couldn't be properly decided by a court; others, like the PUP, wanted those rights included. Loyalists felt they had been discriminated against on the basis of their class by aristocratic, so called 'Big House' unionists and had been advocating for the inclusion of these rights since 1975.

I had drafted the preamble to the advice on the Bill of Rights and included the words: 'The Bill of Rights must value the role of women in public and political life and their involvement in advancing peace and security.' The Agreement had made such a commitment and I added these words of the UN Security Council resolution on Women, Peace and Security. It was key to making the right of women to full and equal political participation more of a guarantee than an aspiration.

To help with this discussion, I invited Albie Sachs – a judge in South Africa's constitutional court – to explain how the Bill of Rights in South Africa had been used to progress laws and policies while ensuring no regression on issues such as health and social welfare. But his arguments fell on deaf ears. Unionist parties remained opposed and at times I felt I was going around in circles.

I set a deadline of 10 December 2008 for delivery of the report, to coincide with the sixtieth anniversary of the Universal Declaration of Human Rights. When we voted on the final advice that December, I stood alongside Tom Duncan, Colin Harvey, Alan Henry, Ann Hope, Colum Larkin, Eamonn O'Neill and Geraldine Rice to show that we had cross-community consensus for the bill. Daphne Trimble, who was connected to the Conservative Party, and the DUP's Jonathan Bell, rejected the advice. Daphne insisted that she would write a minority report but the Commission didn't receive a copy before we finished the advice.

As chief commissioner, I was to present the report of the final advice to the secretary of state and that meant following the protocol that it would not be made public until the handover on 10 December. Daphne Trimble organised her own press conference at the Ulster Unionist Party's offices at Stormont the day before on 9 December. The press conference ran contrary to the Commission's mandate to provide the secretary of state with the report first, and prior to it being made public. I made my views clear to her.

This is what led to Ian Knox's cartoon in the *Irish News* on 11 December, in which he depicted the opposition from Daphne Trimble and Jonathan Bell. In it, I was standing at a sweet counter telling them that it wasn't a pick-and-mix. It summed up my belief: it wasn't acceptable to say 'these rights are mine and those ones are for you'.

I handed over the advice on a Bill of Rights to Minister Paul Goggins – standing in for Secretary of State Shaun Woodward – at a presentation ceremony in the same room in which the Agreement had been signed. It was with enormous pride that I repeated what I had said on Good Friday: human rights are for all. The parties in the Assembly are now around the table again – addressing the issue of a Bill of Rights twelve years after it was sent to Downing Street.

The world has changed since I handed over the advice in 2008 – with the pandemic there is a much greater understanding of people's rights in terms of health and livelihoods. The principle – human rights for all – literally became a matter of life and death, so that no distinction should be made between rich and poor in terms of vaccination. Brexit has also changed the goalposts, given that the Good Friday Agreement made it clear that Northern Ireland citizens had the right to be British or Irish or both. However those rights have yet to be enshrined in law. The delicate balance of East–West, North–South relationships that are at the heart of the Good Friday Agreements have been upset, making an already difficult issue even more of a problem.

I left the Commission in 2011, a year before my term ended. I could see that the Conservative government had no appetite for introducing a Bill of Rights for Northern Ireland. David Cameron had already written a letter to me in 2009, when he was leader of the opposition, stating that a future British Bill of Rights would suffice for Northern Ireland. When he became prime minister in 2010, the Conservatives instigated a review of the Human Rights Act. No report has been produced but the threat remains that human rights will be devalued. When I stood down, I explained to the public that I would continue to defend human rights and equality, and that the government had to be held to account to ensure there would be no regression on protections for the most vulnerable.

The years at the start of the new century were tumultuous both professionally and personally for me. From 2007 to 2014, I faced some of the most difficult times in my life – dealing with the deaths of family and friends and my own diagnosis of cancer.

It was a difficult start to 2007 when I heard the news on 8 January that David Ervine had died. His son rang to tell me as I was getting out of my car, and I was so distraught that I forgot to put on the handbrake. My neighbour then came to the door to tell me that my car had rolled into his.

David and I had become firm friends during the peace process and our friendship only grew stronger as we met crisis after crisis together during the turbulent years after the Agreement. Despite numerous death threats, it wasn't a gunshot that killed David – but it might as well have been. At the age of fifty-three, he died from a heart attack caused by the stress of trying to make the peace process work. On the day of the funeral, Gerry Adams hugged David's widow, Jeanette, on the steps of Rev. Gary Mason's East Belfast Mission. His greeting was welcomed by members of the UVF and UDA who had lined up outside the church. Inside were Tim Phillips from Beyond Conflict in Boston and Tom Moran from New York, along with David's pal who had come all the way from Australia to offer condolences on behalf of its indigenous community. As I paid tribute to my friend from the pulpit, I could see Chief Constable Hugh Orde, Secretary of State Peter Hain, former Taoiseach Albert Reynolds and the DUP's Peter Robinson. People from across Ireland had gathered together – this was the kind of reciprocity that was needed. Gary Mason was there on 27 June 2009 when the UVF and RHC announced their decommissioning of weapons. David would have been so pleased to see what he had been working for finally come to fruition.

My parents passed away within weeks of one another, in the same year that David died. My father was ninety-four years old and my mother was ninety-three. After my father died, my mother told us that her journey was now complete, her work on earth was settled and it was her time to go. It was poignant to hear her say that she was as happy as she could be. She gave me a pen that had belonged to my father and asked me to do a good job with it. The following day, as I held on to her hand, I knew the time had come to let her spirit go free. I spoke at both funerals and it was an honour to pay tribute to them. We were lucky to have had them both for so long, but it only made it harder to let them go.

I had no idea during my time at the Human Rights Commission that when I investigated why the cancer drug, Herceptin, had not been made available in Northern Ireland, that the day would come when I would be in need of it myself. In 2006, I challenged the minister of health, Michael McGimpsey, about putting women's lives at risk because of the postcode lottery – patients in England were prescribed Herceptin through the NHS but there was no such access in Northern Ireland. The Department of Health agreed with the Commission's stance – that its lack of availability was putting women's lives at risk – and agreed to fund it in Northern Ireland.

Years later, in 2013, I came to see how health and human rights worked in practice when I was diagnosed with breast cancer. It still came as a shock, even though I felt something was wrong. The questions came pouring out, and oncologist Seamus McAleer answered them all one by one. How far had it spread? What were the survival rates? What did the treatment involve? I had to find the tigers from inside my soul to cope with the long process of three operations, six months of chemotherapy and five weeks of radiotherapy. The wigs were far in advance of the one Mo Mowlam had had to wear, more stylish but not more comfortable. My sister Mary had also been on the cancer journey so I had some idea of what was coming, but the learning curve was still a very steep one.

I experienced every part of the NHS, from emergency care to acute care, hospital care and community care – and the care was beyond compare. I saw the skills of the paramedics who rushed me to casualty on a busy Saturday night when my heart was taking a pounding as the white blood cells were collapsing. The medics and nurses in their specialist fields literally saved my life. I wrote an article for the *Belfast Telegraph* for breast cancer month to raise awareness and in praise of the NHS. It was the little touches that made the difference: the tea and toast, the smiles, the kind words of reassurance at the lowest points. I remained in isolation because of the risk of infection and for six months I couldn't go to work at the university. I was thankful I could still concentrate on my writing from my bed at home.

Brian, the boys and Mary, along with my good friends, saw me through those lonely months. I had to get used to role reversal – I was the vulnerable one and Rowen, now in his mid-twenties, looked out for me. If every cloud has a silver lining, my son was it. I would have the odd wobble but I'd soon get over it, and remember that life was for living.

When yet another lump turned out to be scarring from the surgery I did a little jig out of the cancer unit. I really was the cat with nine lives during those seven years, surviving clots on both lungs at the end of a long plane journey. I was grounded again – but as with the cancer, once I was back on my feet life went on as normal. The downside was the family history of cancer – my mother, my sister and my brothers. The good part is that we all survived, thanks to the NHS.

The right to an adequate standard of health had been there for me but it wasn't there for my younger sister Noeleen, who took her own life in 2017. I had seen the trail of devastation caused by suicide, but I never thought it would come to my door. During my time in the Assembly, I had chaired the ad hoc committee on mental health to obtain better services for vulnerable individuals. Down the line, I'd discover that Noeleen was one of those vulnerable people.

Her death left Mary and me with many questions. She had worked as a theatre nurse in the Royal Victoria Hospital in Belfast, so it was hard to understand how such an exceptional and caring person had found it so difficult to cope with some of her own challenges.

As a young girl, she was carefree and content, and a gentle soul. Being the youngest, she was 'the special one' – our father's little pigeon, our mother's precious child, Mary's little angel and my darling younger sister. When she came home from her work, our mother saw her as 'a ray of sunshine' because she would take time to sit and listen to her. After she got married, she went to live in Athlone, so we naturally saw a bit less of her, but the three of us remained very close, and took our breaks together two or three times a year.

Noeleen first approached her doctor in the early 2000s to seek help for panic attacks. As she passed through the system, doctors continued to prescribe medication. The dosages increased and she became more reliant on the prescriptions – that became the rock on which she perished. It is well known that during the Troubles in Northern Ireland high doses of benzodiazepine were prescribed to individuals suffering from anxiety. Like so many others, Noeleen felt that there had to be a magic pill that would make her feel well again, especially when she was given assurances that the answer lay in medication. Each consultant gave a different diagnosis – adjustment disorder, attachment disorder, borderline personality disorder – and each was accompanied by a different prescription. The medication made her increasingly drowsy and catatonic, a far cry from the witty, engaged and caring person she really was. When we asked about referrals for talking therapies, we only heard about long waiting lists, with the result that she never received the one-to-one counselling that might have made a difference.

Over time, Noeleen's own resilience and ability to cope disappeared, and it became harder for her to make good decisions. She gave up her work as a nurse and we watched helplessly as she experienced memory loss, irritability and palpitations, and slept only a few hours at night. When funding cuts were introduced in the health service, Noeleen's medication was removed with no back-up support or plan to monitor the withdrawal symptoms, or the anxiety that followed. She felt as though no one was listening to her.

When she didn't improve, she volunteered on occasion to be admitted as an inpatient to hospital. When that happened, it reminded me of the committal process I had seen in places of detention: possessions were checked and an identification bracelet was clasped on the patient's wrist without any explanation. There were empathetic and compassionate care workers – Noeleen had been one of them herself – but she didn't see enough of them. She described herself as 'a china doll, broken in millions of pieces'.

She finally got to see a consultant whom she felt could have provided her with the care she needed, and gave her hope of recovery for the first time. But her request to stay as his patient was ignored and she never got to see him again. She was informed that she was a on a waiting list, but telling a person in crisis about waiting lists is meaningless. Noeleen felt she had been classed as a 'no hoper'.

She came to live with Mary in the last year of her life. Mary and I both tried to advocate on her behalf, but it was the most disempowering experience of our lives. During a hospital admission in that last year, we watched as our sister's life was wasting away. In one hospital we were told to stop spoiling her when we asked if we could supply a mattress cover to make her more comfortable. By then, she weighed only seven stone.

Noeleen called us after that visit and cried as she described how she'd been asked to repeat what she'd been talking about with us. When Mary asked her if she wanted to come home, she replied that she did, as she felt increasingly anxious on the ward.

Mary rang the hospital to say that we were coming back to take her home but the telephone conversation that ensued left us feeling very concerned – if we were being demeaned in this way, how much worse must it be for our very vulnerable sister? We were advised the following day that Noeleen should not leave, even though she had been a voluntary admission. We lived to regret our decision as after that Noeleen felt we had let her down when she needed us most.

She was allowed to come home two days later and was promised that the crisis team would come out to see her, but when she enquired about the visit, she was told that they were having a meeting about her that day and would not be able to come. The following day, Noeleen ended her life by drowning. The last words I said to her were ones that I now regret, telling her she needed to help herself. I realise now that she had heard that so often from others, she didn't need to hear it from me. I never saw her again. She had given up hope and having struggled to find peace, she found it in the only way she could. As I said at her funeral, I hope that she has it now.

It is those of us who were closest to Noeleen who struggle to find some peace now. We had been left to navigate our way through the system, going from A to Z, and back again. From time to time, Mary and I look on the failures in the system, in terms of mental health, but that only makes us angry. If we couldn't find the help we needed, then who can? I had been the patron of CAUSE, a mental health charity, and had seen how volunteers had struggled to find more resources. But, as Mary and I discovered, the most important resource of all – which costs nothing – is the commitment to listen to the patient and their carers with respect and dignity.

14

From the Local to the Global: Sharing the Learning

'Change the name and the story is told about you.'

Horace

My term as chief commissioner at the Human Rights Commission ended in 2011 and I returned to my job at Ulster University. In 2014, I decided to retire and became involved with Trócaire, an Irish overseas development organisation that had invited me to join its board. I also began working with Interpeace, an international peacebuilding NGO, serving on its board for four years and then doing four more as its chairperson. Peacebuilding and development work had always been important to me, and I now had time to get more actively involved.

I knew from my visit to South Africa with the other political parties, in the run up to the Good Friday Agreement, and from visiting Bosnia, that we had much to learn from other experiences of conflict and peacebuilding. As part of my work with Interpeace and Trócaire, I would visit countries throughout Africa to see at first hand how they were resolving their conflicts. In return, I wanted to offer them my experiences of our own successes and wrong turns, in the hope that it would be useful for both parties.

One mistake we had made as political parties in Northern Ireland was not having a process for the implementation of the Good Friday Agreement, including a timetable and targets for the commitments in it. Nine out of ten peace agreements collapse within ten years due to faltering implementation, and we were in danger of doing the same, with ongoing disagreements over the interpretation of what had been agreed. The lesson I learned was 'don't look at where you fell but at where you slipped', that it is just as important to look at what lay behind the issue as the issue itself.

Shortly after the Good Friday Agreement, the Women's Coalition had proposed that the parties should form an implementation committee, but the larger parties were by then in government and didn't believe it was needed. Consequently, aspects of the Agreement remained unaddressed and important issues were either ignored or disputed: the needs of victims and survivors, a Bill of Rights, a Civic Forum, integrated education, measures to tackle social and economic problems and the representation of women.

We should have been asking different questions as parties to the Agreement, such as how conflicts could be aired between the different political/religious communities without these resulting in violence and how an agreed interpretation could be achieved in the new political dispensation. It would have required us to rethink the implementation process in a more cohesive way, but that wasn't a priority for party political opponents and we paid a heavy price as a result.

There were clashes of interpretation over whether the union between Northern Ireland and Great Britain had been settled or whether this would be left to a future referendum to decide. The new political dispensation required the consent of the majority of the people in Northern Ireland and that consent could change in the future. While this had settled the question for nationalists, it had simultaneously made unionists more unsettled. I started to focus on how we might achieve a more settled Northern Ireland, keeping in mind John Hewitt's words in 'An Irishman in Coventry':

This is our fate: eight hundred years' disaster,
crazily tangled as the Book of Kells ...
Yet like Lir's children, banished to the waters,
our hearts still listen for the landward bells.

We still had to deal with the deeply held sectarian divisions in Northern Ireland, most starkly mapped by 'peace walls', although the less visible barriers were also equally divisive. I was reminded of this in Iraq where the Sunnis and the Shiites have also constructed Belfast-style 'peace' walls to protect themselves from neighbours they previously lived alongside happily. The use of concrete and steel to divide or protect people – the narrative varies – was also evident when I took my son Rowen to Jerusalem. As we stood at the city's walls, I explained to him that Christian Crusaders and the followers of Mohammed had both stood in the same spot but that the new brutalist wall that we could see being built was intended to separate Israelis from Palestinians.

On a street in Jerusalem, we observed a soldier, with his wife and children by the hand and a Kalashnikov slung over his shoulder. It was the normalisation of conflict in the very land where the greatest commandment had been written: 'Love thy neighbour as thyself.' This attachment to guns was also to be seen in the Occupied Territories. I experienced that at uncomfortably close hand when I acted as a monitor for the 2005 presidential elections and was forced to dive for cover when live bullets were fired into the air just as the polling stations were closing. The question for me was the same in Northern Ireland: how do we take the gun, that has been used by both traditions for centuries, out of politics?

I have visited the Middle East on a number of occasions, each time gaining greater insight into aspects of peacebuilding. I first went there in 2000 with David Trimble and David Ervine at the invitation of Tim Phillips from the Project for Justice in Times of Transition. David Trimble was to join us in Ramallah to speak about the Agreement, but first he wanted to spend some time with Israeli politicians. This meant that David Ervine and I were left to meet President Arafat, with Palestinian chief negotiator Saeb Erakat and Palestinian National Authority Foreign Minister Nabil Shaath sitting alongside him. They all listened as David Ervine and I spoke about the smiles of the children, in spite of the fact that they were living in harsh conditions in a refugee camp. President Arafat's response to David was unforgettable: 'I have heard about you, the Irish revolutionary, and I am pleased that you have come all this way. Remember our children when you return as we hope one day we will see the same peace that you have managed to achieve.' David thanked the president for hosting the meeting, despite knowing that he had just been mistaken for Gerry Adams. He also told me he would kill me if I ever repeated what Arafat had said. I couldn't help wondering how David Trimble would have responded if he had been there.

I returned to the Middle East with the National Democratic Institute from Washington DC and the Atlanta-based Carter Centre to monitor the presidential election in 2005 and the Palestinian Legislative Council election in 2006. On the first occasion I was sent to Gaza, which meant crossing the Israeli checkpoint at Erez – one of the most heavily fortified border crossings in the world. I watched as two soldiers threw a stinger across the road to stop a car and search the undercarriage from a bunker underneath. The scene was reminiscent of the checkpoints that had existed on our own border and that were being dismantled following the Good Friday Agreement. The blood-spattered walls were another reminder of what happens when soldiers fire indiscriminately at civilians crossing borders. As in Northern Ireland, there were calls in the Middle East for the state to be held accountable for its breaches of international human rights standards. In both contexts too there was also considerable opposition to any effort to hold soldiers accountable for the deaths of innocent people. My experience in Gaza confirmed my commitment to the application of international human rights standards and the importance of independent international inquiries.

On each occasion, we were accompanied by former US President, Jimmy Carter, and I learned much from working alongside this man who had dedicated his post-presidential life to conflict resolution. When Palestinians reported they had been refused entry to post offices designated as their polling station in East Jerusalem, Jimmy Carter took it on himself to personally sort out the problem. I could only imagine the shock on the Israeli post office workers' faces when the former US president turned up at their door.

The elections in the Occupied Territories were democratic, free and fair – essential for the legitimacy and mandate required for political parties generally, but particularly for those formerly aligned to armed groups. I was not surprised when Hamas, the Palestinian Islamic organisation, won the election. Their disciplined 'get out the vote' organisation was as methodical as the systems employed by Sinn Féin or the DUP at home. When I asked one woman why so many women were coming out to vote for Hamas, she replied, 'They provide for our needs'. This was a theme common in each conflict region that I visited; addressing bread-and-butter issues, such as livelihoods, health and education, is as important, particularly for women, as the militarised responses to safety and security.

When Jimmy Carter was asked by the media if Hamas could rise to the challenge of governing Gaza, he replied: 'You are asking a peanut farmer from Atlanta who became the president of the United States that question. When you come to power, you take a different path because you have the responsibility of governing on behalf of all of the people.' It was a prescient point and not just for political leaders in the Middle East.

If the Israeli/Palestinian situation was challenging, the same was true of Colombia when I visited it first in 2001, as part of an international delegation to share experiences on negotiations. During the discussions, the justice ombudsman for Colombia asked if I would visit the local police station where three men – referred to back at home as the 'Colombia Three' – had recently been detained. The ombudsman was keen for me to know that the men were being treated fairly and asked that an armed guard escort me to the prison. I had become accustomed to having an armed guard – as a foreign national I was deemed at risk of being kidnapped – so travel in an armoured car, with outriders and sirens blasting had become the norm. The highly fortified police station was similar to some I had visited in Northern Ireland, although the interior was somewhat different. A statue of the Virgin Mary was in prime position above the desk of the chief of police. When he asked if I was used to seeing similar statues in police stations at home, I didn't know if he was being serious.

I spoke with the three men – Niall Connolly, Martin McCauley and James Monaghan – in the yard, having earlier run the gauntlet of imprisoned men trying to make a grab for me through the bars of their cells. All three men thought they would be home for Christmas. I was less certain, given that they were being associated with FARC (the guerrilla movement in Colombia), and the charges were serious. On my return home, I decided to make a report to the Irish and British governments – who would have been alerted about my visit to the jail by the Colombian authorities – and I also called the men's families to say that all three were in good health. Several years later, after being discharged by a court and while awaiting trial on new charges, the Colombia Three absconded to Ireland. A Colombian special court eventually cleared them in 2020. The judge said that there was no supporting evidence that the three had been part of a terrorist group and a full amnesty was issued.

The eventual Colombia peace agreement in 2016, in contrast to the Good Friday Agreement, tackled the broader issue of truth and justice early on. It provided for the prosecution of individuals in the army and in FARC, and right-wing paramilitaries, for human rights violations and criminal offences. It also agreed mechanisms for investigations and for amnesties where there was insufficient evidence, and it established a special commission to oversee these transitional justice approaches. Such mechanisms spoke directly to the needs of victims, especially children and other vulnerable people who had been kidnapped. Despite the difficulties they experienced during the implementation of their peace agreement, the Colombian negotiators had the courage to face up to these issues while we in Northern Ireland are still struggling to come to terms with different interpretations of the events of the Troubles and contrary positions as to who can be categorised as a victim.

President Santos and FARC's Rodrigo Londoño – more commonly known as Timochenko – signed the peace agreement in Cartagena with a pen constructed from a bullet and engraved with the words: 'Bullets wrote our history. Education writes our futures.' As I watched the jets fly over the stadium in celebration of the men shaking hands on their deal, I hoped that they would be able to turn this promise into action. Unfortunately, current indications don't augur well and once again show that implementation has to be rapid in order to keep faith with the spirit of the agreement.

Dealing with the past in the aftermath of a terrible conflict is such a complex challenge that it requires a multi-dimensional approach. I had tried to explain that to President George Bush when he asked – during the St Patrick's Day event at the White House in 2002 – about the progress we were making in Northern Ireland. I replied that we were learning to understand each other and come to terms with what had happened. But he misunderstood my meaning when he said he couldn't forgive the men from Afghanistan who had planted the bombs on 9/11. I explained that to understand didn't mean to forgive and forget – we couldn't whitewash acts of violence – but in spite of continuing underlying tensions in Northern Ireland we had begun to acknowledge the rationale for others' actions. We were beginning to understand that we needed to adopt a more nuanced approach if we wanted to live together peacefully in a shared land and even that would take time. Gerry Adams and David Ervine were standing in front of me, along with Ian Paisley Snr, David Trimble, John Alderdice and Seamus Mallon, and most of them wouldn't have disagreed.

I met President Bush again in another line-up with party leaders at Hillsborough Castle on 8 April 2003. The president had come to Northern Ireland with National Security Adviser Condoleezza Rice and Secretary of State Colin Powell to meet with Prime Minister Tony Blair. The meeting was crucial as a decision was being made on whether to invade Iraq as a consequence of allegations that Saddam Hussein was threatening states with his arsenal of nuclear weapons. The UN had asked for time to confirm those allegations as starting a war in Iraq would have repercussions around the world. The Women's Coalition agreed that I should give President Bush a letter outlining the need for the UN investigators to do their work, based on the knowledge – drawn from our own experience – that sending battalions of soldiers into a country was easier than withdrawing them afterwards. Arguments were raging about what constituted a 'just war' and I had heard these many times before, both at home and in other conflict situations. In the letter to George Bush I listed the reasons why decisions to go to war had to be considered more carefully, since we did not believe the arguments to be morally acceptable.

When he saw the letter in my hand the president said: 'You again.' He remembered me from our previous exchange in the White House. I said I simply wanted him to read the arguments inside. The letter set out the ethical principles: that all peaceful means of change had to be exhausted; that the issues at stake had to be serious enough to justify the response; that a war that was pursued had to have a reasonable chance of success and not likely to be a protracted struggle that produced a futile outcome; that any violence adopted had to be proportionate to the injustice it was claiming to redress rather than leaving behind a legacy of division; that the proponents of military action had to have substantial support for its adoption – otherwise known as a 'democratic mandate' – and had to be accountable to the people it was purporting to represent; and lastly, that the use of military action had to be part of a minimalist protection strategy, to be used when other means of defence were unavailable, rather than as an aggressive strategy. As I knew only too well by then, violent conflict removes the most basic right of all: the right to life.

President Bush asked why I thought he intended to bypass the UN. I said that all the signs were pointing in that direction and that Tony Blair was already proposing a 'coalition of the willing' to join the US in going to war. President Bush was nose to nose with me when he asked 'Don't you know Saddam Hussein is a rapist, a gangster and a criminal?' The room became hushed at the mention of 'rape'; conversations came to a sudden halt. I told the president that I was an MLA representing South Belfast and the job entailed having to deal with rapists, gangsters and criminals on a regular basis, but I followed due process as bombing them from the air was illegal. Tony Blair moved into the circle to tell the president that he was going to be late for lunch but the president turned back to say, 'I want to have the last word with this woman.' The entourage moved on leaving me speechless.

The night before I had run the gauntlet of protesters arguing that I shouldn't have been meeting with President Bush on the grounds that I was colluding with someone they termed a 'war mongerer.' I stood on a platform that had been built across the motorway to tell the thousands who had gathered there that I had gone into prisons and to all kinds of strange places to talk to people who I had disagreed with and that I was going to talk to the US president if I got the chance. The Iraq war that followed had lasting consequences both for the people there as well as on a global scale. It left me even more convinced that before a political decision is made to put boots on the ground, the ethics need to be fully examined.

When I first visited Bosnia in the autumn of 1998, it reminded me of something a woman in West Belfast had said at the start of the Troubles: 'I have a bitterness in me and a revenge that I know that these people who burned our houses must have had. I have that same bitterness now.'

One person's justice had become another person's grievance – a common feature of conflict. A woman I met in Republika Srpska – the ethnic Serb region of Bosnia and Herzegovina – said that she had felt her bitterness would last forever and that what had helped to change her mind was not to see her neighbour as the enemy and for her neighbour to feel the same way about her. She said she had had to accept the legitimacy of the other side since it was the only way for Bosnians and Serbians to coexist. That resonated for me in the context of British and Irish identities in Northern Ireland.

Bosnians, Serbs and Croats were still arguing over the cause of their conflict – a familiar debate in Northern Ireland. Although I recognised the different scale of the violence that had taken place there, when I heard a Bosnian woman say 'No one has suffered as much as us', I knew I had heard similar at home and in many other conflict regions. Another comment resonated with me: 'I am tired of hearing about hope, give me something more than hope to hold on to'. This was the point that my son Gavin had made on the evening of the Good Friday Agreement when he asked what difference the peace agreement would make. Talk of 'peace dividends' only makes sense when there is change for the better in those communities that have borne the brunt of the conflict.

This was brought home to me when I visited Rwanda in 2019 with Interpeace to meet survivors of the genocide. The scars and suffering were still apparent twenty-five years after the war had ended, and just as they did in Northern Ireland, people here were saying, 'The past is my present.' While I was in Rwanda, the man who was driving me around told me his story. John had watched his family, who were Tutsi, being butchered from a ditch on the opposite side of the road where he lay hidden with his older sister. Both had managed to escape to the local Catholic Church and had lived there for a year, close to where their parents and siblings were buried. When we visited the genocide memorial museum he explained that his family, like thousands of others, had been re-interred at the site a few years earlier. I cried with him when he placed his hand over the names of his mother and father on the headstone; twenty-six other names were listed there, family members who had also been killed alongside his parents. It was a comfort, he said, to have someone to listen to him. He had shared his feelings with his surviving sister, but as she was recently married he didn't want to bother her any more. It was heart-breaking to hear him say that he wouldn't be getting married as he didn't trust himself to be a loving partner given his experiences. The loving hug he gave me when we said goodbye suggested otherwise.

I had laid a wreath at the museum earlier that day on behalf of Interpeace and had been shocked at the exhibits detailing the massacres. It had left me conflicted, as had the conversation with John. I could understand the need for memorialisation but wondered how it would help people to come to terms with long-term trauma or to live in harmony with their neighbours who had perpetrated such atrocities.

It was in Rwanda too that I heard from women about the impact of the violence on them and their struggle to have rape included on the list of indictments at the international tribunal that had been set up by the UN to prosecute those responsible for genocide and other serious violations of international humanitarian law. The women recounted the difficulties they had in just getting to Arusha, in Tanzania, to give evidence and spoke of how they had been retraumatised by the process set up to hear their statements and let down by the lack of support services.

In Muhanga in southern Rwanda, the women talked about how they had been treated as outcasts. As I listened to each of their stories it sounded as if they had been through hell on earth. Clarisse's Hutu husband had been brutally murdered because he had married her, a Tutsi woman. She had escaped death, as had her children, but life was unbearable, as she had had to assume the role of breadwinner in a very disrupted society. She explained, 'I was rejected by my family because I had betrayed their trust by marrying a Hutu man. And my husband's family rejected me because I was the root cause of their son's death.' Women in mixed marriages felt stigmatised, raising children they felt did not 'belong' to one side or the other.

As a consequence of the serious and debilitating impact of the conflict, Rwanda's government had invested its funds – that were supplemented by the EU and the UN – in mental health services. The healing circles that I visited resembled a cooperative movement in which psychotherapists worked alongside victims and survivors. As I knew from personal experience, the system in Northern Ireland would have benefited from a similar approach. The other important feature of healing circles was that they included income-generating activities that allowed the women to be self-sufficient and independent. I could see the pride in their faces when they asked if I would like to take some of their potatoes back home with me.

What I heard in these meetings echoed what I'd heard in Colombia, Syria, Iraq and Liberia. Women said that peace – however defined – was better than open warfare, but they also needed 'freedom from want' and 'freedom from fear'. In any post-conflict societal reconstruction, women needed training, steady employment, and the necessary skills for economic security and independence. However, all too often what I saw was a priority focus on the re-integration of men rather than on women's security and leadership. Twenty years after UN Security Council resolution 1325 on Women, Peace and Security, we should be able to say confidently: 'Nothing about us, without us.' But just as this has proved elusive for the disability movement who first coined the phrase, the women's movement is still seeking a genuine commitment to this principle.

In 2016, when conflicts were raging in Syria, Afghanistan, and Sudan, I addressed, at the invitation of Inclusive Security, the first ever hearing on the role of women in peace and security at the US House of Representatives Committee on Foreign Affairs. In his opening remarks, the committee chairperson said that the 'truly historic panel' was addressing an issue of critical importance and that the benefits of women's participation and the risks of their exclusion in all aspects of governance and peacemaking were too great to ignore. These were encouraging words since many politicians and negotiators in different parts of the world had come to regard the UN Security Council resolution on Women, Peace and Security as a women's issue. But it wasn't a women's issue; it was a security issue.

I told the members of Congress that from my experience across different conflicts, women were a key resource both during situations of conflict and when the violence ends. The priorities they bring to the peace table lay the foundations for a more durable long-term peace. I added that women make an essential contribution through civil society activism as well as at the negotiating table. This was the rationale behind the Women's Coalition's proposal to establish a Civic Forum as part of the Good Friday Agreement. This broader advisory body was shelved as soon as the more established political parties involved in our power-sharing governance arrangement set their minds to dividing up power rather than sharing it out. I often overheard the more traditional politicians say that they weren't interested in listening to what unelected representatives had to say. My response was to point out that violence narrows politics and that it was important to embrace new ways of achieving greater participation. There is a real benefit in creating the space to draw on the insights and networks of community activists, business leaders, spokespersons from various faiths, trade unionists and grassroots organisers, as well as representatives from the women's movement: often, it is among these civic society activists that you will find those who will take the most risks for peace.

Despite the worthy resolutions and debates, I found the representation of women's interests and priorities was often missing from agreements. The 2016 Colombian Peace Agreement was the exception and went much further than the 1998 Good Friday Agreement in declaring: 'We are conscious that the transformation this country needs is not possible without a society that recognises and respects the differences and the historical roots of gender-based stigmatisation and discrimination.' I was aware from my meeting in Bogotá with Elena Ambrosi, on the Colombian government's negotiating team, and with FARC's Tanja Nijmeijer and Victoria Sandino, that there had been pressure for a gender sub-committee – which they managed to achieve – during their negotiations in Havana. Learning from the role that women from civil society had played in the Northern Ireland process, Victoria said, 'We saw how you had made your voices heard and we wanted to do the same'. I was amazed at what I was hearing – I hadn't realised we had made such an impression on women who were negotiating a political transition in their own countries. Sharing the learning had been gathering like a snowball.

When women are at the peace table, and when parallel mechanisms are set up to reflect their concerns, the issues that affect women are more likely to get attention. I knew this from my visits to Gaziantep in Turkey, near the Syrian border, where I met women organising against Assad's regime. A young woman described her sense of abandonment during her incarceration in a male prison and how her name had been deliberately omitted from the list for detainee release because her family wanted to protect her reputation. I'd heard similar stories about the importance families placed on protecting a woman's honour – rather than the woman herself – from young women in Gulu, northern Uganda, who had been kidnapped by members of the Lord's Resistance Army. Even after they had managed to escape from the soldiers, they were stigmatised by their families for bringing 'dishonour' to the community because many of them had been raped and some of them were pregnant or had had children. It is stories such as these that made my friend, UN mediator Gina Torry, insist that ceasefire agreements in Central Africa had to include a cessation of conflict-related sexual attacks. It was somewhat surreal that just as I was struggling to get to sleep under my mosquito net in Gulu, Hillary Clinton appeared on my TV screen introducing a UN resolution on the protection of women and girls from wartime sexual violence in 2008.

I was confirmed in my belief that the political is often personal when I returned to Colombia in 2016 to visit Putumayo, on the border between Colombia and Ecuador. There, women from Mujeres Tejedoras de Vida (Women Weavers of Life) sat down with a group of us from Northern Ireland and spoke of their pain and sorrow, but also of how they had coped, including by working together on a Wall of Truth constructed out of the names of murdered and disappeared women. It was close to midnight, and from the rooftop patio I could see men in the street down below throwing beer bottles, shooting off guns and fighting each other after a national football match. It wasn't 'conflict-related', just toxic masculinity on display; the kind of behaviour that forced women to stay indoors.

It struck me that 'conflict violence' and 'everyday violence' (something that lawyers, diplomats and human rights activists discuss at length) were indistinguishable when it came down to the everyday experience of people trying to live a normal existence with dignity. What was clear from the places I visited was that, in common with Northern Ireland, war and peace are connected through a web of power, with domestic and sexual violence occurring before, during and after war. Even though there is no evidence that there was systematic use of rape as a war crime, in the usual sense of that term, in the Northern Ireland context, the armed patriarchy was, nonetheless, lethally dangerous for women. Female partners forced into submission by paramilitaries wielding guns in Northern Ireland, often in their own families and communities, is an example of this. The coercive control used by men, acting as individuals or in groups, was the same across the world. I have seen how women's bodies have been used and abused in the battle for power – forced sterilisation of East Timorese women by the Indonesian authorities; forced sex on a massive scale in the genocides of Bosnia and Rwanda; forced marriages by the soldiers who kidnapped girls in northern Uganda; guards forcibly abusing and disappearing women and girls in Syria. I came to see how war has the face of a woman.

The question that Jessica Doyle and I addressed in our study on Intimate Partner Violence in Conflict and Post-conflict Societies in 2016 was one that many people were asking: Did peace make any difference to women experiencing domestic violence? That same year, just after their peace agreement, I had asked the same question of the Colombian chief of police as I wanted to know if he had a plan to tackle domestic violence and sexual abuse. He told me he had more serious issues to deal with first. But what he and most of the police chiefs in countries coming out of conflict don't appreciate is that violence is not just limited to the battlefield but is also internalised in the home. Jimmy Carter's book, *Women, Religion, Violence and Power*, made the same point, one that he and I talked about on 8 March 2015 at the Nobel Peace Prize Forum in Minnesota. There, we called on governments around the world to pay more attention to the issues of women, religion, violence and power.

Clearly there is a need for more women as mediators and negotiators to expand the conversation beyond one where the focus remains on matters such as where borders are drawn and who gets control of mineral wealth. Though, as Melanne Verveer stated in her role as US Global Ambassador for Women's Affairs, women activists shouldn't have to go it alone. Alongside support from women mediators, it is crucial that men are convinced of the importance of women's involvement and of the priorities that they set.

I saw how that could be done during my visit with Trócaire to Eastern Congo where 'safe communal spaces' had been created to enable men to ask questions of women without feeling judged. More important was the fact that the men were listening to women's answers. The idea that 'promoting equality was the responsibility of both men and women' had clearly moved into the mainstream when it became the theme of the African Union Women's Conference in Addis Ababa in 2019; the participants – men and women – clicked their fingers in assent every time the phrase was used.

I heard the same determination from Liberian women who visited Northern Ireland in 2009 through the Irish government's Conflict Resolution Unit in advance of the tenth anniversary of UN resolution 1325 on Women, Peace and Security. In Belfast, it was amazing to hear this song from the Liberian women:

No longer men in front
And women at the back,
Together we will walk
Side by side, side by side

The emphasis the UN resolution places on preparatory work for women's participation is still vital. I saw this in practice in Internally Displaced Persons (IDP) camps when I travelled in 2017 to Kachin, in northern Myanmar, where gender awareness capacity-building programmes were being delivered. I have been impressed by the work that Hind Kabawat and Mariam Jalabi are doing to build capacity for women as peace mediators and negotiators in the Syrian Opposition Coalition. They move between holding meetings with women in places near the border with Syria and at the same time network with high-level diplomats at the UN in Geneva and New York to get their message across. The war in Syria has turned into a proxy one and Russia, Iran, Turkey, the USA and the European Union are now among the main players. It is no mean feat to deal with them, along with the players from inside Syria. But Hind and Mariam and the other women on the high negotiating committee never give up hope that one day their work on transitional justice will pay off and that they can return home to a much different country from the one they left behind.

When I started to work with Rajaa Altalli shortly after the war began in 2011, she was trying to bring the voices from civil society to the peace table. I was heartened to hear her say that the Northern Ireland Women's Coalition experience had made her think about what they should be doing and it gave her the idea of setting up the Centre for Civil Society and Democracy. All of these women had been warned that they would have blood on their hands if they became involved in politics and were advised to stick to what they were already doing – providing humanitarian aid. They knew this very experience – of working with displaced people and refugees – provided them with special expertise that they could bring to bear in the drafting of a new Syrian constitution. Hind explained how widows who had been married to men not born in Syria had difficulty applying for passports for their children since the assumption was that only Syrian men could pass on the family name. She said that exile due to war is hard, but the lack of a passport, creating a sense of statelessness, is worse. I saw women putting forward these issues and Staffan de Mistura, in his role as UN Envoy to Syria, insisting on the inclusion of representatives from civil society and a women's advisory group during the UN negotiations in Geneva – that made him the exception rather than the rule. From all this, I have concluded that international systems of rights and accountability need to be effective – for women as well as men – to ensure that individuals, communities and societies can be resilient in the face of conflict.

This work with women in peace processes has also challenged me to ask who is not at the table? Whose voices are not being heard? My friend and colleague from Interpeace, Graeme Simpson, wrote 'The Missing Piece' – a UN report on youth, peace and security. In it, he points out that we have to challenge the stereotype of young men (as a threat with their guns) and young women (as passive victims) and focus instead on their contribution to making change. I couldn't agree more. From my experience in Northern Ireland I knew that ours had been a young people's war, with one third of those killed having been under the age of twenty-four.

At the time of the ceasefires in 1994, nine out of ten children in West Belfast had seen cars hijacked and burned, half had seen people using guns, and one in three had seen a bomb explosion. Rowen was nine years old in 1997 when his teacher asked his class to write about their vision for the future. He wrote: 'I think that people shouldn't have to go to bed at night worrying about murders in their area.' It showed me how young people carry these worries and can become the transmitters of memory.

We need to invest in the idea that they should be listened to and be recognised as the essential change agents of the future. That would be more forward-thinking than the expensive and often counter-productive securitised responses that see young people as a risk or a threat.

Initiatives like Politics in Action, which I joined in 2020, encourage young people from across Northern Ireland to become involved in political discussion. Politics has been the elephant in the classroom, deemed too contentious to discuss by many parents and teachers. Now these young people can come together in small clusters of schools that create spaces for children to learn together about politics with their teachers and facilitators. The discussions also help to address the segregated school system in Northern Ireland – it still saddens me that event today 90 per cent of children attend either a Protestant or Catholic school. Participants in our project come from different traditions and different socio-economic backgrounds and nothing has been off limits in their conversations. Politics in Action is now opening up the discussion to include young people on the other side of the border – a border that, as we have discovered during the recent pandemic, is a fluid one, as more of our young people are also discovering.

I made this point about the fluidity of borders during a recent visit to Cyprus – an island divided north and south, just like ours. Avila and I undertook some workshops in the Turkish and Greek parts of the island, and afterwards we came to the conclusion that the mosquitoes do not make a distinction about which side of the border they are on. Just like climate change, a contagious disease crosses borders. In Beyond Borders, a not-for-profit organisation facilitating international dialogue, a woman from Yemen drew connections between political power-brokers – including the UK – and the proxy war in her country, declaring, 'We are not starving, we are being starved.' Her call for action continues to keep me alert.

I continue to value this work that shares our experience with practitioners from other societies, but the challenges also continue at home. It remains a hard fact that while a peace process can open up opportunities for some, for others it can fail to deliver on expectations. The Good Friday Agreement stated that the governments 'continue to recognise the importance of measures to facilitate the reintegration of prisoners into the community by providing support both prior to and after release, including assistance directed towards availing of employment opportunities, re-training and/or reskilling and further education'. The EU PEACE programmes supported these interventions, but the government was more reluctant to go down that path. It meant that those – most especially on the loyalist side – who tried to follow a political path but didn't succeed became disenchanted with the Good Friday Agreement.

In Northern Ireland, I continue to observe how individuals are using politics as a cover to develop networks of organised crime and criminality. My current work, since 2017, with my fellow commissioners John McBurney, Tim O'Connor and Mitchell Reiss on the Independent Reporting Commission to oversee measures on the disbandment of paramilitary groups has highlighted the fact that the demobilisation process can leave community-level power vacuums that lead to the emergence of criminal gangs, and has made clear the need for effective community policing. In Northern Ireland, some individuals connected to paramilitary groups – the 'bandas criminales' as they are known in Colombia – are able to control lucrative illicit activities. They use their allegiance to paramilitaries to enable them to carry out activities such as extortion, drug trafficking and money laundering. I understood the pattern of behaviour and used the term coercive control from my work on domestic violence to show how paramilitaries were exerting fear and control over their local communities. The term entered our everyday parlance as we began to find ways to challenge paramilitary groups.

The Independent Reporting Commission has applied this unique lens to its work, as we made clear in *The Fresh Start Panel Report on the Disbandment of Paramilitary Groups in Northern Ireland* back in 2016: 'There is a gender dynamic to the issue of disbanding paramilitary groups. The ex-prisoner groups and former paramilitaries we met were almost all men. The "masculinity" issue, attached to the status of being a paramilitary, and the fear of being emasculated through a process of disbandment needs to be understood.'

Seeing how women operate as an early warning system within communities, providing a vital resource for the ending of conflict and criminality, we are able to argue for greater support to be given to women's organisations. Almost one thousand women have taken part in a community transformation programme to date.

I have seen women who do not flinch from confronting paramilitary groups. The McCartney sisters – whose brother Robert was murdered by IRA members on 31 January 2005 – called the IRA out despite being ostracised for doing so by people within their community. After twenty-nine-year-old journalist Lyra McKee's murder in Derry City on 19 April 2019, her friends repainted the landmark Free Derry Corner with the words 'Not In Our Name'. It begs the question as to why we are still dealing with paramilitaries over two decades after the Good Friday Agreement.

I remain frustrated about the extent to which the peace dividend has failed to have the positive impact that I expected on disadvantaged working-class communities. Too many people feel they have been short-changed: the promise of jobs and a decent standard of living didn't materialise. When the rising tide doesn't lift all boats, people, especially young people, can become easily disillusioned, a feeling fuelled if policing is perceived to be inadequate. I have been impressed by the community-based restorative justice initiatives that are making an important contribution to their local communities – so much so that it has led policymakers from other conflict societies to visit Northern Ireland to see whether the model can be adapted to their own situation. But more needs to be done if sections of the community are not to be left feeling increasingly marginalised.

The work I am doing to end paramilitary activity on the Independent Reporting Commission is complex and needs something more sophisticated than the response I am used to hearing: 'Lock them up and throw away the key.' In reply, I try to give the same upbeat response that Mo Mowlam gave about the delay in implementing the Good Friday Agreement: 'No one said it was going to be easy.' The delusion that paramilitarism can be brought to an end by policing alone has endured for more than two decades. It remains a political problem to be resolved by politicians. And that's where leadership comes in.

The day we signed the Good Friday Agreement has been described as a constitutional moment in our history. The referendum that followed taught me that citizens have to be genuinely informed when asked to make decisions that are going to affect their lives. That was not the case in 2016, when the UK voted to leave the European Union. As a result, Brexit has created a fraught situation. A negotiated protocol to enable Northern Ireland to remain in the EU single market for trading purposes (aligned with the Republic of Ireland) has been trailed by one side, predominantly unionists, as undermining the union with Britain and British identity and by nationalists and others as the best possible solution to a bad situation.

Since we are all from a big wide world and we are all connected, our interests are enhanced, not undermined, by being part of an effective, interdependent and multilateral system. Once again, civic and political leaders have to engage in dialogue to rebuild trust between people across and between these isles. This was the catalyst in building relationships east and west, between the people of these islands and the EU, as well as among the people of Ireland, north and south. If I have learned anything from the peace process, it is the importance of acknowledging and respecting a diversity of views that I may not always agree with. It has helped me to look beyond the binary divisions that have long characterised allegiances in Northern Ireland.

There is much that still needs to be delivered but we have come a long way. There are people alive today who may well have gone to early graves had it not been for the Good Friday Agreement. As a mother who raised a family in Belfast during the dark days of the conflict, I value the fact that our children can now go out at night without their families worrying about how – and if – they will come home. A letter that I received a decade after the Agreement filled me with joy. In it, a mother wrote of how her children could now aspire to things that she once could only have dreamed of.

I am grateful that we are increasingly welcoming people from other countries into our demographic mix. Our response to people from other cultures reveals a great deal about the state of our society, the integrity of our communities, and the prospects for our collective future. Islamophobia doesn't disparage just Muslims, racism doesn't demean Black and Asian people alone, xenophobia insults more than immigrants, misogyny hurts more than women. Peter Sutherland made this statement as the UN Special Representative for International Migration and I completely agree with him. We are all diminished by hatred of others and we all have a stake in confronting that hatred. Our greatest challenge in the coming years remains our oldest one – how to live well together.

I have dedicated much of my life to meeting that challenge. That work can be slow and precarious, but I have seen how myriad small, incremental actions can make a difference over time. Change is not down to a single person; it takes a collective effort and I am grateful to have helped to make a difference.

So, when people ask me, 'What difference does peace make?' I say, 'All the difference in the world.' By dint of our achievements, our society now stands on the cusp of a new era. We have been able to craft new tools and institutions to help build a transformative politics and to shape the future that we want to see for ourselves and for our children. With imagination, that future can be glimpsed though, as we see more than twenty years on from the Agreement, there are still risks and forces that spawn the old demons of fear and threaten the building of trust.

As I reflect on where I am now, it's clear that I owe much to my early years. I loved being in the thick of things – perched on a barstool chatting to the cattle dealers, chasing after the stray sheep and running on the cross-country team with a bunch of hardy schoolgirls. The direction I have taken also comes from my mother's wish to keep the peace and my father's desire that I should stand up for myself. Noeleen's struggle to find peace of mind and Mary's determination to walk again after her car accident showed me that being at peace comes from the inside. The social and political movements in which I became involved have also left a lasting imprint on my life. I am one of the long-flight birds and will battle on, standing up and speaking out for women's rights, peace and equality.

Acknowledgements

It wasn't an easy task to write this book, since my work as an academic has trained me to aim for objectivity in my writing. And yet when it came to writing this memoir, I had to do the opposite – recalling events from where I stood. Patsy Horton's guidance as editor shaped the book and I greatly appreciate her multi-tasking and professional skills. Valuable assistance also came from Helen Wright who applied order, sequence and discipline at every stage, and made the process an enjoyable one. The publication was supported by a grant from the Arts Council of Northern Ireland, which has made its own important contribution to politics and the arts over many years, as indeed has Blackstaff.

I am most grateful to Avila Kilmurray for recalling our shared experiences, also published in her book *Community Action in a Contested Society: The Story of Northern Ireland*. A heartfelt thanks goes to Avila and Brian Gormally for their generosity and kindness, and for casting a critical eye wherever it was needed. A special thanks to Mike Morrissey, Frank Gaffikin and colleagues in the social science faculty at Ulster University and the Transitional Justice Institute. I am particularly grateful to Celia Davies and Fionnuala Ní Aoláin for their assistance with research applications for my work on domestic violence. Friend and colleague Margaret Ward and colleagues at Queen's were also most supportive. I am grateful to the University of Chicago's Pozen Human Rights Centre as it was there that the seeds for the book were first planted. Back home, Susan McKay's encouragement ensured that I got on with it.

I valued and appreciated long-time friend Tony Novosel's guidance, advice and thoughtfulness throughout. Jane Gordon and David Russell sent speedy responses, as did Tim O'Connor, to requests for occasional clarification. A special thanks to Sandra Peake and Alan McBride at WAVE, to Noelle Collins at Women's Aid and to the many victims and survivors who readily gave of their time. I am especially grateful to Kate Fearon who generously put at my disposal the accounts from her book, *Women's Work: The Story of the Northern Ireland Women's Coalition* and to Renée McKinty for her work on the archives. I was also able to draw on *Wave Goodbye to Dinosaurs*, the PBS and BBC documentary produced by Abigail Disney's Fork Films and Trevor Birney's Fine Point Films. I owe a special word of thanks to its director, Eimhear O'Neill. Deep gratitude goes to all my friends in the Women's Coalition, most especially Ann McCann – a peace-keeper in every sense of the word.

The exchanges with staff and fellow board members at Interpeace, particularly Martin Acked and Necla Tschigri, were more than helpful. RoseMarie FitzSimons and I became constant companions as she worked on her film *The Art of Peace Making*. Our travels together led to many productive conversations on women and peacebuilding. I was fortunate to have friends from further afield who also provided assistance, in particular Melanne Verveer, Catherine Shannon and Carmen Suro-Bredie, and Tim Phillips at Beyond Conflict. Tom Moran and Olga Reisman, sadly now deceased, were by my side for years. Wise counsel also came from John McGettrick and Olivia O'Kane as well as from my fellow commissioners on the Independent Reporting Commission: John McBurney, Tim O'Connor and Mitchell Reiss. They had to listen to my tales and never once complained.

Above all, the care of my family has been beyond compare. Brian, Gavin and Rowen encouraged me to write this memoir and provided the support to see it through. My sister Mary was there every step of the way and I couldn't have written this book without her. The nourishment of body and soul that she provided kept me going, and the greatest thanks of all is owed to her.

Glossary

Alliance Party. Cross-community political party founded in 1970. John Alderdice was the party leader at the time of the 1998 Agreement. Alliance supported the Agreement.

B Specials. Members of the Ulster Special Constabulary, disbanded in 1970.

Belfast Agreement. More usually known as the Good Friday Agreement, the result of the peace negotiations on Good Friday, 10 April 1998.

CIRA (Continuity Irish Republican Army). Republican paramilitary group, founded in 1986, became active after the Provisional IRA ceasefire in 1994. Opposed to the 1998 Agreement.

Combined Loyalist Military Command. Established in 1991 as an umbrella group for the main loyalist paramilitary organisations. Supported the 1998 Agreement.

Conservative Party of Great Britain. John Major was the party leader at the time of the 1998 Agreement.

Cumann na mBan. Women's republican organisation formed in 1914.

Dáil, (Dáil Éireann). Lower house of the Irish Parliament in Dublin.

DUP (Democratic Unionist Party). Founded in 1971. At the time of writing, the largest unionist party in government in Northern Ireland. Rev. Ian Paisley was its leader from 1971 to 2008. Opposed the Agreement in 1998.

Fianna Fáil. Political party in the Republic of Ireland, founded in 1921.

Bertie Ahern was the party leader, and taoiseach, at the time of the 1998 Agreement.

Fine Gael. Political party in the Republic of Ireland, founded in 1933. John Bruton was the party leader at the time of the 1998 Good Friday Agreement.

Gaelic Athletic Association (GAA). All-Ireland sporting organisation promoting traditional sports, including Gaelic football and hurling.

Garda Síochána. Police service in the Republic of Ireland.

Good Friday Agreement. See Belfast Agreement.

ICTU (Irish Congress of Trade Unions). Northern Ireland Committee is based in Belfast.

INLA (Irish National Liberation Army). Republican paramilitary group formed in 1974 in a split with the Official IRA. Political links to the Irish Republican Socialist Party. Supported the 1998 Agreement.

IPLO (Irish People's Liberation Organisation). Republican paramilitary group formed in 1986 in a split with the INLA.

IRA (Irish Republican Army). Formed in 1919. Split into two in 1969/70 into Provisional IRA and Official IRA. Supported the 1998 Agreement.

Labour (Northern Ireland). Not to be confused with the Labour Party in Great Britain. Malachi Curran was party leader, participated in the multi-party peace negotiations 1996–1998 and supported the 1998 Good Friday Agreement.

Labour Party (Great Britain). Tony Blair was party leader, and prime minister, at the time of the 1998 Agreement.

LVF (Loyalist Volunteer Force). Split with the Ulster Volunteer Force over the UVF's support for the peace process. Opposed the 1998 Agreement.

MLA (Member of the Northern Ireland Legislative Assembly). Official title of the 108 members elected to in the first Northern Ireland Assembly in 1998.

NICRA (Northern Ireland Civil Rights Association). Founded in 1967 to campaign for civil rights in Northern Ireland.

Northern Ireland Executive. Headed up by First Minister, Deputy First Minister and ministers in charge of government departments with powers devolved to it from Westminster following the 1998 Agreement.

Northern Ireland Office (NIO). British government department set up under Direct Rule by the Westminster government in 1972 to administer Northern Ireland. Continues to hold responsibility for constitutional matters and national security following the devolution of powers to Northern Ireland Assembly.

NIWC (Northern Ireland Women's Coalition). Cross-community political party founded in 1996. Monica McWilliams and Pearl Sagar were joint party leaders at the time of the 1998 Agreement. NIWC supported the Agreement. Dissolved in 2006.

Orange Order. Protestant fraternal organisation named after King William of Orange, founded in 1795. Loyal Order parades take place yearly around 12 July (The Twelfth). Opposed the 1998 Agreement.

Patten Report. Based on the findings of the Commission on the future of policing in Northern Ireland and named after its chairperson.

Provisional IRA. Also known as the Provisionals or most frequently the IRA. Formed out of a split with the Official IRA in December 1969. Supported the 1998 Agreement.

PUP (Progressive Unionist Party). Pro-Union left of centre political party founded in 1979. Hughie Smyth was the party leader at the time of the 1998 Agreement, which the party supported.

Real IRA. Republican paramilitary group. Formed in late 1997. Political links to the 32-County Sovereignty Movement. Opposed the 1998 Agreement.

Royal Ulster Constabulary (RUC). Northern Ireland's police force from 1922 to 2001. Renamed the Police Service of Northern Ireland (PSNI) following the implementation of the Patten Report's recommendations.

SDLP (Social Democratic and Labour Party). Nationalist political party supporting Irish unity achieved through non-violence and constitutional politics. John Hume was the party leader at the time of the 1998 Agreement. The SDLP supported the Agreement.

Sinn Féin (SF). Republican political party in government in Northern Ireland. Gerry Adams was the party's leader from 1983 to 2018. Sinn Féin supported the 1998 Agreement.

Stormont. Location of Parliament Buildings, the Northern Ireland Assembly, and Castle Buildings where the 1998 Agreement was signed.

Taoiseach. The prime minister of the Republic of Ireland.

UDA (Ulster Defence Association). Largest loyalist paramilitary organisation, founded in 1971 and proscribed in 1992. Supported the 1998 Agreement.

UDP (Ulster Democratic Party). Loyalist party, political counterpart of the Ulster Defence Association (UDA) and the Ulster Freedom Fighters (UFF). Gary McMichael was the party leader at the time of 1998 Agreement. UDP supported the Agreement. Dissolved in 2001.

UKUP (United Kingdom Unionist Party). Pro-Union party founded in 1995. Robert (Bob) McCartney was party leader. UKUP opposed the 1998 Agreement. Dissolved in 2008.

Ulster Unionist Council. Governing body of the Ulster Unionist Party until its powers were transferred to the UUP Executive in October 2007.

UUP (Ulster Unionist Party). Formerly the main unionist party governing Northern Ireland from 1921 to 1971, linked to the Conservative Party with which it had an electoral alliance from 2005 to 2012. Principal aim is to maintain the constitutional link with Great Britain. David Trimble was the party leader at the time of the 1998 Agreement. UUP supported the Agreement.

UVF (Ulster Volunteer Force). Loyalist paramilitary organisation. Founded in 1966, and named after the original UVF of the early twentieth century. Supported the 1998 Agreement.

Index